In Missouri's Wilds

In *Missouri's* *Wilds*

St. Mary's *of the* Barrens *and the* American Catholic Church, 1818 to 2016

Richard J. Janet

American Midwest
Truman State University Press
Kirksville, Missouri

Cover art: Aerial View of the Barrens. Courtesy of DeAndrei's-Rosati
Memorial Archives, DePaul University, Chicago, IL.
Cover design: Lisa Ahrens

Library of Congress Cataloging-in-Publication Data

Names: Janet, Richard J., 1955– author.
Title: In Missouri's wilds : St. Mary's of the Barrens and the American
  Catholic church, 1818 to 2016 / Richard J. Janet.
Description: Kirksville, Missouri : Truman State University Press, [2017] |
  Series: American Midwest | Includes bibliographical references and in-
  dex. Identifiers: LCCN 2017000960 (print) | LCCN 2017038615 (ebook) |
  ISBN 9781612481999 | ISBN 9781612481982 (alk. paper)
Subjects: LCSH: St. Mary's of the Barrens Seminary (Perryville, Mo.)—His-
  tory. | Catholic theological seminaries—Missouri—Perryville—History. |
  Vincentians—Missouri—Perryville—History. | Catholic Church—Missou-
  ri—Perryville—History. | Perryville (Mo.)—Church history.
Classification: LCC BX915.P45 (ebook) | LCC BX915.P45 J36 2017 (print) |
  DDC 282/.778694--dc23
LC record available at https://lccn.loc.gov/2017000960

Contents

List of Illustrations | vii

Preface and Acknowledgments | ix

PART 1: BEGINNINGS TO 1818

Chapter 1: Vincentians, the Barrens, and the
American Catholic Church | 3
Chapter 2: Founding of St. Mary's of the
Barrens | 19

PART 2: AN ERA OF BOUNDLESSNESS AT THE
BARRENS, 1818–1847

Chapter 3: Frontier Leadership | 35
Chapter 4: Policies and Problems | 61

PART 3: AN ERA OF FRAGMENTATION AND
CONSOLIDATION, 1847–1888

Chapter 5: Second-Generation Leadership | 81
Chapter 6: Civil War and Aftermath | 101

PART 4: THE BARRENS TRIUMPHANT, 1888–1962

Chapter 7: Revival and Growth | 127
Chapter 8: Conforming to New Demands | 167

PART 5: DECLINE AND FALL OF ST. MARY'S OF THE BARRENS, 1965–2016

Chapter 9: Closure and Controversy | 215

Chapter 10: Conclusion | 244

Works Cited | 253

Index | 269

About the Author | 277

ILLUSTRATIONS

1. St. Vincent de Paul (Courtesy of DeAndrei's-Rosati Memorial Archives, DePaul University, Chicago, IL, hereafter DRMA) | 10

2. Diorama of Saint-Lazare (Courtesy of DRMA) | 13

3. Panoramic View of Perryville, Missouri (Library of Congress Prints and Photographs Division) | 15

4. Louis William Valentine DuBourg (Courtesy of St. Louis University Archives) | 23

5. Felix De Andreis (Courtesy of DRMA) | 26

6. Joseph Rosati (Courtesy of DRMA) | 37

7. John Timon (courtesy of Archives of the Diocese of Buffalo) | 38

8. Rosati Cabin (Courtesy of DRMA) | 57

9. First Seminary Building (Courtesy of DRMA) | 59

10. Stephen Vincent Ryan (Courtesy of DRMA) | 86

11. Abram Ryan (Courtesy of Father Abram J. Ryan Archive, Belmont Abbey College) | 87

12. Barrens Campus Pre-1913 (Courtesy of DRMA) | 94

13. Thomas J. Smith (Courtesy of DRMA) | 132

14. Barrens Campus Pre-1913 (Courtesy of DRMA) | 135

15. Church Façade (Courtesy of DRMA) | 141

16. Barrens Campus Post-1913 (Courtesy of DRMA) | 166

17. Cyril LeFevre (Courtesy of DRMA) | 168

18. James A. Fischer (Courtesy of DRMA) | 180

19. Farm Buildings (Courtesy of DRMA) | 181

20. Novitiate Building (Courtesy of DRMA) | 183

21. Academic Building (photo by author) | 188

22. Aerial View of the Barrens (Courtesy of DRMA) | 220

23. Church of the Assumption Today (Courtesy of DRMA) | 245

24. Apostle of Charity Residence (photo by author) | 249

PREFACE AND ACKNOWLEDGMENTS

St. Mary's of the Barrens holds both professional interest and personal meaning for me. As a historian, I am drawn to the historical significance of "the Barrens." The history of the old seminary represents a fascinating story worthy of retelling as well as a compelling case study for the analysis of broader trends in the American Catholic experience. Personally, my life has intersected with the Barrens at various points. I was born in the shadow of the Barrens, raised and educated in nearby Vincentian parishes, and served on the faculty of the college seminary in the 1980s. The place loomed so large in my mind that I was driven initially to understand the seminary's closing and resulting controversy, which led to an article on the "decline and fall" of the Barrens. That study, generously supported by the Vincentian Studies Institute, inspired the present project on the broader historical sweep of the Barrens, again with VSI support.

As I researched and reflected on the history of St. Mary's of the Barrens, it became clear to me that its story could only be understood in the fuller context of the American Catholic story over the past two centuries. As a result, an "institutional history" broadened into an extended essay on the reciprocal relationship between an isolated southern Missouri seminary and the "bigger" story of American Catholicism. What follows is a kind of hybrid history combining the story of the Barrens, fascinating and important in its own right, with general trends in the history of the American Catholic Church.

I could have written a different book. The Barrens deserves a detailed chronicle of its history, highlighting its lesser-known characters, seemingly minor events, and quirks of historical development. Some of those details have been explored in articles and informal studies by Vincentians and others over the past decades. I have enjoyed reading those stories, and hope more of them follow. I tried to include some of those elements, but often sacrificed the details of the Barrens story in order to identify broader points of correlation with the American Catholic experience. If I distorted or undervalued the details of the Barrens story along the way, I am truly sorry.

For one reason or another, this project took much longer to complete than I originally anticipated. The longer it took, the more debts I assumed to people and institutions who contributed to my work. I am deeply thankful to the following friends, and for the many others who assisted me that I might fail to acknowledge.

First and foremost, I am grateful for the long support of the midwestern Vincentian community and the many individual Vincentian priests and brothers who have befriended and encouraged me over many years. The Vincentian Studies Institute at DePaul University offered grant support, hospitality, and research assistance during my trips to the archives at the Richardson Library on DePaul's Lincoln Park campus. Father Edward Udovic, CM, senior executive for University Mission at DePaul; Father John Rybolt, CM, Vincentian scholar-in-residence and authority on all things Vincentian; and Nathaniel Michaud, director of publications for the VSI, proved unfailingly helpful and patient over the course of my work. The staff of the De Andreis–Rosati Memorial Archives in the special collections department of the Richardson Library, especially Morgen MacIntosh Hodgetts and Andrew Rhea, went above and beyond the call of duty to field my requests and answer my questions. Special thanks, as well, go to my friend Father Bill Hartenbach, CM, who opened the files at the Midwest Provincial Offices of the Congregation to me during his tenure as provincial superior. Father Raymond Van Dorpe, CM, present-day provincial superior, fielded my questions about the current status of the Barrens and the Vincentian community with prompt authority and good grace. The late Father Louis Derbes, CM, shared his insights and knowledge of source materials as house archivist at the Barrens campus.

At Rockhurst University, I have been aided by receipt of a sabbatical leave of absence and collegial advice and support, especially from Faith Childress, chair of the Department of History, and Bill Stancil, theologian and director of the Rockhurst University Press. Ellie Kohler of the Rockhurst University Greenlease Library helped me run down hard-to-find texts and sources through interlibrary loan.

Thanks to the faculty and administration of Kenrick-Glennon Seminary in St. Louis, who listened and offered insightful comments on my work during my delightful sabbatical experience on that campus in the fall of 2015. Thanks also to Trish Erzfeld and Barb Sparkman of the Perry County Historical Society, who shared the resources of the society and helped me track some elusive sources in their collection and the Perry County Courthouse records. I am also indebted to Barbara Smith-Mandell of the Truman State University Press, who oversaw the publication of this work from intial query to final release.

Finally, thanks and apologies are due to my family, including my children (Damien and Shannon, Jonathan, Clare and Brian, Sam, and Ben) and my young grandsons (Jonathan, Will, and Nicholas), who hope to never hear the acronym "SMOB" again. My wife, Susan, has lived with this project, and with my fascination for the Barrens, for longer than she should, and her inspiration and patient encouragement are largely responsible for the completion of the book.

Of course, any problems or errors with my research or interpretation are entirely my own.

Richard J. Janet
Kansas City, Missouri

Part I

Beginnings to 1818

Chapter One

VINCENTIANS, THE BARRENS, AND THE AMERICAN CATHOLIC CHURCH

Sweet St. Mary's of the Barrens in Missouri's wilds,
thy children never can forget thee!

—Abram Ryan, *A Crown for Our Queen* (1882)
The Case for the Barrens

The history of American Catholicism might well be written in the story of abandoned buildings and closed institutions. The Catholic landscape is dotted with such historical artifacts, victims of shifting demographics, dwindling resources, and new ideas yielding new models and more buildings and institutions better suited to new realities. The social and cultural changes that closed outdated institutions and opened new ones define the history of American Catholicism. Growth and contraction, a struggle for necessary resources, new concepts better adapted to changing cultures (both within and outside the Catholic Church)—all shape the contours of the Catholic story. The varied institutions spawned by those forces reflect the nature of the Catholic experience.

Some Catholic institutions lasted longer than others. Those that operated longer reveal more of the story, for their survival and adaptation to changing circumstances speak eloquently to trends in the broader Catholic culture. St. Mary's of the Barrens Seminary in Perryville, Missouri lasted longer than most Catholic institutions, and its fortunes provide important insights into the history of American Catholicism.

The story of St. Mary's of the Barrens is little known today. From the perspective of the twenty-first century, the Barrens appears a historically insignificant place—a small, midwestern Catholic seminary founded in 1818 by a group of mostly Italian clerics in an isolated settlement in rural southeastern Missouri. Relatively ignored by historians, its utility occasionally questioned by its own sponsoring religious community, the Barrens suffered from an identity crisis throughout its history. That crisis contributed to the ebbs and flows in the fortunes of the Barrens, as reflected clearly in the decades following the Civil War and in the discussions surrounding what to do with the large campus after the final closure of the seminary in 1985.

And yet, the Barrens was arguably the first American institution of higher learning established west of the Mississippi River, and just the fourth Catholic seminary founded in the fledgling American Catholic Church. According to one historian, it may have been the most stable of the seminaries founded before 1833.[1] The Barrens was the motherhouse of a Catholic religious order (the Congregation of the Mission, popularly known as Lazarists in Europe and Vincentians in the United States) destined to establish parishes, schools, and seminaries throughout the American continent, including present-day DePaul, Niagara, and St. John's (NY) Universities. The Barrens trained numerous leaders of the nineteenth-century American Catholic Church, including bishops in St. Louis, New Orleans, Monterey–Los Angeles, Galveston (TX), Pittsburgh, Toronto, and Buffalo. The founders of the Barrens made important contributions to the mission church in the United States. Their experience reflected the difficulties of Old World immigrants in the vast and often bewildering American frontier. Vincentian missionaries described a land of immense spaces, teeming plant and wildlife, often bewildering local cultures, and harsh extremes of weather and climate. They noted the difficulties of missionary work, and sometimes simple survival, in a land far removed from

1. McDonald, *Seminary Movement in the United States*, 56.

their normal means of support and oblivious to the customs of cultivated, Catholic Europe. As its role changed, the Barrens adapted. It developed new works, shed its old functions, and mutated in response to the needs of the Vincentian community and the American Catholic Church.

Despite these facts, the story of the Barrens remains obscure, a testament to the eccentricities of its history and locale. Catholic institutions in the growing cities of the eastern seaboard, including New York, Boston, Philadelphia, and Baltimore, crowd the pages of Catholic histories. Outside the east, New Orleans, St. Louis, Cincinnati, and even Bardstown (Kentucky) eclipse the Barrens in historical memory. St. Mary's of the Barrens suffers from its isolated location, uncertain history, and, perhaps, the modest ambitions of its Vincentian patrons. From almost the foundations of the institution, questions arose about its status and utility. Was it too isolated from the centers of population and missionary activity in the vast Louisiana Territory? Was the locale unhealthy? Was the surrounding community supportive? Was the culture of rural Missouri too foreign to the European founders of the Barrens? Were scarce resources well spent on such an uncertain enterprise?

As the Barrens struggled to survive and grow amidst such questions, it developed a distinctive identity reflecting the interplay of its founders and its surrounding environment. While the larger Catholic Church established itself in the urban centers that drew large numbers of Catholic immigrants, the Barrens remained a singular rural outpost surrounded, outside the Barrens Settlement, by an often-indifferent territory. What Catholic institutions that existed in the region were founded, or re-founded, by the Barrens Vincentians. Resources were begged or borrowed, often directly from Catholic and Vincentian foundations in Europe. The first generation of European Vincentians struggled to accommodate themselves to the unique cultural environment of the area and to grow distinctly American roots in a settlement known for its backwoods American character.

Even as the Barrens developed its unique identity, it reflected significant themes in the history of early American Catholicism. Most surveys of American Catholic history emphasize similar themes and patterns, including the inauspicious beginnings of the Catholic Church in the colonial and early republican eras as it struggled to establish and maintain an identity in a predominantly Protestant American culture.[2] By the middle of the nineteenth century, the American Catholic Church grew—first slowly, then dramatically—in the wake of immigration from Catholic Europe, contributing to the development of a Catholic institutional network and leadership structure. This trend reached its apogee in the immediate post–World War II era, as Catholic institutions thrived and American Catholics began to share more proportionately in the postwar boom. The era of confident progress and triumphalism was challenged in the 1960s by broad cultural changes in American life, which combined with the Second Vatican Council to usher in a new period of challenge for American Catholicism. Over the past fifty years, the very nature and bases of Catholic identity have been called into question in an increasingly homogeneous and secular American culture.

Within these broad and generally recognizable historical stages, scholars have identified significant tensions in the American Catholic community. Many historians acknowledge the challenges of Americanization, as the Catholic Church struggled to define itself in a cultural environment vastly different from, and indifferent or even hostile to, the European Catholic patterns to which most church leaders were accustomed.[3] As the church grew, new problems and opportunities arose. Rapid institutionalization provided, for some scholars, the "plausibility structures" necessary for the maintenance of a growing Catholic community.[4] For others, rampant institutionalization threatened the vibrant culture underlying Catholic resurgence, especially given the growing Romanization of the Catholic Church following the defeat of Americanism at the

---

2. For recent histories of the American Catholic experience, see Hennesey, *American Catholics*; Dolan, *American Catholic Experience*; Gillis, *Roman Catholicism in America*; Morris, *American Catholics*; Crews, *American and Catholic*; Fisher, *Communion of Immigrants*; and Varacalli, *Catholic Experience in America*.

3. On the historical relationship between Catholic and American ideals, see McGreevy, *Catholicism and American Freedom*.

4. See Berger, *Sacred Canopy*; and Varacalli, *Bright Promise, Failed Community*.

turn of the twentieth century. Political differences complicated American Catholic history, as the church struggled to thrive in a democratic, egalitarian society so different from Old World ecclesiastical experiences. In the post–World War II and Vatican II era, scholars detect a variation of the Americanist challenge in the struggles for individual autonomy experienced by increasingly educated, assimilated Catholics in conflict with the corporate, communitarian, and authoritarian tendencies of the official Catholic Church.

The history of St. Mary's of the Barrens parallels the trends identified in the broader history of American Catholicism. The Barrens experienced an early history of trial and hardship, followed by an era of consolidation, and capped by a post–Vatican II period of crisis and reformulation. In the process, the Barrens reflected many of the same tensions that characterized the broader American Catholic Church—efforts to adapt to the new American cultural environment, the challenges of managing a growing institution, and later struggles over individual autonomy in a new cultural and ecclesiastical climate.

In general, the American Vincentians at the Barrens proved readily adaptable to American circumstances. Often against the wishes of the order's Superior General, the Barrens operated a "mixed" seminary, combining diocesan, Vincentian, and lay students; assumed debts in typical American fashion as a means of financing and expanding operations; purchased slaves to work the farms; and commissioned missionaries to far-flung territories distant from any established Vincentian house.

The challenges of later nineteenth- and twentieth-century institutionalization proved a double-edged sword at the Barrens. The growth of the Vincentians in numbers and works, including the establishment of new parishes and schools, and the appointment of a number of Barrens faculty and alumni to episcopal seats, drew Vincentians temporarily away from their motherhouse after the Civil War. Continued growth, however, led to the division of the American Vincentian community into separate eastern and western provinces, with the Barrens restored as western provincial headquarters, and a period of renewed vitality ensued after 1888. In the first half of the twentieth century, the Barrens grew as a variety of activities centered at the site and the educational program was standardized and professionalized. Finally, the diverse aspirations of individual Vincentians in the later twentieth century, reflected in disagreements within the Vincentian community at its General Assembly of 1968/69 and the efforts of regional Vincentian communities to reexamine their commitments in the 1970s, contributed to the final closing of the seminary in 1985.

Particularly germane to the experience of the Barrens, the renowned Catholic historian Philip Gleason has identified important trends in the history of Catholic colleges and seminaries. Gleason suggests that such institutions moved from an initial stage of "boundlessness" in which, despite physical challenges, all things seemed possible, to a middle nineteenth-century period of "consolidation" during which definite boundaries and limits were established.[5] That period of consolidation and later twentieth-century triumphalism was, in turn, challenged by broad cultural changes, the spirits and reforms of the Second Vatican Council, and socioeconomic challenges to American Catholic institutions in the late twentieth and early twenty-first centuries. Gleason also posits that early American Catholic colleges, including the Barrens seminary, "began in a condition that strikes us now as peculiarly amorphous and undifferentiated" from other Catholic organizations, only to move toward greater "differentiation and specialization," resulting in today's complex of Catholic institutions of higher education.[6] The experience of the Barrens college and seminary, from the amorphous mixture of lay and clerical students in its early years to its evolving curriculum and its struggle to attain professional accreditation in the twentieth century, neatly reflects Gleason's model.

Begun as both a dream (Bishop William DuBourg's vision of a training ground for generations of priests in the new Louisiana diocese) and a compromise (planned first for New Orleans, then St. Louis, and moved to the Barrens Settlement when settlers there offered DuBourg land and money for his new seminary in

---

5. See Gleason, "Boundlessness, Consolidation and Discontinuity Between Generations."
6. Gleason, "From an Indefinite Homogeneity."

exchange for the services of resident priests), St. Mary's struggled through much of its early history. Throughout its early years, the Barrens, like other early American Catholic institutions, faced daunting challenges regarding finances, personnel, ecclesiastical authority, identity, and relations with the surrounding culture. The apostolic works of the Barrens were constantly molded by the demands of the day and the needs of an immigrant and minority Catholic population. At numerous times, Vincentian leaders considered abandoning their original outpost and, indeed, a dark period (1866–86) ensued when the seminary and lay college were removed from the grounds of the Barrens, leaving the site without apparent direction or purpose. When the early years of struggle and accommodation ended, new generations sought a consolidation of gains in a more confident American Catholic Church, only to face contraction in the uncertain climate of post–Vatican II changes in emphases and morale, and declines in popular interest and religious vocations, ending in the definitive closing of the Barrens seminary in 1985.

Over the past quarter century, St. Mary's of the Barrens and the American Vincentian community have faced daunting new challenges that required reorientation of community goals. Changes in the social and cultural climate of the American Catholic Church, combined with the declining number of active clerics and the pressing practical need to care for aging priests and religious, have directly affected the fortunes of almost every established Catholic institution in the United States. At the Barrens, unused property was sold or leased, expensive and outdated older buildings were destroyed, and a major retirement center for senior Vincentians was constructed, often in the context of heated disagreements among a community divided over the practical demands of contemporary religious life and a long-established heritage and historical identity.[7] For American Vincentians, the closing of the Barrens seminary marked (for better or worse) the end of a rich and eventful era.

7. See chap. 9 following; Janet, "Decline and Fall of St. Mary's of the Barrens, Part One"; and Janet, "Decline and Fall of St. Mary's of the Barrens, Part Two."

The Identity of the Barrens

The recent changes at the Barrens resulting from these disagreements highlight the difficulty of defining the institution historically.[8] Given its uneven historical development and numerous transmutations, identifying the Barrens has proven elusive even for its sponsoring community. Just what was—and is—St. Mary's of the Barrens?

Founded in 1818 in present-day Perryville, Missouri, St. Mary's of the Barrens is the American motherhouse of the Congregation of the Mission, an order of priests founded by St. Vincent de Paul in 1625 to educate clergy, conduct parish missions, and serve the poor of early modern France. By agreement with the newly consecrated Bishop William

1. St. Vincent De Paul
A portrait of Vincent de Paul (1581–1660) from the frontispiece of the 1664 biography by Louis Abelly. Vincent founded the Congregation of the Mission and remained the spiritual inspiration for the Vincentian family of priests and sisters as they spread throughout the globe, including the Vincentians who migrated to the Barrens in 1818. Canonized in 1737, Vincent is venerated as the "Apostle of Charity."

DuBourg, who recruited Vincentians in Rome for his new diocese in 1815, the Vincentians came to the Barrens to establish a seminary to train diocesan priests for the vast Louisiana Territory. At the same time, the seminary also educated candidates for admission into the Vincentian order, creating a tension common among "mixed" seminaries (combining diocesan and religious order can-

---

8. Janet, "Decline and Fall of St. Mary's of the Barrens, Part One," 177.

didates) in the early United States. To support the seminary, St. Mary's opened a lay college for secular boarders and a day school for local commuters.

By agreement with the Catholic settlers of the Barrens, the priests of St. Mary's operated a parish church on the grounds of the seminary. As an extension of their parish work, the Vincentians of the Barrens traveled throughout the local area and to lands as far distant as Texas to found Catholic mission outposts and new parishes for Catholics long deprived of the services of resident clerics. By the mid-twentieth century, these early mission efforts were continued in the "motor missions" conducted out of the Barrens that brought Vincentians to largely non-Catholic areas in southern Missouri to explain Catholic beliefs and doctrines.

As the motherhouse and largest single community of Vincentians in America, the Barrens served as the first provincial headquarters and domicile for the Vincentian visitor (provincial superior) and, with the division of the American province in 1888, as the central house for the new western province of the order. The extensive lands attached to the seminary became an important farm worked by Vincentian brothers (and, early in its history, African American slaves owned by the community) for the support of the entire establishment.

Over the years, additional works attached themselves to the Vincentian motherhouse—a shrine to Our Lady of the Miraculous Medal in the impressive seminary/parish Church of the Assumption at the Barrens and, eventually, the Miraculous Medal Association, a sophisticated fund-raising organization created to encourage popular devotion to the image of the Virgin Mary as she appeared to the French Daughter of Charity Catherine Labouré in 1830; spiritual and catechetical outreach efforts like the Religious Information Bureau and the Catholic Home Study Service, which grew out of the domestic missionary activities of the priests of the Barrens; a retirement center for the care of retired and debilitated Vincentians; museums housing historical and cultural artifacts collected by or donated to the Barrens over its long history; a retreat center for local parishes and prayer groups; and, most recently, an educational extension campus administered by a local community college.

Influences on the Barrens

In all its various works and manifestations, St. Mary's of the Barrens developed a unique character forged by the interaction among the Vincentian charism, the needs of a developing American Catholic Church, and the culture of Perry County, Missouri. The spirituality of St. Vincent de Paul, the seventeenth-century Gascon peasant-priest who became the social conscience of early modern France, focused on a humble commitment to serving the spiritually and materially poor.[9] "Let us love God, my brothers, let us love God," Vincent famously advised his followers, "but let it be with the strength of our arms and the sweat of our brows."[10] Committed to service and the revitalization of the French Church in line with the Counter-Reformation principles enunciated by the sixteenth-century Council of Trent, Vincent's community staffed country parishes, schools, and orphanages; conducted parish missions and special retreats for ordained clergy; and eventually administered an extensive social welfare agency through its massive headquarters at the old Saint Lazare monastery in Paris. The Vincentians and the Daughters of Charity grew quickly in numbers and influence but remained content to learn from, and even subordinate themselves to, the needs of both the populace they served and the more renowned and powerful benefactors and religious communities with whom they coexisted. Like most other Catholic religious orders, the fortunes of the Vincentian community waxed and waned with the politics of the day, especially during the chaotic years of the French Revolution and Napoleonic era. Indeed, the initial Vincentian mission to the United States coincided with the revival of the order's European status after the fall of Napoleon Bonaparte. Over the course of the nineteenth and twentieth centuries, the congregation in the United States grew dramatically, reaching a height of over

9. On Vincentian spirituality, see Ryan and Udovic, *Vincent de Paul and Louise de Marillac*; and Renouard, "Itinerary and Elements of Vincentian Spirituality." The Vincentian Studies Institute promotes the study of Vincentian history and spirituality through its numerous publications and programs. See a description of its activities on the website of the Office of Mission and Values at De Paul University.
10. Vincent de Paul, *Correspondence, Conferences, Documents*, vol. 11, *Conferences*, 32.

2. DIORAMA OF SAINT LAZARE A scale-model of the headquarters of the Congregation of the Mission of the Mission as it appeared in 1783 by the Chicago artist Jeffrey Wrona. Saint-Lazare was sacked by a revolutionary mob in July 1789 and soon after was taken over by the revolutionary government. The Vincentians themselves fled France and established their headquarters in Rome, from which they came to the United States.

eight hundred priests and brothers by 1960 with responsibility for parishes, schools, seminaries, and universities scattered over four American provinces.

The American Catholic Church remained a minority denomination throughout the colonial era and the early years of the American republic. Widely scattered American Catholic communities faced challenges of social discrimination and the lack of adequate numbers of clergymen, parishes, and schools. American bishops struggled to address these vexing problems, which only grew with the influx of European Catholic immigrants by the middle of the nineteenth century.[11] The Vincentians and other Catholic religious communities were pressed into parochial service by Catholic leaders, and they often struggled to accommodate the needs of the growing American Catholic Church in the context of what they perceived as an alien American culture. The broader needs of the church often intruded, for better or worse, on the development of the Barrens over a two-hundred-year period.

The Barrens Settlement, later Perryville, was a relatively young outpost in early nineteenth-century Upper Louisiana. Founded by English Catholic migrants from Maryland via Kentucky, the earliest settlers of the Barrens secured Spanish land grants in what both the Spaniards and the Americans, after the Louisiana Purchase in 1803, administered as the district of Sainte Genevieve. These settlers named their new home "the Barrens" for reasons

---

11. On the experience of lay Catholics in a "priestless" environment, see O'Toole, *Faithful*. On the struggle of early American Catholic seminaries, see White, *Diocesan Seminary in the United States*. On anti-Catholicism in the early republic, see Massa, *Anti-Catholicism in America*.

3. PANORAMIC VIEW OF PERRYVILLE, MISSOURI
The original Barrens Settlement, founded by Isidore Moore in 1803, developed into the village of Perryville, which became the seat of Perry County in 1821. The largely agricultural community grew from a population of 177 in 1850 to 1,708 in 1910 (shortly before this photo was taken from the roof of the courthouse in 1913), and 8,225 in 2010.

unclear to historians.[12] Later German immigrants accentuated the tendencies of the frugal farmers, trappers, and salt-miners of the original Barrens Settlement. One historian described early Perry County as a "religious haven in the trans-Mississippi West" given the religiosity of its early settlers, both Catholic and (mainly German Lutheran) Protestant.[13] While some early Vincentians commented on the virtues of the Barrens citizenry, others emphasized the isolation of the area and the perceived unhealthiness of its topography and climate.[14] Echoes of this criticism can be detected as late as the 1980s, when a report by a consulting psychologist linked perceived psychosexual issues among the student body to the isolated environment of the freestanding rural seminary, and

12. While sources differ on the origins of the name "Barrens," the historical geographer Walter Schroeder notes that the term was "not transferred from Kentucky," the previous homeland of many of the settlers of the region, but referred generically to grasslands or prairie, like the area of southern St. Genevieve district (west of the marshy bottomland near the Mississippi River) where Isidore Moore led his extended family in 1803/4. Schroeder notes that the term was used as early as 1805 to refer to this community of settlers as opposed to the "open landscape"; Schroeder, *Opening the Ozarks*, 389.
13. O'Rourke, *Perry County, Missouri*.
14. The early American writer/politician Henry Brackenridge described the area of the Barrens as he found it in his 1814 trip through the region as "scarcely fit for tillage, badly watered, with woods of a poor and straggling growth"; Brackenridge, *Views of Louisiana*, 202.

another report by a St. Mary's faculty member called for a new "collegial and collaborative [formation] model that provides a context for personal growth and spiritual formation" (a context, by implication, found lacking at the Barrens).[15]

In a sense, the Vincentians and the Barrens seemed made for each other—the unassuming followers of the humble Vincent and the modest farmers seeking a rural American haven. The relative isolation of the Barrens was valued by some as a benefit in the spiritual formation of clerical students, and its location on the edge of a relatively churchless frontier afforded numerous opportunities for missionary work by priests and students. From its earliest provision of priests to established settlements like Ste. Genevieve and St. Louis, to its pioneering evangelization of southern Missouri, its expansive mission establishments stretching as far as Texas, through its activities as a hub of motor mission activity in the 1930s and '40s and its continued service to parishes today, the Barrens capitalized on its location to become an important center of mid-American Catholicism for almost two hundred years. However, a number of early Vincentians felt drawn to what they saw as the richer missionary fields of St. Louis or Lower Louisiana. Over the decades, most American Vincentians spent at least part of their years of educational and spiritual formation, and often part of their active ministry, at St. Mary's and many expressed conflicted emotions about the old motherhouse and its surrounding community. In a real sense, the Barrens was home to generations of Vincentian students and clerics, with all the accompanying tensions and ambivalence connected to being home.

Of course, the location of the Barrens influenced its adaptation to American culture and mores. Established by Italian and French clerics on the edge of an old French district organized under Spanish land laws, populated by predominantly Anglo-American Catholics and later German immigrants, the Barrens grew into a distinctly American settlement by the middle of the nineteenth century. Complications over the legality of land deeds in the

---

15. MW Province Files—Lipsmeyer, "Students of St. Mary's Seminary," and Brusatti, "Current State of Transition in the Church."

decades following the American purchase of the Louisiana Territory limited land transfers in the area.[16] Contact with overwhelmingly American settlements like Cape Girardeau to the south and the predominance of small farms defined the economic climate of what became Perry County. The priests of the Barrens adapted to these social and economic circumstances, operating a lay school and farm, purchasing (and accepting gifts of) additional properties, expanding facilities, purchasing slaves, and securing loans in a manner quite foreign to their European superiors. The norms of the Vincentian order called for flexibility in responding to the immediate needs of the Catholic Church. That flexibility was evident at the Barrens, where practical necessity often triumphed over doctrinaire principle, and the Vincentians proved adept at accommodating cultural and economic change. At the same time, the Vincentians avoided political and intellectual entanglements, and few were implicated in the Americanist and modernist controversies of the early twentieth-century Catholic Church. In that respect, the spirit of the order neatly coincided with the essential conservatism of rural southeastern Missouri to create an institution that avoided extremes and contented itself with "silent service . . . [and] a low profile in the American Church."[17]

The history of St. Mary's of the Barrens, while exhibiting some unique characteristics reflecting its sponsoring religious order and local community, represents a microcosm of the American Catholic Church and a case study for the transformation of a religious community in a changing world. The Barrens story is one of struggle, hope, uncertainty, and adaptation, much like that of institutional Catholicism and the American Catholic community in general. An

16. To fortify Upper Louisiana against the encroachment of first Britain and then the young American republic, both France and Spain offered free land grants to prospective settlers. After the Louisiana Purchase in 1803, recipients of these grants faced difficulties in holding their claims given sometimes inconsistent measurements, forgeries, and shoddy record keeping. The US government established commissions to adjudicate disputes over these claims. Extended disputes often tied up the use of land for years. On Spanish land grants in Missouri, see Foley, *Genesis of Missouri*; and Reda, *From Furs to Farms*, 60–63. On Perry County, see *Spanish Land Grants of Our Own Perry County, Missouri*.

17. Editorial Staff, "American Vincentian Experience," 433–35.

understanding of the experience of St. Mary's of the Barrens over the last two hundred years provides important glimpses into the life of the American Catholic Church, the Vincentian religious order, and the small Missouri community that the Barrens called home.

Chapter Two

FOUNDING OF ST. MARY'S OF THE BARRENS

> I find myself quite consoled, although I sense that in America great blows are being prepared against us. Those who do not have to go tremble for us, but I feel peaceful and full of courage and confidence that the Lord will smooth out all difficulties.
>
> —Felix De Andreis to Vincenzo De Andreis, Demonte (18 March 1816)

The traditional historical narrative of Catholic beginnings in colonial America and the early republic stresses the hardships faced by a minority church in a generally hostile prevailing culture.[1] Catholics were few and far between in the early United States, even as events in Europe inspired a growing trickle of immigrants before 1830. Joseph Varacalli identified a number of key themes that defined the "less than auspicious beginnings" of Catholicism in the early United States, among them the small population of Catholics and lack of a "developed organizational network of parishes and institutions and few priests"; the hostility of the majority Protestant culture; and the influence of events in Europe, particularly the French Revolution, in driving Catholic immigrants while concurrently exacerbating "even further

---

1. For a brief popular outline of the historical experience of Catholics in the United States, see Brekus, "Catholics in America."

the tenuous situation of Catholics in America." As a result, what pockets of Catholics there were in the early American republic tended to be essentially "unchurched" and free to develop "highly irregular and syncretic versions of the faith," including numerous practical accommodations with their Protestant neighbors. Even so, as Catholic immigrants came to the shores of America—and estimates show that the Catholic population grew to a quarter million even before the great influx of Irish immigration after 1840—American Catholic leaders, often of foreign extract themselves, demonstrated practical genius in nurturing an organizational network in less than ideal conditions.[2]

This was particularly true in the trans-Appalachian West, where the nature of frontier life precluded the development of central religious authority until well into the nineteenth century. As John Dichtl asserted, "Extreme scarcities of priests, scattered parishes and missions, an absence of supporting institutions (e.g. convents, seminaries, schools), and persistently short supplies of financial resources and devotional, liturgical, sacramental, and catechetical materials beset the Catholic Church into the early decades of the nineteenth century."[3] Frontier Catholicism, lacking even the meager resources and urban hubs of the Eastern seaboard, proved even more "irregular" in its organizational patterns and demanded even more of its leaders. European-born priests recognized the difficulties of missionary work on the American frontier. Many of them were trained in the ultramontane atmosphere of revolutionary Europe to uphold high ideals regarding church authority and their own priestly duties. They looked to Europe, as Michael Pasquier noted of French missionaries after 1789, for guidance in their work among what they regarded as "heretical Protestants, lapsed Catholics, savage Indians, and miserable slaves" but eventually realized the difficulty of their position as arbiters of faith in a strange new land.[4] The tension between the high standards of Old World Catholicism and the practical conditions of the American frontier was felt by many

2. Varacalli, *Catholic Experience in America*, 25–30.
3. Dichtl, *Frontiers of Faith*, 4.
4. Pasquier, *Fathers on the Frontier*, 5–6.

priests of the period, and contributed to the growth of a unique American Catholic culture.

The traditional narrative, therefore, has been somewhat modified by newer historians, "untouched (and unscathed) by the experience of the Catholic ghetto," who offer new perspectives on the fortunes of early American Catholicism while still focusing on how Catholics "took responsibility for their religious identity in climates that were culturally hostile and institutionally poor," in the process giving birth to a Catholic community "unlike anything found anywhere else in the Catholic world."[5]

The founding of St. Mary's of the Barrens underscored many of these historiographical points. Its establishment was triggered by the religious turmoil created during the French Revolution and Napoleonic era. Its sponsoring bishop lacked resources, inspiring almost desperate measures to recruit priests and beg materials for the founding of his seminary. The local community that welcomed the new establishment represented a pocket of Catholic settlers anxious for a more regular religious life. The priests of the Barrens clung to Old World traditions while adapting to bewildering conditions. The Barrens leaders, meanwhile, responded creatively in forging a unique Catholic outpost in the wilds of frontier Missouri.

Revolutionary Precursors

The upheavals of the revolutionary era in Europe affected countless individual lives, institutions, and historical forces, including those that conjoined to establish St. Mary's of the Barrens Seminary on the American frontier in 1818. The story of the Barrens begins with the changes in the fortunes of the European Vincentian community, the altered career path of the French churchman William DuBourg, and the movement of Anglo-Catholic settlers from Maryland into Kentucky and, eventually, southeast Missouri.

Before 1789, the Congregation of the Mission, along with their sister community the Daughters of Charity, served as the

5. Farrelly, "Catholicism in the Early South."

unofficial social conscience and virtual welfare agency of early modern France.[6] In his own lifetime, the saintly Gascon peasant Vincent de Paul became counselor to royalty and, despite his humble protestations, superior to a growing community of male and female religious committed to the spiritual reform and physical relief of a society torn by rigid class divisions and economic disparities. From its massive house at Saint Lazare in Paris, the Congregation provided both spiritual and economic succor to increasingly desperate hordes of Parisians.

All that came to a crashing halt in the early hours of 13 July, 1789, when Saint Lazare was raided and sacked by a mob whose attention turned the next day to the more famous storming of the royal prison-fortress of the Bastille. The superior of the Congregation, Cayla de la Garde, fled for his life, eventually landing in Rome where he spent the remainder of his life. The community itself was abolished in France along with most other religious orders that opposed the revolutionary Civil Constitution on the Clergy in 1791. Emperor Napoleon reinstated the Vincentians at the behest of Pope Pius VII in 1804, only to outlaw it once more in 1809 during a quarrel with that same pontiff. The order was finally welcomed back by the restored Bourbon monarchy in 1816 and established a new Saint Lazare on the rue de Sevres on the Left Bank, which continues to serve as the Congregation's motherhouse to this day. In the meantime, the Vincentians established their headquarters at Monte Citorio in Rome, where they conducted missions for the local clergy and weathered the storm of revolutionary and ecclesiastical politics.

Before the French Revolution, Louis William Valentine DuBourg, born in 1766 to an affluent planter family in the French colony of Santo Domingo, seemed destined for a distinguished career in the French Catholic Church.[7] Educated at the renowned College de Guyenne in Bordeaux, where academic success won him plaudits

---

6. On the history of the Vincentians, see Poole, *History of the Congregation of the Mission, 1625–1843*. Five volumes of a projected six-volume series on Vincentian history have been published in English by New City Press; see Rybolt, *Vincentians*.
7. See Melville, *Louis William DuBourg*.

and encouragement toward an eccle- siastical career, DuBourg studied at the seminary of Saint-Sulpice and was ordained a priest in 1790. His work at the *petit seminaire* at Issy earned DuBourg a growing reputa- tion as a talented teacher and administrator, but the arrest of Louis XVI in 1792 forced him to flee Paris for Spain and, ultimately, the young American republic. DuBourg spent the next eighteen years in Baltimore, where he formally entered the Sulpician order and served as rector of Georgetown Academy. He left Georgetown in 1798 amid financial struggles and established the new St. Mary's College in Balti- more, Maryland.

4. LOUIS WILLIAM VALENTINE DUBOURG
DuBourg (1766–1833) fled France for the United States and was named bishop of Lou- isiana in 1815. As bishop, DuBourg recruited the Vincentians for his frontier diocese and directed them to build their seminary at the Barrens Settlement in Missouri. He returned to France in 1826, becoming bishop of Mon- tauban and archbishop of Besancon before his death.

By 1812, DuBourg came to the attention of the American pri- mate John Carroll and was appointed apostolic administrator for the Louisiana Territory, the vast lands on the western frontier beyond effective Catholic administrative con- trol. Disorder reigned in the Louisiana Catholic Church, caused by a combination of the confusion arising from shifting political and ecclesiastical jurisdictions; the intrigues in New Orleans of the Spanish Capuchin Antonio de Sedella, who opposed the new arrangement in ecclesiastical organization brought about by the Louisiana Purchase; the acute shortage of clergy in the territory; and the imminent threat of invasion by English forces during the

War of 1812. In 1815, DuBourg traveled to Rome to explain the situation in Louisiana to Vatican officials. His intentions were either to obtain the resources and personnel necessary to administer this large and complex land, or else to resign his position. He also planned to request a division of the territory for ecclesiastical governance, with Upper Louisiana transferred to the jurisdiction of the relatively new diocese of Bardstown, Kentucky. However, authorities in Rome persuaded DuBourg to accept consecration as bishop of the entire Louisiana diocese on September 24, 1815. Thereafter, the new bishop's focus became recruitment of priests to serve his fledgling American diocese.

Meanwhile, groups of English-speaking Maryland Catholics, dissatisfied with their persecuted status in Maryland in the eighteenth century, sought opportunities to claim western lands after the American Revolution. A number of Maryland Catholic families settled in Kentucky, where they came to the attention of Spanish authorities in Upper Louisiana. Eager to attract Catholic families to their territories west of the Mississippi River, the Spanish government offered generous land concessions to Catholic settlers. One group of Kentucky Catholics, led by Joseph Fenwick, was enticed by Spanish offers and established a settlement at the mouth of Brazeau Creek along the banks of the Mississippi River as early as 1797. Another prominent Maryland-Kentucky Catholic leader named Isidore Moore explored lands along both banks of the Mississippi in the 1790s, eventually securing land grants to an area on the Spanish side of the river (where he and his followers could freely practice their religion and own slaves) in 1801. Moore later admitted that personal differences between Fenwick and him led to his decision to found his own settlement to the immediate northwest of the Fenwick settlement. Moore's land was removed from the river bottoms and featured prairie-like grasslands, ideal for the growth of small farms and a tight-knit community.[8]

"Above all," wrote the historical geographer Walter Schroeder of the cohesiveness of the Barrens settlers, "it was . . . Catholicism that

8. Schroeder, *Opening the Ozarks*, 388–89.

gave them their greatest distinction."[9] The devoutly Catholic Barrens settlers were served intermittently by priests from more established communities in Kentucky, Ste. Genevieve, or St. Louis. One of those priests, the last of an aborted Trappist American mission near Florissant named Marie Joseph Dunand, tended the Catholic settlers of the Barrens before 1814.[10] Impressed by the piety and simplicity of the settlers, Dunand encouraged them to build their own log cabin church and to seek their own resident pastor.

Coming Together

While in Rome in 1815, Bishop DuBourg resided at the Vincentian house at Monte Citorio at the recommendation of Cardinal Lorenzo Litta, prefect of the Congregation for the Propagation of the Faith, with whom DuBourg dealt closely during his Roman mission.[11] The Vincentians served as spiritual directors and faculty for students of the Propaganda, and DuBourg was impressed by individual Vincentians at Monte Citorio, most particularly by the young priest Felix De Andreis. De Andreis, born in 1778 in Piedmont, was a rising star in the Congregation, recognized for his intellectual promise and zeal. He spent his early years in the order dodging revolutionary and Napoleonic authorities and nursing a frail physical constitution, until he was assigned in 1806

9. Ibid., 392.
10. See Dunand, "Diary." During the French Revolution, displaced members of the "reformed" Cistercians from the abbey of La Trappe left France for Switzerland and other parts of Europe. A small group moved to the United States, establishing itself eventually in Kentucky. A splinter group from Kentucky, including Dunand, moved to Cahokia, Illinois, and Florissant, Missouri, in 1809, returning to France after many difficulties and the fall of Napoleon in 1814. Dunand and a few others remained in the American Midwest. See Garraghan, "Trappists of Monks Mound."
11. For details of DuBourg's Roman negotiations and the events surrounding the founding of the Barrens, see Personnel Files, DRMA—Souvay—Rosati, *Memoire sur l'establissement de la Congregation de la Mission aux Etats-Unis d'Amerique*, composed by then-Bishop Rosati around 1839 (original manuscript in the Congregation's Roman archive, copy in DRMA). Rosati's memoir has been translated into English by Stafford Poole, CM, as "Recollections of the Establishment of the Congregation of the Mission in the United State," and published in six installments in the *Vincentian Heritage Journal* from 1980 to 1984. See also Poole, "Founding of Missouri's First College"; and Easterly, *Life of Rt. Rev. Joseph Rosati.*

5. FELIX DE ANDREIS
DuBourg's prized recruit, the talented De Andreis (1778–1820) became the first superior of the Vincentian mission to the United States. Remaining at DuBourg's side in St. Louis, De Andreis never set foot at the Barrens, although he was buried there in 1820; his grave may be found inside the Church of the Assumption.

to the Vincentian headquarters at Monte Citorio. DuBourg met with De Andreis and easily (De Andreis had long voiced a desire to join a foreign mission) convinced him of the need for missionaries in the American Catholic Church. However, the permission of the leadership of the Congregation was required before De Andreis or other Vincentians could join DuBourg's American venture.

Carlo Domenico Sicardi, vicar general of the Vincentians since 1804, sympathized with DuBourg but refused to allow his confreres to leave Rome. Sicardi maintained that the Congregation, intermittently suppressed in France since the Revolution and divided in its internal structure, lacked sufficient numbers for additional works outside its mission activities in Rome. Father De Andreis, in particular, could not be spared in light of his value to the foundation at Monte Citorio.

Undeterred by Sicardi's refusal, DuBourg laid his case before Pope Pius VII. Pius was concerned that DuBourg should remain in his Louisiana post and personally approached Sicardi regarding the transfer of De Andreis and other Vincentians to America. The Vincentian leader insisted that De Andreis must remain at Monte Citorio if the order was to fulfill its mission of ministering to the

Propaganda and conducting retreats for the Roman clergy, a mission personally assigned to the Vincentians by Pius years earlier. The Pontiff relented and sent word to DuBourg that De Andreis would not be available for the American mission.

Still, the newly consecrated bishop of Louisiana persisted, approaching his friend Cardinal Ercole Consalvi, Vatican secretary of state and an influential advisor to the pope. Consalvi interceded on DuBourg's behalf and persuaded Pius to approach Vincentian authorities once more. At this juncture, the persuasive diplomat Consalvi met with Sicardi in late September 1815, negotiating the number and manner of regulation of the Vincentians that Sicardi agreed to send to DuBourg's new American diocese. Plans were made quickly for departure, and on October 14 the Vincentian missionaries met with Pope Pius to receive his blessing and instructions regarding their new mission. The original recruits included Fathers De Andreis, his former student Joseph Rosati, John-Baptist Acquaroni, and students Joseph Pereira, Leo Deys, and Anthony Boboni. While De Andreis remained in Rome until December to collect contributions for the establishment of a seminary in Louisiana and necessary items for the mission, the remainder of the group departed for Marseilles on October 21.

The relationship between Bishop DuBourg and the Vincentians was outlined in a contract drafted by Sicardi and Consalvi and signed by the bishop on November 17, 1815. This contract stipulated that the main responsibility and charge of the Vincentians would be the establishment of a seminary to train priests for the Louisiana diocese, while assuming pastoral responsibilities for Catholics in the territory "so long destitute of spiritual assistance."[12] The order would be governed by its own rules; would reside, as much as possible, in a central house; and would receive assignments from their own superior. Any parishes and missions maintained by Vincentians would be administered by Vincentian authorities, and would be relinquished when a sufficient number of diocesan clergy became available. These stipulations proved significant in the course of the

---

12. "Foundation Contract 17 November 1815," trans. Frederick J. Easterly and reprinted in Rybolt, *American Vincentians*, 451–54.

Vincentian efforts to further their educational and pastoral missions on the American frontier.

The small band of missionaries was reunited on January 24, 1816, at Toulouse, where they rested before again separating for the trip to Bourdeaux. At Bourdeaux, the Vincentians conducted missions and began to study French in preparation for their arrival at New Orleans. By now, the group consisted of eight priests (including De Andreis and Rosati), three students, and the Vincentian brother Martin Blanca.[13]

On April 24, 1816, the group received a letter from DuBourg informing them that he would not personally accompany them to America but would follow later, and announcing his decision to change the episcopal residence from New Orleans to St. Louis.[14] The seminary must naturally be located near the bishop's residence, so the group must undertake the study of English, the preferred language of Upper Louisiana. This surprising revelation resulted in the loss of at least two members of the band, cowed by the prospect of learning a complex new language.

The remaining party, under the leadership of De Andreis, departed for the United States aboard the American brig *Ranger* on June 12, 1816. During the voyage, the missionaries adhered to Vincentian norms regarding community life, with regular religious ceremonies, reflection, and instruction. They landed in Baltimore on July 26, where they remained at St. Mary's Seminary until early September. At that time, they began the arduous journey to Bardstown, Kentucky, the home of DuBourg's friend and confrere Bishop Benedict Flaget, via Pittsburgh and down the Ohio River to Louisville.[15] Flaget advised the route through Kentucky, where the

---

13. For details of the journey to America, see Rosati, "Recollections," pts. 1–3.

14. Turmoil in the Church in New Orleans, traditionally attributed to the Spanish Capuchin friar Antonio de Sedella ("Pere Antoine"), who disputed DuBourg's authority, contributed to DuBourg's decision to relocate his see city. See Carmel, "Problems of William Louis DuBourg, Bishop of Louisiana, 1815–1826."

15. Flaget's life mirrored that of his friend DuBourg—he was born in France in 1763, was educated and ordained into the Society of St. Sulpice, and served as a seminary professor before leaving his homeland with the onset of the Revolution. Flaget traveled to America with DuBourg in 1792 and taught at Georgetown during DuBourg's presidency before embarking on the western missions. He became the first bishop of

Vincentians could remain in preparation for the eventual establishment of a Louisiana seminary closer to St. Louis. Arriving at
Bardstown in November 1816, the group was welcomed by Flaget
into his community at St. Thomas Seminary and spent the next
two years studying English and French, joining in the life of the
Bardstown seminary, and preparing for their own establishment in
Upper Louisiana.[16]

On October 1, 1817, Bishop Flaget, accompanied by De Andreis,
Rosati, and Brother Martin Blanca, left Bardstown for St. Louis to
inspect conditions there prior to DuBourg's arrival. Flaget found the
condition of the church and attitudes of the people of St. Louis less
than desirable, but managed to raise some money and enthusiasm
among Catholics regarding their new bishop.[17] Flaget and Rosati
traveled back to Bardstown after the completion of their mission,
leaving De Andreis at Ste. Genevieve, the leading settlement of the
old French lead mining district just south of St. Louis, to serve as
pastor for the next three months.

While the group was still in St. Louis, a deputation from the Barrens Settlement called on Bishop Flaget. Father Dunand had con-
tacts with the Kentucky bishop, whom he introduced to the Barrens
during a previous missionary trip. Dunand had undoubtedly heard
from Flaget of plans to establish a new Catholic diocese in Louisiana
and of the difficulties in New Orleans that necessitated relocation of
the diocesan see to St. Louis. "When I learned that M. DuBourg, the
newly chosen Bishop of Louisiana, intended to establish his See in
the state of Missouri," Dunand wrote, "that piece of land on which
the church of my good Americans had been built seemed to me
most appropriate for an institution. Persuaded that nothing would
contribute more to perpetuating the good in this parish than an
educational institution, I decided to propose to them that they buy

---

Bardstown, Kentucky, in 1808 and remained bishop when the see city was transferred
to Louisville in 1841. He died in Louisville in 1850. See biographies of Flaget by his
coadjutor and successor, Spalding, *Sketches of the Life, Times, and Character of the Rt. Rev.
Benedict Joseph Flaget*; and Schauinger, *Cathedrals in the Wilderness*.
16. Rosati, "Recollections," pt. 3, 51–52.
17. Rothensteiner, *History of the Archdiocese of St. Louis*, 1:258–59.

the full depth of their land for this purpose."[18] The Barrens settlers offered Flaget's group an old Spanish land grant of 640 acres for the site of the proposed seminary.

DuBourg arrived at Bardstown on December 2 and ten days later began the journey to St. Louis. Arriving at his new see on December 28, he spent the next few months attending to the church and bishop's residence. Another delegation from the Barrens arrived and formally offered the bishop land for the establishment of the seminary. Encouraged by favorable reports from Flaget and Father Stephen Badin,[19] Bishop DuBourg visited the Barrens Settlement in late March 1818 in company with Father Dunand. The bishop found the land, climate, and population suitable for his needs and agreed to construct his seminary at the Barrens. The people, in turn, promised to share in the work of construction and to contribute a sum of $7,500 over the next five years for the maintenance of the Catholic clergy.

DuBourg wished to complete the seminary and bring his prized recruits over from Bardstown as soon as possible. He arranged to have a priest from Bardstown with a background in architecture draw up plans for the Barrens seminary and supervise construction. However, DuBourg was disappointed in his plans for an early completion of the seminary and, instead, sent for Rosati (acting superior in De Andreis's absence) and his band in July 1818, planning to house them in temporary quarters in Ste. Genevieve. Rosati led his charges down the Ohio River and up the Mississippi to the Barrens, where they landed on October 2, 1818, to an enthusiastic reception by DuBourg and the settlers of the Barrens. Arrangements were made to house the missionaries at a place owned by Mrs. Sarah Hayden only two miles from the site of the proposed seminary, hoping that work at the seminary would be

18. Dunand, "Diary," 48–49.
19. Stephen Badin was born in France in 1768 and was a Sulpician seminarian when the French Revolution forced his migration to the United States with DuBourg and Flaget. He was the first Catholic priest ordained in the United States (1793) and was an active missionary throughout Kentucky, Indiana, Michigan, and Illinois. He died in Cincinnati in 1853 and his remains were later transferred to the University of Notre Dame, which he had favored with a generous grant of land in 1841. See Schauinger, *Stephen T. Badin.*

accelerated with the clergymen on site and the students assisting in construction.

Rosati was most impressed by the location and inhabitants of the Barrens. "The missionaries," Rosati wrote, "were very edified by the exactitude with which . . . prayers had been said. Later it was learned that these customs were general, that the presence of strangers did not prevent these Catholics . . . from carrying out those acts of their religion with a holy liberty and independence. They invited their guests, who generally were not Catholics, to join in their prayers."[20] With De Andreis, superior of the American Vincentian mission, required at Bishop DuBourg's side in St. Louis, Rosati became acting superior of the Barrens community. De Andreis conducted a novitiate for the Vincentians in St. Louis until 1819, while Rosati served as acting superior, professor, pastor, and, with the death of De Andreis on October 15, 1820, official superior of the Congregation of the Mission in the United States.

Meanwhile, the missionaries, temporarily established in the Hayden house, attempted to reconstruct Old World seminary life as nearly as possible. When it became obvious that the seminary building was still far from completion, several temporary cabins were built at the construction site to house the growing congregation. Rosati moved his group into the cabins in June 1819. One of the largest cabins served as "the University." One corner housed philosophy and general literature while other sections served as a tailor's shop and "shoemaker's department." The dining room was in a smaller adjoining cabin, but "when the rains feel heavy, several of the inmates preferred to remain dry, though supperless, rather than rush through rain and storm to buy too dearly a scanty supper."[21]

The small missionary band that founded St. Mary's of the Barrens Seminary in 1818 faced daunting challenges. Finally established at an isolated locale after an arduous and protracted journey, forced unexpectedly to learn a difficult new language, their leader ensconced in St. Louis at the service of the bishop, his young protégé made to assume multiple tasks at the Barrens,

20. Rosati, "Recollections," pt. 4, 110.
21. Timon, "Barrens Memoir," 53.

the seminary building unfinished with primitive living conditions, faced with establishing some kind of regular routine consistent with Vincentian norms while also serving a long-neglected
Catholic community—the roots of the Barrens took hold in these
unpromising circumstances. Reflecting the culture of the Catholic
Church in the New World, and the circumstances of the Barrens
Settlement, St. Mary's would grow from these uncertain beginnings to motherhouse of missionaries and bishops over the next
quarter century.

Part 2

*An Era of Boundlessness
at the Barrens,
1818–1847*

Chapter Three
FRONTIER LEADERSHIP

> The growth of the Congregation in America in the midst
> of all these vicissitudes was truly amazing.
>
> —Joseph Rosati (1839)

In two important articles published in the last decade, the renowned
Catholic historian Philip Gleason offered a rich paradigm for the
contextualization of the history of Catholicism in the early American republic.[1] Gleason argued that the early history of Catholic
institutions in the United States (ca. 1790–1850) was characterized
by a movement from amorphous, ad hoc, dynamic growth to more
regularized and differentiated development. Gleason adopted the
language of Herbert Spencer, who described the process of biological
evolution as a movement from "indefinite, incoherent homogeneity" to "definite, coherent heterogeneity" among biological species,
to describe the growth of American Catholicism. Early American
Catholic institutions, including schools and colleges, moved from
a state of homogeneity, in which they were largely undifferentiated
from each other and interdependent, to one of heterogeneity by
the middle of the nineteenth century, when institutions became
more clearly defined and differentiated in their functions and
governance. In the process, Gleason, borrowing from the ideas of
American cultural historian John Higham, suggests that the spirit

---

1. Gleason, "Boundlessness, Consolidation and Discontinuity Between Generations";
and Gleason, "From an Indefinite Homogeneity."

guiding Catholic historical development—and, perhaps, the leadership styles demanded by that spirit—changed from one of "boundlessness," in which all things were possible (or necessary, given the strict limitations on available resources) and occasionally audacious decisions were made by pioneering bishops, to one of "consolidation," in which more careful episcopal leaders sought to manage Catholic growth in a more standardized manner in order to stabilize Catholic institutions.

Gleason supported his main arguments regarding the "boundlessness" of early American Catholic seminary development and the transition from "indefinite homogeneity" to the increasingly differentiated status of Catholic colleges through a brief historical review of several factors influencing institutional histories. Those factors include an early generation of visionary leaders who confronted challenges in an often creative and improvisational manner; a tendency to consider the needs of the church in a holistic fashion and to respond to those needs by adapting institutions according to circumstances, so that colleges and seminaries often became multifaceted Catholic centers serving the various needs of the local Catholic community; an accompanying flexibility of organization and policy resulting in "mixed" institutions combining lay and clerical students as well as various instructional levels, hybrid curricula, and intermixing of Catholic and Protestant students; an ambivalent relationship to American culture, resulting in later criticisms and calls by some commentators for a more Americanized Catholic Church; and the persistence of a variety of frustrating problems growing out of the ad hoc nature of Catholic growth.

The early history of St. Mary's of the Barrens Seminary in Perryville, Missouri, certainly reflected important elements of Gleason's conceptual framework. Founded in 1818 as an outgrowth of Bishop William DuBourg's missionary efforts for his vast Louisiana diocese, "the Barrens" grew from unpromising roots in an isolated region seventy-five miles south of St. Louis to become what Gleason described as a "staging area for the Church's expansion" and "all-purpose center of Catholic life" for the diocese.[2] In the process, St.

2. Gleason, "From an Indefinite Homogeneity," 61–62.

Mary's reflected the "mixed" nature of early Catholic colleges, as it combined seminarians with lay college students, Catholics with Protestants, practical with classical curricula, and various levels of instruction.

The early leaders of the Barrens also reflected the pioneering spirit observed by Gleason, a spirit that necessitated situational decisions combining Catholic institutions in a manner frowned upon by European superiors and emphasizing practical considerations and needs over ecclesiastical niceties.[3] Of course, the dynamic spirit conditioned by the harsh circumstances facing early American Catholic institutions often spawned tension and controversy— over the occasionally irregular nature of seminary studies, the intermingling

6. JOSEPH ROSATI
Native of the Kingdom of Naples and friend of De Andreis, Joseph Rosati (1789–1843) sailed with the first group of Vincentians to the United States. Rosati led the contingent that established St. Mary's of the Barrens Seminary, became superior of the Vincentians and DuBourg's vicar after the death of De Andreis, and served as first bishop of St. Louis from 1827 to 1843.

of seminarians and lay collegians, the relationship between bishops and religious communities, and the differences in perspectives between first- and second-generation Catholic leaders.[4]

St. Mary's of the Barrens experienced both the exuberance and the challenges inherent in this transition from "boundlessness to consolidation" in the American Catholic Church. The French

3. Gleason, "Boundlessness, Consolidation and Discontinuity Between Generations."
4. Ibid., 599–612.

7. JOHN TIMON
The American-born Vincentian who studied and taught at the Barrens embarked on missionary trips throughout the Mississippi River valley and Texas, and became first visitor (superior) when the American mission was elevated to provincial status in 1835. Timon proved an energetic and aggressive leader and was appointed first bishop of Buffalo, New York, in 1847.

Sulpician Bishop William DuBourg and Vincentians Felix De Andreis, Joseph Rosati, and John Timon courageously laid the groundwork for the Barrens, overseeing its early establishment and growth from near-desperation to successful mission center. In the process, they also suffered the criticisms incited by their decisions—decisions that, as Gleason generalized of most early American seminary leaders, reflected a "ragged informality" designed to address the "pastoral needs of the pioneer era."[5] At one point in its early history, those decisions threatened to close the Barrens, and a later generation of American Vincentian superiors indeed opted to remove seminary operations from St. Mary's in the name of stabilization and "consolidation." But, in the interim, especially over the quarter century from 1818 to 1847, St. Mary's of the Barrens experienced an "era of boundlessness" in which talented and visionary leaders established a beachhead of Catholicism in southeast Missouri despite significant practical and cultural limitations.

5. Ibid., 600–601.

The Leadership of the Early Barrens

The first decades following the establishment of St. Mary's of the Barrens Seminary in 1818 were eventful ones for the Vincentian mission and the American Catholic Church. At the Barrens, the early Vincentian pioneers struggled to develop a stable institution that met the often rigorous expectations of the Congregation for discipline and uniformity while also addressing the real needs of Bishop DuBourg's immense diocese. The lack of priests to serve a territory vast in distance but sparse in Catholic settlements, the difficulties in physically building a motherhouse and seminary, problems of finances and debt, the need to maintain Vincentian discipline in a hybrid environment and amid the transfer of priests to service in area missions, evidence of anti-Catholic bigotry in the surrounding territory, and sometimes strained relations with diocesan authorities complicated the situation at the Barrens.

Fortunately, the Barrens community was well served by a number of talented and energetic leaders in the first half of the nineteenth century who stamped the American mission with their distinctive virtues and qualities. Men like William DuBourg, Felix De Andreis, Joseph Rosati, and John Timon achieved heroic status in the history of the Vincentians in America through their efforts on behalf of the Barrens and the Catholic community in Upper Louisiana. Indeed, their work drew the attention of the broader Catholic Church—Rosati and Timon became pioneer bishops in St. Louis and Buffalo and the cause for the canonization of De Andreis was promoted within a century of his death.[6] The clerical founders of the Barrens were among the "first rate men" admired by midcentury observers for their talents and commitment to the American mission.[7]

Bishop DuBourg's main contributions to the history of the Barrens, aside from his initial recruitment of Italian Vincentians for the Louisiana diocese, included the decision to move his episcopal

6. See "Decree of the Sacred Congregation of Rites, 1918," in De Andreis, *Frontier Missionary*, 30–35, for a summary of De Andreis's life and the initial investigations proposing his canonization.
7. Gleason, "Boundlessness, Consolidation and Discontinuity Between Generations," 590–91, quoting an 1860 article by Jeremiah W. Cummings, "Our Future Clergy."

see to St. Louis and to involve Vincentian missionaries in disparate activities throughout Upper and Lower Louisiana. DuBourg was intimately involved in the details surrounding the establishment of the Barrens, from the selection of the site to the layout of the buildings and organization of the curriculum.[8] Indeed, his willingness to intervene in affairs directly touching on the Barrens until his return to France in 1826, for better or for worse, became a recurring theme in the early history of the institution.

DuBourg's uneven historical legacy is addressed by his twentieth-century biographer, who quoted a contemporary eulogy of the bishop approvingly. "In the name of heaven he set out 'as a giant to run the way' . . . if we follow the man, the priest, the bishop, through so many responsible and trying relations, we will not stop to examine the imperfections of frail humanity; they all vanish before this galaxy of brilliant and virtuous deeds, like spots in the firmament swallowed up in the gorgeous light of the mid-day sun."[9]

By all accounts, Felix De Andreis, first superior of the Congregation of the Mission in the United States and leader of the missionary band that founded the Barrens seminary in 1818, was an extraordinary man.[10] From his birth in Piedmont in 1778 to his death in St. Louis, friends and coworkers commented on his intellectual gifts and personal charisma, as well as his remarkable piety and humility. His extant letters reveal a sensitive spirit, alive to the numerous practical demands of active ministry, eager for new knowledge, modest to a fault, and full of spiritual zeal in the mold of Saint Vincent de Paul. According to one account, he was nearly denied admission to the Vincentian order because of his poetic sensibility, which seemed incompatible with the "simple and familiar" routine of normal Vincentian work among the poor, uneducated Catholics

---

8. "Nothing escaped him," Joseph Rosati wrote later. "He went into the smallest detail about anything that could be useful to his beloved seminary," including the shipment of two hundred apple trees to the Barrens with instructions on how and where to plant them; Rosati, "Recollections," pt. 5, 117.

9. Melville, *Louis William DuBourg*, 2:961–62.

10. On De Andreis, see Rosati, *Life of the Very Reverend Felix De Andreis*; De Andreis, *Frontier Missionary;* and SMOB Records, DRMA—History: General Histories, 1906–1968—Bozuffi, "Servant of God."

of nineteenth-century Italy.[11] A more recent assessment of his personality, based on close examination of his letters, acknowledged an "inquiring and restless mind" given to fits of melancholy and depression.[12]

De Andreis became the superior of the small band of missionaries who landed in Baltimore in 1816 ahead of Bishop DuBourg and eventually found their way into Missouri by 1818. When the bishop finally arrived in Missouri in December 1817, De Andreis accompanied him to St. Louis, and he lived and worked there until his death in October 1820. In St. Louis, De Andreis served as vicar-general for the vast Louisiana diocese as well as superior of the Vincentian mission, most of whose members remained in Bardstown until late 1818. Living in difficult conditions in a crowded rectory, with constant health concerns, overwhelming pastoral duties (including the responsibility to teach in both French and English), and a lack of both the books and the Vincentian colleagues that nurtured him, De Andreis managed to build a strong base for both DuBourg's diocesan establishment in St. Louis and a permanent Vincentian house, ultimately at the Barrens.

De Andreis's main concern was always for the development of the Vincentian American mission. While he never visited the Barrens, he remained its titular superior and advocate until his death. His reports to Rome focused on the needs and progress of the fledgling seminary. He constantly worried about the scattering of Vincentians across Upper Louisiana, which violated Congregation rules for community life and prayer. At one level a very idealistic man who could dig in his heels in maintenance of church laws and discipline, he was faced with practical demands that stretched his understanding and patience. He tried to make a virtue of necessity, telling his former superior Bartolomeo Colucci, "I am overwhelmed when I think of the grace of having been called to these missions, and I really cannot explain what I feel about it. I say only that if I do not become holy I would be even worse than

11. SMOB Records, DRMA—History: General Histories, 1906–1968—Bozuffi, "Servant of God," 17.
12. Rybolt, "Three Pioneer Vincentians," 157, 155.

a demon since the opportunities to practice the most beautiful Christian virtues even heroically are so beautiful, so frequent, so urgent, so attractive, so incomparable. In our houses in Europe I would never have had opportunities like these."[13] But he missed the familiar environment, intellectual stimulation, and camaraderie of his former life. In many ways, De Andreis was unsuited for missionary work. He was too fragile, too sensitive, too torn between his commitments to high ideals and his compassion for the needs of the people at hand. That tension was expressed in his ambivalence regarding slavery—which he abhorred but was forced to accept as a practical expediency—and the Indians he wished to serve, whom he praised for their simplicity, innocence, and spiritual capacity but criticized for their primitive habits.[14] Indeed, De Andreis's efforts to balance ideals with practical reality would be reflected throughout the history of the Barrens and the early Vincentian missions in America. It is, perhaps, the primary tension evident in Vincent de Paul's own efforts to accommodate practical necessity while retaining high ideals and spiritual rigor.

De Andreis finally succumbed to his physical ailments and died in St. Louis on October 15, 1820. His death was felt most keenly at the Barrens. "The loss of this holy man could have ruined the establishment of the Congregation in America, of which he was the founder, the Superior, the support, the soul and the life," wrote Rosati. "His great virtues and talents had won the esteem and veneration of his confreres, who looked on him as their father. After his death they regarded themselves as orphans."[15] De Andreis's role extended beyond the spiritual, however. He stoutly defended Vincentian interests in the new American mission, and acted as an important go-between with (and potentially calming influence on) the sometimes impulsive Bishop DuBourg.

DuBourg wrote a moving tribute to his vicar-general in a circular letter to the clergy of Louisiana, calling De Andreis "the hope and

---

13. De Andreis to Bartolomeo Colucci, CM, Rome, 27 April 1818, in De Andreis, *Frontier Missionary*, 209.
14. De Andreis to Carlo Domenico Sicardi, CM, Rome, 24 February 1818, in De Andreis, *Frontier Missionary*, 192.
15. Rosati, "Recollections," pt. 4, 138.

support of the Louisiana mission." The Vincentian historian John Rybolt concurs: "[De Andreis] suffered enormously to help us flourish. His saintly life gave strength to many of his students, preparing them effectively for the life he would never share. There would not be a Vincentian community in this country without him."[16]

Joseph Rosati, born to a noble family in the picturesque mountain village of Sora in the Kingdom of Naples on January 12, 1789, took vows in the Congregation of the Mission in 1808, was ordained in 1811, and became attached to De Andreis at Monte Citorio thereafter.[17] Rosati accompanied his mentor as virtual second-in-command of the American Vincentian mission and, while De Andreis served in St. Louis as Dubourg's vicar, Rosati led the Barrens through its first struggling months. On De Andreis's death, Rosati was appointed superior of the American Vincentian missionaries with extraordinary authority to make decisions on the ground, for "God wants you at the head of that work which he makes it clear is dear to Him."[18]

For the next ten years Joseph Rosati led the Barrens community. Leadership of the Barrens meant teaching and directing Vincentian and diocesan seminarians, serving as pastor of the Barrens church, overseeing missionaries sent from the Barrens to nearby settlements, and supervising ongoing construction activities at the site. At the same time, Rosati was appointed vicar-general of the Louisiana diocese to replace De Andreis, adding substantial travel up and down the Mississippi River to check on the fledgling Catholic outposts of the territory. In 1822, the same year he founded the lay college at the Barrens, adding to his responsibilities there, Rosati was appointed vicar-apostolic of the newly established vicariate of Mississippi and Alabama but managed to avert that assignment. Two years later, however, Rosati was elevated to coadjutorship of the diocese of Louisiana, becoming DuBourg's lieutenant with right of succession to the bishopric.

Despite his additional diocesan duties, Rosati continued to play an active role in affairs at the Barrens, defending the establishment

16. Rybolt, "Three Pioneer Vincentians," 158.
17. On Rosati, see Easterly, *Life of Rt. Rev. Joseph Rosati.*
18. Rosati, "Recollections," pt. 4, 139.

of the lay college, commissioning Fathers Jean-Marie Odin and John Timon for mission work throughout Missouri and Arkansas, and planning for the construction of the new Barrens church. Rosati occasionally found himself at odds with Bishop DuBourg over matters pertaining to the Barrens and the administration of the Upper Louisiana section of the diocese. Their disagreements over the relocation of the seminary to lower Louisiana and the timing of the proposed division of the diocese contributed to DuBourg's resignation as bishop of Louisiana during his visit to Europe in 1826. Roman authorities responded by dividing DuBourg's former territory into two dioceses (New Orleans and St. Louis) and appointing Rosati temporary administrator of both sees. When letters eventually reached Rosati informing him of Rome's decision to appoint him to the New Orleans diocese, Rosati demurred for reasons both personal and touching on the needs of the American Vincentian mission.[19] He wrote to Father Antonio Baccari, Vincentian vicar-general in Rome that, while the material comforts and prospects for success in New Orleans might be superior to St. Louis, he preferred "to eat cornbread and to be poor the rest of my life rather than to have all my comforts in Louisiana."[20] Once again, Rome complied and Rosati was appointed first bishop of St. Louis (including the states of Missouri, Arkansas, western Illinois, and points west to the Rocky Mountains) in March 1827. He remained administrator of the New Orleans diocese until the episcopal appointment of his Vincentian confrere Leo de Neckere to that see in 1829.

As the Barrens grew in these years, the workload increased on the new bishop, but a permanent replacement for Rosati at the Barrens was not appointed until 1830, allowing the bishop's final move to his see city in St. Louis. Among Rosati's last direct contributions to the Barrens was his transfer of land deeds registered in the name of the bishop to the Vincentian community, involving a complicated series of transactions given Missouri statutes forbidding the endowment of a religious establishment.[21]

19. Rosati, "Recollections," pt. 6, 125.
20. Easterly, *Life of Rt. Rev. Joseph Rosati*, 94.
21. Editorial Staff, "Survey of American Vincentian History," 35–36.

As bishop of St. Louis, Rosati compiled an enviable record of expansion and accomplishment. The first permanent cathedral, still standing on the Mississippi River bank, was completed in 1834. Jesuit priests, originally recruited by DuBourg, were assigned to work among the Indian tribes and to staff the male academy that grew into St. Louis University. Orders of religious sisters and lay brothers were drawn to St. Louis to open schools, hospitals, and orphanages. Under Rosati, St. Louis became a beacon of mid-American Catholicism.[22] Of course, Rosati's early recognition of the lack of resources for the Missouri Catholic Church also proved correct, and he compiled an unenviable load of debt that was left for his successor to address.

Bishop Rosati was also an active participant in the national affairs of the American Catholic Church. He helped recruit and consecrate new bishops and played leading roles at the first four Councils of Baltimore. When Rosati undertook a fund-raising trip to Europe in 1840, his former classmate Pope Gregory XVI charged him with a diplomatic mission to Haiti on behalf of the Holy See. Rosati traveled back and forth between Haiti and Rome in an ultimately unsuccessful effort to finalize a concordat with the unstable Haitian republic.[23] During an 1841 trip to Haiti, Rosati stopped over in the United States to consecrate Peter Richard Kenrick (brother of the Philadelphia bishop Francis Kenrick) as his handpicked coadjutor bishop, a move that paid dividends for St. Louis during Kenrick's fifty-five-year tenure as bishop. In the course of his European travels, Rosati also provided invaluable service to his own religious community as mediator between the quarreling French and Italian branches of the Vincentians.[24] His health weakened in the process of these varied and tedious negotiations, and Rosati died in Rome on September 25, 1843.

Joseph Rosati looms large in the history of the American Vincentians and the American Catholic Church in general. Beginning

---

22. See Rahill, "St. Louis Under Bishop Rosati," 495–519; and Rybolt, "Joseph Rosati, CM."
23. Poole, "Diplomatic Missions of Bishop Joseph Rosati."
24. Rybolt, "Joseph Rosati, CM," 401–2.

with his leadership at the Barrens, Rosati displayed the talents that marked him for advancement and prominence in the American Catholic Church. In a recent assessment of Rosati's legacy, John Rybolt credits Rosati with effectively founding the Congregation of the Mission in the United States through his wise practical leadership, broad historical perspective, lively personality, and national prominence. Rosati emerges in this portrait as a "multi-faceted personality who put order and purpose into the Mission."[25] William Barnaby Faherty described Rosati as "an outstanding pastoral bishop" who exhibited all the qualities necessary for leadership in the missionary American Catholic Church: "organizational ability, zeal, order, discipline, dedication and bounce."[26] Rosati stamped these characteristics onto the early history of St. Mary's of the Barrens at a crucial period in the history of the new institution.

In 1831, the Roman Vincentians sent Father John Tornatore to the Barrens to relieve Rosati of his duties as superior. Tornatore was, in one respect, an impressive recruit for the Barrens. Born in Piedmont in 1783, he came from a family that included a number of Vincentian priests and entered the novitiate of the Congregation in 1803. After ordination, he worked primarily as a theology professor at Monte Citorio. Tornatore had a solid reputation for rigorous adherence to the rules of the Congregation and had served as assistant to the Roman vicar-general Antonio Baccari. On the other hand, Tornatore was an already experienced administrator, set in his ways and ill-fitted to adapt to the demands of a frontier mission. He had trouble learning English, and his determination to follow rules bordered on scrupulosity. Nevertheless, Rosati had long sought Tornatore's appointment, and gratefully acknowledged his arrival in a letter to Superior General Dominique Salhorgne. "In Father Tornatore we have an excellent superior for our seminary, a good director for our novices, and a strong support of the observance of our rules."[27] Salhorgne's response rather oddly, and perhaps prophetically, included the "condition" that Rosati "be pleased to keep

25. Rybolt, "Three Pioneer Vincentians," 161.
26. Faherty, "In the Footsteps of Bishop Joseph Rosati," 290–91.
27. Easterly, *Life of Rt. Rev. Joseph Rosati*, 126.

always the high surveillance over all our confreres and that nothing important will be done until after consultation with you."[28]

As it turned out, Tornatore's administration proved problematic for the Barrens. Although he did see the construction of the new church through to completion and commissioned Odin for an important European fund-raising tour, old problems festered and new ones emerged at the still young establishment. The problem of mixing lay collegians, diocesan seminarians, and Vincentian trainees at the Barrens was exacerbated by the new superior's predilection for following the letter of the law. Numbers decreased in the college, to the financial detriment of the entire institution. The American Vincentian mission ran up a debt, enormous for the time, of 60,000 francs (roughly equivalent to $300,000 today).[29] The Vincentian brothers attached to the Barrens raised complaints about the state of the house, and tensions increased with now Bishop Rosati over pastoral appointments and the maintenance of diocesan clerical candidates at the Barrens.[30] Tornatore responded to the internal problems of the Barrens community "with repressive measures" consistent with his personality and Old World sense of order.[31] As a result, a number of brothers and lay students left the community, and even a few priests departed for Louisiana without permission.

Jean-Marie Odin[32] felt these problems keenly, and during his European sojourn in 1835, he conveyed his feelings to Vincentian authorities. At the 1835 General Assembly of the Congregation, the leaders of the Vincentian community acted on Odin's recommendations. The Assembly issued a number of decrees pertaining to the American mission, including the replacement of Tornatore by

28. Rosati, "Recollections," pt. 6, 142.
29. Timon, "Barrens Memoir," 79.
30. Editorial Staff, "Survey of American Vincentian History," 34.
31. Ibid.
32. Odin (1800–1870) arrived at the Barrens in 1822, was ordained in 1824, and almost immediately set out on mission trips throughout southeast Missouri, Arkansas, and Texas. Rosati and Timon relied on Odin greatly while they were distracted by affairs outside the Barrens. Odin was named vicar apostolic of Texas in 1842, bishop of Galveston in 1847, and archbishop of New Orleans in 1861. See Foley, "Missionaries Extraordinaire"; and Bayard, *Lone Star Vanguard*.

Father John Timon, who would become superior of the Barrens and visitor of a newly erected American Vincentian province.[33]

John Timon was born of Irish immigrant parents in Conewago (present-day Hanover), Pennsylvania on February 12, 1797, and moved with his family to St. Louis in 1819.[34] Influenced by Felix De Andreis, Timon joined the Vincentian community at the Barrens, where he was ordained in 1825. After his ordination, he served on the faculty of the Barrens and endured the hardships of the early years at the fledgling institution. Even before his ordination to the priesthood, Timon had joined his friend Odin on mission trips throughout Illinois, southern Missouri, and Arkansas beginning in 1824.[35] Timon's own "Barrens Memoir," written sometime after 1859, recounts his experiences as a pioneer missionary traveling from the Barrens to often remote settlements and enduring the vagaries of extreme weather, dangerous travel, Protestant bigotry, scant resources, and underserved Catholic populations.[36]

Even though he was described as a "retiring, sensitive little man, hardly five feet in height,"[37] Timon earned a reputation as a zealous and confident preacher and capable administrator. After Rosati's elevation to the bishopric of St. Louis and during the unfortunate administration of Tornatore, Timon apparently played a leading role in making the state of the Barrens known to the new bishop and requesting financial assistance and the transfer of the deeds of the Barrens property.[38]

Backed by the entire Barrens community, Timon successfully opposed the order of the General Assembly of 1835 to suppress the lay college. In the meantime, the new visitor worked hard to restore order to the mission, improving the financial conditions of the Barrens through more regular collection of tuition revenue and acquisition of new property and luring wayward Vincentians back

33. Easterly, *Life of Rt. Rev. Joseph Rosati*, 141.
34. On Timon, see Deuther, *Life and Times of Right Reverend John Timon*; and Riforgiato and Castillo, *Life and Times of John Timon*.
35. See Foley, "Missionaries Extraordinaire."
36. See Timon, "Barrens Memoir."
37. *Dictionary of American Biography*, s.v. "Timon, John."
38. Timon, "Barrens Memoir," 66.

to the central mission at the Barrens. Timon's dynamic leadership paid dividends for the Barrens. Student enrollment, both in the lay college and the seminary, increased. An influx of new clerics from Europe swelled the ranks of the Barrens community. Finances improved as well, and Timon gained a reputation for financial acumen (his friend Ramsay Crooks of the American Fur Company provided Timon with important advice) and fund-raising ability. Timon's 1837 European visit yielded benefits in new recruits and 10,000 francs in contributions to the American mission.[39]

Of course, success also brought renewed challenges and controversies for the Barrens and its superior. The recurrent problem of mixing lay collegians with diocesan seminarians and Vincentian candidates continued to plague the institution, as did the additional debt taken on by Timon even as the financial situation generally improved. The personnel of the Vincentian mission was spread thin, especially with the assumption of new seminary apostolates throughout the United States and the maintenance of parishes and missions surrounding the Barrens. Among the most delicate of the problems faced by Timon and the Barrens community was its relationship to Bishop Rosati in matters pertaining to control of the seminary, fees for diocesan seminarians, and the assignment of Barrens personnel to posts far removed from the seminary. Timon alludes to the "painful and trying scenes" with Rosati over these issues, and a compromise was worked out in 1837 that allowed Vincentians to continue service in area parishes so long as they were accorded time to attend to their community obligations at the Barrens. Timon acknowledges that he "refused several parishes which the good bishop pressed on [me]" but accepted others "under rules that left the visitor more free."[40]

Invariably, the tensions created by the dynamic leadership of Timon incited criticisms of the visitor. Timon acknowledged that "several members, almost all of whom since left the Congregation, had greatly misrepresented affairs to the motherhouse." In such circumstances, Timon determined that "a change was needed, and

---

39. Ibid., 84.
40. Ibid., 83.

that, as it could not be done in the way he had wished, it was well to let it be done in the way that providence decreed."[41] And in 1847, Providence seemed to intervene by way of an offer of an episcopal appointment to the newly erected see of Buffalo, New York. Timon accepted, and for the next twenty years he compiled an enviable record of success in establishing Catholic schools, orphanages, hospitals, and parishes and as an ardent spokesman for the Union during the Civil War.

The leadership of John Timon represents perhaps the height of the "boundlessness" phase in the history of the American Vincentians and the Barrens. Timon directed the Barrens and his religious community through a period of growth and national prominence, but at the expense of internal tension and overcommitment. Described by contemporaries as a humble man, Timon's writings, including his "Barrens Memoir," reflect a confidence and tendency toward self-promotion that might be excusable given his reflections on the strides made by his community at the Barrens. As he wrote, "He [Timon] found the Congregation scattered, discontented, almost disbanded, without property but with heavy debts. He left them numerous, and, unless as to what is hinted, possessing large property quite unencumbered, and with less debt than at his commencement."[42]

In his assessment of Timon's contributions to American Vincentian history, John Rybolt emphasizes Timon's American mindset and willingness to adapt to American conditions, the growth in numbers under Timon's leadership that allowed Vincentians to live in community and so preserve an important element of Vincentian life, and Timon's emphasis on education (even at the expense of more traditional Vincentian works like parish missions).[43] If De Andreis provided the spiritual roots for the Barrens and Rosati nurtured its early growth, Timon elevated the Barrens to greater heights and national prominence.

The early leaders of the American Vincentian mission, and especially of the Barrens, conformed to Gleason's model of creative,

41. Ibid., 105.
42. Ibid.
43. Rybolt, "Three Pioneer Vincentians," 165.

dynamic, and adaptive figures who met the many challenges of the early nineteenth century through policies of "boundlessness" and improvisation. Of course, it is easy to romanticize these pioneer leaders and their heroic qualities. As the collaborators on the "popular history" of the American Vincentians observed, "different periods of history called for different forms of leadership: creativity at one time, consolidation at another" and "even the great leaders of the early days made mistakes."[44] But the fact remains that the Barrens was served well at a critical time in its early history by a cadre of talented clerics who understood the challenges of the era and met them with a combination of resolve and adaptability.

An Undifferentiated Institution

Like many other early American institutions, the role of St. Mary's of the Barrens was more expansive than limited. The Barrens was, essentially, what the local bishop—in consultation with the superior of the Barrens, who in this early period was usually the bishop's vicar—said it was. This dynamic identity allowed the Barrens and other seminary colleges in the United States to adapt to the circumstances of a missionary church that was long on needs and short on resources.

The original contract worked out between Bishop DuBourg and the Vincentian congregation and signed in November 1815 reflected both the charism of the Vincentian community and the needs of the vast Louisiana diocese. The "essential condition" of the contract directed that the missionaries would "go out with him [DuBourg] as subjects of the Congregation of the Mission, to form an establishment in his diocese, discharge the different functions appertaining to their institute, and especially to found a seminary as early as possible."[45] While the contract called for the Vincentians to reside as much as possible in community, it recognized the urgent needs of DuBourg's diocese and allowed for the modification of the normal formation program and the establishment of

44. Editorial Staff, "American Vincentian Experience," 437.
45. Rybolt, *American Vincentians*, 451.

mission parishes in accordance with the discretion of the superior of the mission.[46]

Of course, the impatient DuBourg had his own plans for his newly recruited missionaries, which included the elevation of De Andreis, the superior of the Vincentian American mission, to the status of diocesan vicar-general. Indeed, De Andreis filled various roles in St. Louis. He directed a few novices in the episcopal residence in the manner described as a "domestic" or "household" seminary typical of the early American Catholic Church.[47] De Andreis also tended the cathedral church, serving the needs of Catholic families in the diocesan capital. "I am here with the bishop," he wrote, "and temporarily filling the office of vicar-general, pastor, missionary and a little bit of everything. To put it better, I am ruining all these occupations, since I am convinced that I am good for nothing."[48]

Early in 1818, De Andreis wrote to the Italian Vincentian vicar-general Carlo Sicardi regarding the Barrens, "it will be very difficult for me to place the house that we are going to erect in a few months on the same footing as those in Italy. In this country we must be like a regiment of cavalry, or mobile infantry, needing to run here or there whenever the salvation of souls may require our presence. . . . I believe that the Congregation is for the Church, and not the Church for the Congregation."[49] De Andreis's willingness to assume a variety of posts, drawn from his experience of the Vincentian charism and his understanding of American Catholic conditions, set the tone for the American Vincentian mission, the fortunes of the Barrens, and the activities of his immediate successors as Vincentian superiors. Rosati and Timon assumed similar roles, combining their work at the Barrens with their responsibilities as vicars-general of the diocese of St. Louis. As a result, the Barrens, always envisioned by DuBourg as a foothold of Catholicism in

46. Ibid., 452–53.
47. Gleason, "Boundlessness, Consolidation and Discontinuity Between Generations," 597.
48. De Andreis to Francesco Antonio Baccari, CM, Rome, 3 September 1818, in De Andreis, *Frontier Missionary*, 229.
49. De Andreis to Carlo Domenico Sicardi, CM, Rome, 24 February 1818, in De Andreis, *Frontier Missionary*, 192.

religiously primitive territory, was confirmed as more than a diocesan seminary and American motherhouse of the Congregation of the Mission. To meet the needs of a desperately impoverished local church, the Barrens essentially sacrificed a coherent identity in favor of the "indefinite homogeneity" typical of early American Catholic institutions.

As a seminary, St. Mary's of the Barrens pursued the Vincentian tradition of rigor and commitment to uniformity, adapted to the often harsh circumstances of a largely indifferent American culture that offered few amenities or privileges. To complicate matters further, the Barrens operated as both a diocesan seminary, created to train priests for the bishop of Louisiana/St. Louis, and an internal seminary of the Vincentian order, designed to form candidates for the Congregation of the Mission. As a diocesan seminary, the Barrens operated from 1818 to 1842 (when diocesan seminarians were transferred to St. Louis) under increasing tension with the local bishop.

As a seminary of the Congregation of the Mission, the Barrens offered the full range of educational and spiritual formation required of Vincentian trainees—a full five-year program until ordination combining philosophical and theological studies.[50] The Vincentian novitiate,[51] first established under De Andreis in St. Louis, moved to the Barrens in 1820, where it remained until 1841. The Vincentian theological seminary ran a full course at the Barrens from 1818 until it too was moved to St. Louis in 1862. Over the course of its first twenty years of operation, the combined Barrens seminary trained, according to one report, 120 seminarians, 45 of whom were ordained to the priesthood in that period.[52]

One of the most immediate effects on the seminary of its interdependent relationship with the local church was economic. The original agreement with the Barrens settlers included a grant of 640 acres, contribution of labor for the construction of the seminary, and a subscription of $7,500 for the maintenance of the Vincentian

---

50. Poole, *History of the Congregation of the Mission*, 88.
51. The novitiate was and is a period of introduction and orientation to the traditions and spirituality of the religious community.
52. "Notice," *Annales de la Congregation de la Mission* 4 (1838): 92.

clerics at the seminary and attached parish church. But Rosati recognized quite early that the economic circumstance of the Barrens
settlers, who were hardy, self-sufficient farmers but always strapped
for cash, precluded any real financial commitment to the seminary
community.[53] Meanwhile, DuBourg had few resources to spare and,
indeed, complicated the economic problems of the Barrens by his
reluctance to contribute to the support of the diocesan seminarians
at the school. As a result, the seminary was forced to adopt a variety
of expedients to maintain itself, including the use of student labor
to complete the original buildings, the purchase of a mill on the
Saline Creek, and the enlargement of an early garden into a working
farm. Even these measures failed to provide for the needs of the Barrens community, and the Vincentians resorted to the use of credit
to maintain their establishment. Economic necessity, then, turned
a seminary into a would-be self-sufficient agricultural community
and debtor institution.

Economic necessity also influenced the decision to open a lay
college at the Barrens. The college was founded in 1822 and empowered by the state of Missouri to grant degrees in 1831 (making it
the oldest chartered institution of higher learning west of the Mississippi River).[54] Like seminaries, early American Catholic colleges
developed in an undifferentiated fashion and were not the independent, autonomous schools of today. Indeed, Catholic colleges
were tied closely to seminaries up to the mid-nineteenth century.
According to Gleason, "college and seminary developed hand in
hand, and with the strongest kind of encouragement from the bishops. The college half of the arrangement was vital, not only because
it funneled clerical prospects into the seminary but also because it
brought in funds to support the seminarians. . . . But the benefits
did not flow in one direction only; the college-seminary relation-

53. While Rosati praised the fertility of the site and the qualities of the Barrens settlers,
despite their relative poverty, Timon complained about the "tract of unfertile land, 640
acres, that cost $800, *promises* of help for building, little of which were fulfilled; and
this, under a perpetual obligation, which a capital of $100,000 would scarcely pay;"
Timon, "Barrens Memoir," 51 (emphasis in original).
54. St. Louis University, founded as St. Louis Academy in late 1818, was chartered by
the state of Missouri in 1832.

ship was a symbiotic affair."[55] Seminaries provided teachers for the colleges, colleges provided funds for the seminaries. Throughout its existence (1822–66), the Barrens college retained its "homogeneous" character and close identification with the seminary and other works at the Barrens.

Of course, the development of the Barrens was driven by more than economic necessity. The very real spiritual needs of the Barrens Settlement occasioned the establishment of parochial institutions on the Barrens grounds. In Europe, the Vincentians considered their main works to be the conduct of parish missions, clerical retreats, seminary education, and foreign missions. While the administration of parishes was not unheard of, it was generally not a preferred apostolate for the congregation. The 1815 contract with Bishop DuBourg acknowledged that "the urgent necessities of those souls so long destitute of spiritual assistance, require that the missionaries should exert their zeal in going through the several settlements to instruct and assist them."[56]

By the terms of the contract, the Vincentians reserved the right to accept or reject parishes as a community, and any parochial obligations accepted were to be administered according to the will and direction of the Vincentian superior, not the bishop. This demand occasioned tension between the American Vincentians and the local ordinary (DuBourg and Rosati) in the first decades of the American mission. However, practically speaking, the Vincentians recognized the need for the care of souls very early upon their arrival in Missouri, and the Vincentian superior was also vicar-general of the diocese with responsibilities for the broader spiritual health of the region.[57]

Of course, the Catholics from the Barrens Settlement who offered land and labor to Bishop DuBourg for the new Louisiana seminary were motivated primarily by the desire for resident clergy in their community. For over a decade before the arrival of the

---

55. Gleason, "From an Indefinite Homogeneity," 58.
56. Rybolt, *American Vincentians*, 452.
57. These early frontier "parishes" were more or less informal gatherings of Catholics for sacramental purposes, often without a resident priest and considered "missions" by itinerant clergymen.

Vincentians, the settlers had lobbied ecclesiastical authorities for a resident priest in place of the occasional missionaries who visited them from larger frontier Catholic outposts. Construction of a Barrens church was begun even before the arrival of the Vincentians and after 1819 the superiors of the Vincentian mission served as de facto pastors of St. Mary's Parish, with assistance from the other seminary priests and students. From 1819 to 1848, Rosati, Tornatore, and Timon in turn supervised the American Vincentian mission, administered the seminary and college, and pastored the parish church at the Barrens.

The population of the parish grew rapidly, mirroring the growth of the area after the admission of Missouri into the Union in 1821 and the subsequent establishment of Perry County with its seat in what became known as Perryville, Missouri.[58] The growing numbers of parishioners rendered the original 1814 log church inadequate, and the church was expanded in 1819 in the course of construction of the seminary. In 1825, the log church was again expanded with a new sanctuary and a separate log cabin sacristy (known as "Rosati's Cabin" and still extant on the old seminary grounds). By this time, the Vincentians determined to build a proper worship space on their seminary campus, and Brother Angelo Oliva was sent from Rome to supervise the long process of constructing a stone church in Tuscan Renaissance style roughly modeled on the Vincentian church of Monte Citorio in Rome. The cornerstone of the edifice was blessed in 1827 but a determination not to incur debt delayed the construction process. Finally, the Church of the Assumption, reduced to a one-third scale model of Monte Citorio, was consecrated by Bishop Rosati amid great pomp and splendor in October 1837. By that time, the Barrens complex included a free school for the male children of Barrens settlers (supported by subscription and occasional donations to the seminary), a girls' school under

---

58. De Andreis estimated a Catholic population of the Barrens at eighty families in 1818; a report in the *Annales de la Congregation de la Mission* estimated a total Catholic population of three thousand in 1837; and, extrapolating from official census figures, a figure of 2,500 Barrens parishioners by 1840 seems appropriate; Rybolt, *Frontier Missionary*, 179; *Annales de la Congregation de la Mission* 4 (1838): 92; and "Perry County Population Figures 1830–1990," 76.

8. ROSATI'S CABIN
While the settlers and seminarians of the Barrens worked on a larger seminary building, the Vincentians operated out of a number of small log cabins on the seminary campus. Popularly known as "Rosati's Cabin," this structure served as sacristy to the church and still exists on the Barrens campus today.

the leadership of the Sisters of Loretto (1823), and a new cemetery (1836). The once struggling settlement bereft of clerical services had become a true Catholic center by 1840.

The pastoral needs of the territory outside the vicinity of the Barrens also commanded the attention of the Barrens priests. From the time that De Andreis assumed temporary control of the old parish at Ste. Genevieve in 1817, Vincentian missionaries spread throughout the area seeking pockets of Catholic settlement. Rosati recognized the need for Catholic evangelization in Upper Louisiana after decades when even Catholic settlements lacked pastors or missionaries. In 1824, he commissioned Odin and Timon to begin mission trips south of the Barrens, recognizing "that [because] a great many families dispersed throughout the vast and extensive portions of this Diocese especially committed to our care have been these many years destitute of every kind of spiritual assistance for want of clergymen, we have thought it our duty to afford them that spiritual comfort which is now in our power."[59] As a result, the Barrens became the nerve center of missionary efforts in southern Missouri, Illinois, Arkansas, and as far as Texas over the next quarter century.[60]

The pastoral commitment of the Barrens Vincentians did not stop at diocesan borders. The growth of the Barrens under John Timon in the late 1830s brought requests from American bishops for the Vincentians to staff and direct new apostolates far removed from the Barrens motherhouse. American bishops approached the Vincentians with offers to establish new seminaries or assume control of existing institutions. Over a ten-year period beginning in 1838, Timon accepted Vincentian responsibility for seminaries in Plattenville (Louisiana), Rose Hill (New York), Philadelphia, Bardstown (Kentucky), and Cincinnati while refusing offers for Nashville, Pittsburgh, Vincennes (Indiana), Emmitsburg (Maryland), Charlottetown (Canada), and Richmond. "The bishops of this country," Timon wrote his superiors at the time, "as if by a preconcerted move, are offering us their seminaries."[61] For a short time, the Barrens became the virtual motherhouse of American seminaries, although the experience proved relatively short-lived as conflicts with bishops over control and money, the hostility of the diocesan clergy, and the lack of qualified personnel to fill these numerous posts led the Vincentians to withdraw from most of these commitments over the course of the following decades.[62]

By midcentury, the Barrens had also become something of a greenhouse for the cultivation of American Catholic bishops. The erection of new dioceses to administer the growing numbers of Catholics in the country created a demand for educated leaders, and prominent among the candidates for the new bishoprics were Vincentians from the Barrens, beginning with the appointments of Rosati to St. Louis in 1827 and Leo de Neckere to New Orleans in 1830. By the 1840s, Vincentian authorities were engaged in a

59. Personnel Files, DRMA—Souvay—Rosati, "Testimonial Given to Rev. J.M. Odin, CM," 8 September 1824.
60. For an account of early Vincentian missionary activities in southeast Missouri, see Janet, "St. Mary's of the Barrens Seminary and the Vincentians in Southeast Missouri."
61. Poole, "Brave New World," 144–45.
62. Ibid.

9. First Seminary Building

The two-and-a-half-story original home of the Barrens seminary, which was moved from its initial site adjacent to the church in 1850 to make way for a larger brick administrative/priests building. The original building served many functions before it was finally demolished in the 1920s.

constant struggle to keep their best American members from being
co-opted into the episcopacy, even threatening at times to withdraw all their members from the United States if American bishops
did not cease to promote Vincentian candidates for open bishoprics. Among Vincentians who spent time at the Barrens, either as
students or as faculty, and were considered for episcopal promo-
tion were Joseph Paquin, John Baptist Raho, and John Bouillier in
the early 1840s. While these nominations were averted, over the
next twenty-five years, a number of Barrens priests were appointed
as American bishops—Timon to Buffalo in 1847, Jean-Marie Odin
to Galveston in 1847, Thaddeus Amat to Monterey, California in
1853, John Lynch to Toronto in 1859, Michael Domenech to Pittsburgh in 1860, and Stephen Vincent Ryan to Buffalo in 1868.

   Begun as a seminary to train priests for Dubourg's underserved
diocese, the Barrens became, in turn, an unofficial shadow chan-
cery for the diocese of Upper Louisiana and St. Louis, motherhouse
of the Congregation of the Mission (and provincial headquarters
after the elevation of the American mission to the status of an
independent province in 1835), lay college, parish and elementary school, mission center, taproot for new seminaries and bishoprics, and economic/cultural center for the Barrens Settlement.
The assumption of the diocesan vicariate by the Barrens superiors beginning with De Andreis complicated the development of
the seminary, which grew necessarily to meet its own needs for
economic self-sufficiency as well as the needs of the local community, the diocese, and the broader American Catholic Church.
Philip Gleason describes this as the "foothold function" of early
American Catholic colleges, which became the "initial base[s]" for
the development of the broader Catholic community and virtual
"all-purpose center[s] of Catholic life."[63]

63. Gleason, "From an Indefinite Homogeneity," 61–62.

Chapter Four
POLICIES AND PROBLEMS

It was little of books that we learned here . . . but much
of nature and kindly companionship combined with a
certain manliness which was to stand us in good stead
when battling with the rough frontier life of after days.

—William Clark Kennerly, *Persimmon Hill* (1948)

The willingness of the Vincentians to accept the shifting identities of their motherhouse in its early years was reflected in the often-flexible policies adopted at the Barrens. Even before their arrival in Missouri, Bishop Flaget advised the Barrens missionaries "not to attack certain customs of the country, which were not wrong in themselves, nor opposed to the gospel or the laws of the Church, but merely different from the customs of Europe. A certain amount of toleration is laudable and if it had always been observed by other missionaries, many scandals would have been prevented."[1] De Andreis took this counsel to heart and, as mentioned, determined to base his decisions as superior on the premise that "the Congregation is for the Church, and not the Church for the Congregation."[2]

Physical conditions at the Barrens necessitated a high degree of practicality and compromise. The earliest band of missionaries

1. Rosati, *Life of the Very Reverend Felix De Andreis*, 138–39.
2. De Andreis to Carlo Domenico Sicardi, CM, Rome, 24 February 1818, in De Andreis, *Frontier Missionary*, 192.

determined to maintain a regular schedule of instruction and spiritual formation as circumstances allowed, even during their travels from Europe to Missouri. But the Barrens offered few amenities, and the group was forced to improvise as best as possible. In lieu of a completed seminary building, the original band was housed in temporary quarters at the home of the widowed Sarah Hayden. With Rosati as rector, the small group quickly altered the borrowed home "so as to suit as much as possible the ordinary exercises of a seminary," including the transformation of a part of the front porch into a chapel "enclosed with a partition made of interwoven tree branches in the form of a basket, which was coated with well kneaded earth mixed with straw . . . [and] hung with white bed sheets."[3] When the Hayden home eventually proved inconvenient given its distance from the site of the old log church and seminary construction site, the community transferred temporarily to some log cabins nearer the campus.

Meanwhile, clerics, students, and local volunteers alike worked to build a more permanent and impressive multistory frame house for the community. Rosati described the various activities of the seminary band, "cutting, sawing and transporting the supplies they needed . . . rolling, piling up and burning the tree trunks when they were clearing the fields . . . [bringing] stone for the construction of the house and church . . . [making] roofing shingles and . . . in a word, doing every kind of work when their help was asked."[4] In such an environment, new arrivals who possessed practical skills—like the indefatigable Brother Martin Blanca, the stonemason Angelo Oliva, and the physician-priest Francis Cellini—were especially prized.

Even as the Barrens stabilized physically, economic and cultural circumstances continued to demand practical accommodation. Among the most distinctive accommodations made by early American Catholic institutions as analyzed by Gleason was their hybrid nature and "mixed" population. For colleges and seminaries, that meant mixing not only lay and clerical students but

3. Rosati, "Recollections" pt. 4, 113.
4. Rosati, "Recollections" pt. 6, 109.

Catholics and Protestants and various age levels in a manner foreign to European experience.[5]

European Vincentian leaders were already suspicious of the mingling of diocesan and Vincentian seminarians at the Barrens, and the establishment of a lay college in 1822 did little to allay those concerns. The college accepted its first four local students in 1822, who shared the recently completed "University" building that housed clerics and seminarians. As the original building was enlarged, collegians were "immediately and completely separated from the clerics and at length that part of the establishment took on the form of a regular college," with its own rules and regulations.[6] From this humble beginning, the lay college grew impressively, counting 130 students in 1830 and, even after the defections during the Tornatore years and the confusion surrounding the 1835 decree of suppression, 100 students in 1837.[7] Students came from the surrounding area and from points south and east, with a significant contingent of Louisiana students drawn to the Catholic college upriver.

Rosati defended the establishment of the lay college in his later recollections of the Barrens, explaining that "although the principal object of the establishment was the ecclesiastical education of students destined for the sanctuary, still they were obliged to accept other boys for whom there was no other means of education in the area."[8] He cited the lack of adequate local religious and practical instruction available to secular students, and the "shock" of Protestants who complained that the Barrens evidently sought "no involvement with the public good." He portrayed the college as a moral imperative and instrument of service and evangelization, "a means of doing good and saving souls" consistent with the spirit of Vincent de Paul. Only after these arguments did Rosati cite the financial benefits of the college, "without which they [the seminarians] could not have been either accepted or

5. Gleason, "From an Indefinite Homogeneity," 57–60.
6. Rosati, "Recollections," pt. 5, 105.
7. Poole, "Educational Apostolate," 292; *Annales de la Congregation de la Mission* 4 (1838): 93.
8. Rosati, "Recollections," pt. 5, 104.

supported," and the role of the college in providing prospective recruits for the seminary.[9]

Practical accommodations were also made regarding the curriculum of the Barrens college and seminary. Like most European and American colleges at the time, the Barrens offered the equivalent of a combined high school and collegiate curriculum, including languages (Latin, Greek, English, French, German, Italian, Spanish), mathematics, science (chemistry, astronomy, geology), history, logic and philosophy, music, and theology. While Tornatore opposed the teaching of worldly subjects like "music, drawing and gymnastic exercises," Bishop Rosati and John Timon encouraged instruction in these disciplines.[10]

In his history of the early settlement of the Mississippi Valley, former Barrens collegian Firmin Rozier, scion of a distinguished Ste. Genevieve family and prominent local politician, noted the establishment of the Barrens college, which "acquired a great reputation in the West and was conducted by persons of intellect, virtue and learning, who afterwards acquired national reputations."[11] However, William Clark Kennerly, nephew of General William Clark and a noted soldier and frontiersman in his own right, remembered less the academic reputation of the college during his student days than its relative tolerance—"The discipline was not very rigid; we were allowed to smoke at any and all times, and the smoke from the black cigars which we bought outside the grounds was often so thick that one could hardly see across the room"—and the kindliness of the Vincentians (whom he misidentified as Jesuits!)—"It was little of books that we learned here from the good Jesuits but much of nature and kindly companionship combined with a certain manliness which was to stand us in good stead when battling with the rough frontier life of after days."[12]

At the Barrens seminary, students undertook a traditional curriculum of philosophical and theological studies, together with the

9. Ibid., 107.
10. Ibid., 143.
11. Rozier, *Rozier's History of the Early Settlement of the Mississippi Valley*, 126.
12. Kennerly, *Persimmon Hill*, 83.

"study of geography, history, mathematics," and a special emphasis on the Latin, Greek, French, and English languages. According to Rosati, "It was not enough to have the rules of these languages learned in class, but they were also required to practice them during their daily recreations. The rule required that English be spoken at recreation one week, French another, and finally during the third week Latin."[13] Rosati was also known for his enthusiasm for Catholic ritual and music, and "ceremonies and chant . . . were not looked on as trifles or matters of indifference" at the Barrens.[14]

Vincentian seminaries in Europe were noted for their emphasis on uniformity and rigorous discipline. However, according to Stafford Poole, the Congregation's seminaries were less intellectual and academic, and noted more for their pastoral orientation, in line with Vincent's emphasis on practical education suited to the needs of the time and the mission.[15] The commitment to the study of languages and liturgical rites at the Barrens reflects this tendency toward the practical and pastoral. Perhaps one reason why so many American bishops appealed to the Vincentians to operate their diocesan seminaries was this combination of rigor and practicality, which suited the needs of the pioneer American Catholic Church.

The unique situation of the Barrens, and the American Vincentian mission in general, and efforts to adapt historic norms to American circumstances were reflected in Timon's regulations to govern the newly erected American province after 1835. Among the innovations initiated by Timon were slightly later rising times at Vincentian houses, more days off for the faculty (including an official holiday to observe the Fourth of July), and a refreshing concern for the personal health of priests and their charges (evidenced by the demand for more careful preparation of "fresh and nutritious" food).[16] These changes were undoubtedly inspired by Timon's own experience of the lean early years at the Barrens, which a later

13. Rosati, "Recollections, " pt. 6, 110–11.
14. Ibid.
15. Poole, *History of the Congregation of the Mission*, 96.
16. Editorial Staff, "Survey of American Vincentian History," 43.

chronicler described: "The record of those days spells toil and trial and much resignation. They fared frugally, went scantily clad, and endured with extreme difficulty the rigors of the climate, unused as they were to extremes of heat and cold."[17]

Even in a climate of hardship and practical accommodation, Rosati and Timon were careful to note that regularity was maintained in the face of challenging circumstances. "It should be observed here," Rosati later recounted, "that in spite of the difficulties of a rather rough beginning, the discomfort of an uncomfortable and cooped up dwelling, the multiplicity of occupations, the distraction of the works of the house and the countryside, the commotion made by the workers, the care of a parish that was growing daily, all the exercises of the Community, the novitiate and the seminary were always followed in their turn by everyone and presided over by the Superior in person."[18] Timon noted the same of his own tenure at the Barrens, "When he [Timon] assumed the government, and for some years before, there had been no repetition on Sundays [Repetition of Prayer, a Vincentian tradition of sharing the insights of personal prayer with confreres in community], no office of the little hours of the day, no lecture for brothers on Sundays and holidays, no humiliation [confession of faults], no asking to be warned in chapter, no missions, no cases of consciences [case studies in moral theology]. All this, whilst he was superior at the Barrens, was changed."[19] Even as they adapted to the circumstances of the Barrens, the leaders of the seminary adhered to what they perceived as the foundational values of the Vincentian community.

Americanization

By the middle of the nineteenth century, as the number of Catholic immigrants to the United States grew, critics like the New England Catholic convert Orestes Brownson were calling for a more thorough-going assimilation of Catholic institutions into American

---

17. Rothensteiner, *History of the Archdiocese of St. Louis*, 1:380.
18. Rosati, "Recollections," pt. 6, 108.
19. Timon, "Barrens Memoir," 105.

culture.[20] Gleason cited the campaign for Americanization waged by *Brownson's Quarterly Review*, and especially a series of articles pertaining to American Catholic seminaries, as characteristic of the midcentury era of "consolidation" and its critique of existing Catholic culture.[21] In those articles, liberal American Catholic clergymen like William J. Barry and Jeremiah W. Cummings advocated for specific reforms in seminary education, including the abandonment of the old "mixed" college-seminaries, the establishment of "minor" (i.e., college prep or high school) seminaries to increase American vocations, and the "the importance of developing a national clergy—a body of Catholic clergymen whose American birth and education would constitute the ideal preparation for pastoral service to an American flock."[22] For Gleason, this reform campaign, highlighting the issue of Americanization as a prominent element in the historical development of Catholic institutions, represented a shift from the era of boundlessness to one of stabilization and consolidation. The degree to which institutions like the Barrens were, or were becoming, "American," therefore, became a crucial issue in the story of early American Catholicism.

The earliest missionaries at the Barrens expressed a broad curiosity, and confusion, about their new American homeland. De Andreis was amazed by the climate and culture he encountered in the New World. His letters describe a magnificent and often bewildering land of immense space, abundant wildlife (including such exotic specimens as rattlesnakes and ticks), extremes of climate and weather, expensive essentials, indifferent Protestant cultures, and treacherous travel.[23] Others, especially among the later group

---

20. See Carey, *Orestes A. Brownson*; McGreevy, *Catholicism and American Freedom*; and Gleason, "Boundlessness, Consolidation, and Discontinuity Between Generations," 588–92.
21. Gleason, "Boundlessness, Consolidation, and Discontinuity Between Generations," 588–92.
22. Ibid., 590. Cummings argued that "it requires a great effort and unusual grace on the part of an American to feel at home with a clergyman different from himself not only in religion but in his feelings, interests, manners and even in his speech"; Cummings, "Our Future Clergy," 503–4.
23. De Andreis to Francesco Antonio Baccari, CM, Pro-Vicar General, Rome, 26 April 1819, in De Andreis, *Frontier Missionary*, 280.

of recruits to the Barrens, struggled to learn the intricacies of the English language and American manners. The resulting tensions provoked sporadic outbreaks of Protestant bigotry in the local community, enflamed by cultural as well as theological differences. Timon's memoirs abounded with stories of Protestant antipathy during his frequent missionary trips outside the Barrens.

The tension was reflected most keenly in the attitudes of the brothers attached to the Barrens, who proved indispensable for their efforts in building the Barrens and securing the economic foundations of the house. The work of the brothers brought them into close contact with the local Barrens population (and, hence, the temper of the secular culture of the day). A group of brothers believed that the Barrens community should have left Missouri for Lower Louisiana in 1825, when DuBourg proposed a new and apparently richer locale for the seminary. Under Timon's leadership, they continued to complain about the extremes of climate, the infertility of the soil, and the poor living conditions at the Barrens.[24] The discontent of the brothers was undoubtedly stirred by the democratic climate of the New World, and some among them came to resent the dominance of their ordained confreres and felt that their work, and input into community affairs and decisions, was underappreciated.

But these cultural tensions were tempered by three important factors in the history of the Barrens—the prudence inherent in Vincentian spirituality, the history and influence of the Barrens Settlement, and the leadership of American-born John Timon. Vincentian spirituality emphasized humility and deference, qualities—alongside willingness to sacrifice for the advancement of the apostolate—that inspired an acceptance of the prevailing environment and cultural accommodation. "Vincentian formation once put a high value on the virtue of prudence," in the words of the editors of *The American Vincentians*, "defined not in its classic scholastic sense of choosing appropriate means to a specified end but with a strong connotation of caution bordering on timidity."[25]

24. Editorial Staff, "Survey of American Vincentian History," 34.
25. Editorial Staff, "American Vincentian Experience," 436.

Such values would not have inspired active resistance to American norms and cultures, despite personal confusion and bewilderment.

The culture of the surrounding community also contributed to the assimilation of the seminary. The Barrens Settlement (later Perryville) was a relatively young outpost when the Vincentians arrived in 1818. The early inhabitants of the Barrens Settlement were first and foremost farmers, generally disinterested in the lead mining activities to the north outside the old village of Ste. Genevieve. "Apparently," as Walter Schroeder observed, "not a single Barrens resident moved to the mining communities. . . . Neither did these agriculturists get involved in fur or river trade or in salt making. Their commitment to agriculture with slaves was near total."[26] The other distinguishing characteristic of the early Barrens settlers was their Catholicism. For these Catholic farmers, "the seminary and lay college were not just educational institutions, but also, in the dearth of merchants and other stores between Ste. Genevieve and Jackson, became a commercial center and the true central place of the Barrens, before the county seat of Perryville functioned as one [ca. 1826]."[27] Later German immigrants (Catholic and Lutheran) to the area accentuated the conservative tendencies of the farming community.

Finally, the powerful influence of John Timon directed the process of Americanization at the Barrens. Born in rural Pennsylvania in 1797 and elevated to the episcopacy by 1847, Timon's story is in many ways a very American tale. As superior of the Barrens, Timon focused on adapting "European Vincentian ways to the American scene."[28] Timon's own account of his leadership of the Barrens highlights the drama of his missionary trips through rural mid-America and his efforts to capitalize on the American economic boom to improve the finances of his community. He also proved willing to accept new apostolates far removed from the Barrens, so that the Vincentians became a truly America-wide religious congregation. John Rybolt's assessment of Timon speaks to his Americanizing propensities:

26. Schroeder, *Opening the Ozarks*, 392.
27. Ibid., 393.
28. Rybolt, "Three Pioneer Vincentians," 163.

It is clear to me that Timon's great contribution to the
growth of the Vincentian community was that he was
American born, and that consequently his decisions
arose from an American mindset. Although familiar with
European models and with the spiritual tradition medi-
ated through De Andreis and Rosati, Timon, even more
than Rosati, acknowledged the need to adapt to American life. The province became American, and gradually
grew in numbers of other American-born members.[29]

The combination of traditional Vincentian spirituality, close
contact with the distinctly American Catholic population of the
Barrens Settlement, and the influence of John Timon facilitated the
process of cultural assimilation at the Barrens. Of course, tensions
and inconsistencies persisted as American Vincentians sometimes
struggled to accommodate American circumstances and values
in areas like the maintenance of community life, daily schedule,
travel, dress, use of tobacco and alcohol, finances, and personal values.[30] Those accommodations and accompanying tensions played
out over the broader course of American Vincentian history and
"would not be totally exorcised until after Vatican II."[31] However,
during the early history of the Barrens, the spirit of the Congregation neatly coincided with the essential conservatism of rural southeastern Missouri to create an institution that avoided extremes and
contented itself with "silent service . . . [and] a low profile in the
American Church."[32]

Persistent Problems

Dynamic leadership, shifting identities, flexible policies, and a
propensity toward Americanization did not, of course, prevent
problems from arising at the early Barrens. While some of these
problems were systemic, owing to the chronically desperate early

29. Ibid., 165.
30. Editorial Staff, "American Vincentian Experience," 446.
31. Ibid., 448.
32. Ibid., 436.

circumstances of the institution, others were more particular, reflecting the eccentricities of the setting. Most, however, could generally be subsumed under three categories: finances, personnel, and authority. The early Barrens was plagued by a chronic lack of funds, a shortage of well-trained and adaptable priests and brothers, and tensions over the exercise of jurisdictional authority and external demands. As Gleason observed of other early American Catholic institutions, these problems often spawned additional concerns as leaders responded to pressing needs with a "ragged informality" that exacerbated internal and external pressures for conformity or additional compromise.[33]

The early American Vincentian mission was begun on "a hope and a prayer" as DuBourg scoured Europe for missionaries and resources.[34] The original contributions from European sources sustained the initial band of missionaries for a time, but the mounting expenses of establishing a Catholic foothold in largely non-Catholic frontier territory proved daunting. The original patrimony provided by the Barrens settlers, including the 640-acre land grant and promise of labor, was complicated by contractual and circumstantial factors, as well as the reality of the lack of capital in the Barrens community.[35] DuBourg was unable to help substantially and further complicated matters by his failure to compensate the Vincentians for the maintenance of diocesan seminarians.[36]

Given the conditions, the early seminary struggled to sustain itself economically through its agricultural activities and commercial relations with the surrounding community. As a result, the Barrens community depended on fund-raising efforts, often undertaken by the missionaries on return trips to Europe. Vincentian superiors in Italy proved helpful, as did grants from the Society for the Propagation of the Faith (established in Lyons in 1822), the

33. Gleason, "Boundlessness, Consolidation, and Discontinuity Between Generations," 600.
34. All early American Catholic seminaries faced severe financial problems, leading one historian of the movement to characterize their history as "a story of constant struggle against poverty"; McDonald, *Seminary Movement in the United States*, 56.
35. Editorial Staff, "Survey of American Vincentian History," 35–36.
36. Timon, "Barrens Memoir," 51.

Austrian Leopoldine Society (established in 1829), and the Bavarian Ludwig *Missionsverein* (established in 1838).[37] Even these efforts, and the steady growth of the Barrens under Timon's leadership, proved insufficient, and the subsequent recourse to borrowing money spurred concerns both within the Barrens and among European Vincentian superiors. The relative impoverishment of the community incited recurrent complaints about the inhospitable nature of the area and the need to relocate elsewhere.

The chronic lack of funds to support the Barrens was accompanied by a similar dearth of personnel to maintain the many ongoing works of the seminary-college-parish-mission center. In his memoirs, Rosati recalled the early days at the Barrens:

> The country was new. The diocese, even newer than the country, had just been born. Everything was still to be created, everything had to be organized. There was a certain number of parishes to provide for, others to be established, and missionaries to be sent to visit the Catholics scattered over those vast regions. There was, then, a great need for workers and it was impossible to bring together all the priests of the Congregation in the same place. Mr. Rosati was all alone at the seminary.[38]

New members from Europe occasionally augmented the ranks of the motherhouse, with a contingent including the invaluable Father Francis Cellini arriving as early as January 1819.[39] By 1828 the Barrens community, according to Rosati, numbered four priests, eight brothers, sixteen seminarians, and thirty college students. But, before his departure in 1826, DuBourg continually lured missionaries away from the Barrens (especially for Lower Louisiana), as

37. Rybolt, "Seminary Education in the Louisiana Territory," 6.
38. Rosati, "Recollections," pt. 4, 118.
39. Francis Cellini was a native of Ascoli in east central Italy and a recently ordained Vincentian priest when he traveled to America. Priest, physician, agronomist (he planted vegetable gardens and fruit orchards at the Barrens), amateur architect (he designed the parish church in Fredericktown, Missouri), and missionary pastor (in Missouri, Illinois, and Louisiana), Cellini later became Rosati's vicar-general for the diocese of St. Louis. He died in 1849.

did Rosati on becoming bishop in 1827. Rosati acknowledged that the comings and goings of Vincentians from the Barrens "always caused a kind of disorder in the community and some distressing changes."[40]

Growing numbers of European clergymen sometimes presented different challenges. Early American bishops recognized the problems caused by "missionary adventurers" and "floaters" who moved, like clerical mercenaries, from one institution or diocese to another, or, even worse, immoral priests who created scandals in the nineteenth-century Catholic Church.[41] The Barrens was indirectly touched by one such scandalous figure. Angelo Inglesi was ordained by DuBourg in 1820 and was rapidly promoted in the Louisiana diocese. By 1823, it was discovered that Inglesi was an impostor with no verifiable clerical education who had married in Quebec and was often seen at social functions, even after his ordination, in lay garb behaving inappropriately. DuBourg was devastated by these revelations, which were uncovered by Bertrand Martial, one of the bishop's harshest critics in the New Orleans Church.[42]

More commonly than scandal, some Barrens clerics proved a poor fit for their positions. Angelo Boccardo was sent to America to relieve Rosati of his burden as superior of the Barrens in 1827, but, on disembarking at the port of New Orleans with $2,000 in contributions for the seminary, dropped his luggage in the Mississippi River and returned to Europe in distress despite Rosati's desperate pleas to remain.[43] As mentioned, when a permanent replacement for Rosati did arrive in the person of John Tornatore in 1830, his scrupulous adherence to the letter of the law caused disruption in the house and fanned discontent among some Barrens residents. Other new arrivals proved simply eccentric or naïve to the conditions of the New World. The Milanese priest John Rosetti arrived at the Barrens in 1819 with a small group of protégés intent on establishing their own missionary order, only to abandon their

---

40. Rosati, "Recollections," pt. 6, 119.
41. Gleason, "Boundlessness, Consolidation, and Discontinuity Between Generations," 593, 603.
42. Melville, *Louis William DuBourg*, 2:585–92, 745.
43. Easterly, *Life of Rt. Rev. Joseph Rosati*, 97.

plan within a short time.[44] Finally, in a near-comic interlude, one young "subdeacon, very pious but also very attached to his own opinion, believed that he had for a long time been favored with supernatural lights" and "raised up by God to go convert the Jews in Asia," only to be disabused of his notions by his more practical-minded superiors.[45]

Authority issues also complicated business at the Barrens. Clashes with the bishop over the assignment of Barrens priests to missions and parishes were common, as were attempts to move the diocesan seminary away from the Barrens. A major disagreement occurred in 1825, when DuBourg proposed the establishment of a new seminary in Lower Louisiana. The idea of a seminary for the southern part of the territory was not new, but the struggles of the Barrens complicated the opening of a new institution that might draw scarce resources from the Missouri seminary. Rosati was surprised when Bishop DuBourg "proposed to his coadjutor that he [Rosati] go there himself with the entire Community and leave one priest with some young cleric at the Barrens." DuBourg argued that Lower Louisiana represented "a very much more important" part of the diocese than Missouri, and could support a seminary and the Vincentian mission with greater ease.[46] Rosati answered that abandoning the Barrens after its early struggles to establish itself would devastate the Catholic Church in Upper Louisiana. Vincentian authorities successfully opposed the move, citing the danger of running up additional debt to establish a new seminary, the small number of priests that made it impossible to maintain two houses, and the injustice of abandoning Upper Lousiana, "a country where there is such immense fruit to harvest."[47]

The impulsive DuBourg was disappointed by the Vincentians' refusal to leave the Barrens for the richer state of Louisiana. "I have said Fiat to the deliberation of your Council. Having few years to

44. Rosati, "Recollections," pt. 4, 128. Five members of the band eventually joined the Vincentian community, including three ordained priests and two brothers.
45. Ibid., 126–28. The young man "left the diocese at the beginning of the year 1820."
46. Rosati, "Recollections" pt. 6, 115–16.
47. Melville, *Louis William DuBourg*, 1:87.

live I will probably not see the extinction of the Diocese. And if I see it, I will have nothing for which to reproach myself."[48] The bishop's efforts to bolster Lower Louisiana, given the agreement a year earlier to divide the diocese by 1827, fueled suspicions that he was systematically sabotaging prospects for the church in Upper Louisiana in favor of the southern portion of his vast diocese, which he coveted for himself. While DuBourg eventually relented, the disagreement spilled over into larger debates about the wisdom and timing of the division of the Louisiana Territory into two dioceses. Rosati hoped the creation of a separate St. Louis diocese would enhance efforts to keep Vincentians in central houses close to the Barrens. DuBourg argued that the timing was inopportune given the lack of priests and that the division must be postponed.[49]

As early as 1838, Bishop Rosati proposed to move the diocesan seminarians to a location in St. Louis while keeping students studying for the Vincentian community at the Barrens. The establishment of a St. Louis seminary would accomplish several goals: first, the problem of financing seminarians would be addressed through the construction of rental houses on property purchased by the bishop in the Soulard area of southern St. Louis; second, the interminable problem of "mixing" diocesan and Vincentian seminarians (Rosati admitted in a private letter that such intermingling "brings about the loss of vocation for a good number of young ecclesiastics") would be resolved through the removal of diocesan students; and third, the location of a seminary in St. Louis would fill the need for additional priests in the city.[50] The move also reflected a sentiment, privately repeated by Rosati's coadjutor bishop Peter Kenrick, that, "As an Ecclesiastical Seminary it [the Barrens] has proven an entire failure, and this is felt by none more sensibly than by the Superiors themselves."[51] Rosati extolled the virtues of his seminary plan in a pastoral letter in April 1839, but financial considerations and the bishop's departure for

---

48. Ibid., 2:744.
49. Easterly, *Life of Rt. Rev. Joseph Rosati*, 89.
50. Ibid., 177.
51. Rybolt, "Kenrick's First Seminary," 141.

Baltimore and Europe, leaving behind mounting debts and the ruins of construction for the new establishment, doomed Rosati's dream. Kenrick took up the challenge, however, and by October 1842 transferred diocesan seminarians and some Vincentian clerics from the Barrens to the Soulard Addition. In 1848, the seminary was relocated to a site farther south in the Carondelet district and for the next ten years the school was run under diocesan control without Vincentian involvement. By 1859, however, the Carondelet seminary was closed and St. Louis diocesan seminarians were transferred to St. Vincent's College in Cape Girardeau, where they remained until the opening of the new Kenrick Seminary at 19th and Cass Street in 1893.[52] These moves left the Barrens as a purely Vincentian establishment with an attached lay college, although the establishment of St. Vincent's College in Cape Girardeau in 1843 under Vincentian control was originally meant to divert lay students from the Barrens.

Deliberations over the fortunes of the Barrens and the relocation of seminarians and/or lay collegians elsewhere were calculated partly to allay the continual fears of European Vincentian superiors, who opposed the "mixed state" of the Barrens. In 1835, the General Assembly of the Congregation issued a number of decrees pertaining to the American mission: 1. suppression of the lay college at the Barrens given its declining numbers and inherent problems of discipline and intermingling with seminarians; 2. a requirement that the St. Louis diocese pay fees for each diocesan seminarian at the Barrens; 3. construction of a separate building for the Vincentian community to minimize the intermingling of candidates for diocesan and Vincentian orders; 4. limits to the number and locale of missionary priests sent from the Barrens and requirements that they adhere to Community rules as members of the sole Vincentian house in America; and 5. replacement of Tornatore by Father John Timon, who would become superior of the Barrens and visitor of the entire American Vincentian mission.[53]

The decrees of the General Assembly triggered a crisis both at

---

52. Ibid., 154–55.
53. Easterly, *Life of Rt. Rev. Joseph Rosati*, 141.

the Barrens and in St. Louis, where Rosati objected strenuously to the financial impositions required for education of diocesan seminarians. Timon accepted the appointment as superior, but delayed the implementation of the other decrees, especially regarding the fate of the Barrens college. The newly appointed superior general of the Congregation, Jean-Baptiste Nozo, finally lifted the decree of suppression, relented on payment of diocesan fees for seminarians, and modified restrictions on the activities of college faculty-seminarians.

Finally, as we have seen, American church leaders began what seemed an incessant campaign to draw Vincentians away from the Barrens to assume control of other diocesan seminaries or to accept appointments as bishops of new dioceses. Rosati and Timon were hard-pressed to respond to these requests and to balance the health of the Barrens against the broader needs of the American Catholic Church. Despite its relative isolation and lack of resources, the early Barrens faced numerous demands from its local bishop, European superiors, and American church leaders.

Conclusion

The era of "indefinite homogeneity" at the Barrens ended by 1850. Timon's elevation to the leadership of the new American province encouraged growth at the Barrens, but also led to the thinning out of Vincentian personnel as the order assumed responsibility for new seminaries throughout the United States. The transfer of diocesan seminarians to St. Louis in 1842, and of some lay collegians to St. Vincent's College in Cape Girardeau in 1843, signaled the end of an era at the Barrens. Timon's own elevation to the bishopric of Buffalo in 1847 marked the definitive finale of the "era of boundlessness" at St. Mary's of the Barrens, when the Vincentian community built a seminary, lay college, parish church, and local mission center in relative isolation and against tremendous odds. As the early American republic grew and the Louisiana Territory was divided into numerous states, with waves of Old World immigrants provoking a corresponding nativism, as financial schemes were born and often died on the vine, and as American culture began a fragmentation into sectional divides, St. Mary's of the Barrens developed into a frontier Catholic center with various interconnected works in the spirit of American boundlessness. The first thirty years of the Barrens witnessed heroic efforts in the face of often overwhelming cultural, physical, and financial challenges. Felix de Andreis, Joseph Rosati, and John Timon—spiritual father, practical leader, and native son—established the Barrens as a haven of Catholic possibilities in the wilds of frontier Missouri.

Part 3

An Era of Fragmentation and Consolidation, 1847–1888

Chapter Five
Second-Generation Leadership

> It cost much to sunder the ties of affectionate attachment
> and hallowed recollection that bound us to the old
> homestead, the cradle and nursery of our community in
> this country.
>
> —S. V. Ryan (1862)

After 1840, waves of European immigration and westward expansion fueled broad demographic and economic growth in the United States. At the same time, divisions deepened over issues of slavery, states' rights, and paths to economic development, leading eventually to the bloody Civil War. After that conflict, the United States continued its impressive growth in the context of lingering sectional and cultural differences that would define the country for the next century.[1]

The American Catholic Church experienced similar trends of growth and division. A large number of new immigrants, from places like France, southern Germany, Ireland, and Italy, were Catholic. The growth in the Catholic population led to standardization of Catholic governance and institutional development, moving the church away from its former "boundlessness" toward more

---

1. See Wineapple, *Ecstatic Nation*, for a lively account of this tumultuous era in American history, focusing on national expansion, the events leading to the Civil War, and shifting social/cultural expectations that finally occasioned compromise among political factions and geographical sections.

clearly defined roles and models. Growth, however, also spawned reaction, from the broader non-Catholic population in the form of nativism and internally in the development of Catholic divisions, which deepened during the Civil War. Patrick Carey acknowledges these tensions: "From the rise of Andrew Jackson to the end of the Civil War, American society experienced a new age of intellectual ferment, social and religious reform, economic and cultural disruption, conflicts over slavery, and religious and racial antagonisms that challenged the country's republican fiber and tested its own ideals."[2] These broader American tensions contributed to a "series of crises" within the American Catholic community. The church grew from a small minority sect to a large denomination built around immigrant masses and centralized through increasingly elaborate parochial and ecclesiastical structures. At the same time, American Catholics confronted the challenges of internal development and external prejudice.[3]

The pattern of growth and fragmentation evident in American and Catholic development since the middle decades of the nineteenth century was reflected in the historical experience of Perry County, Missouri, and St. Mary's of the Barrens. Perry County grew, fueled by an influx of French Catholics and German Lutherans. The Barrens Settlement gave way to the village of Perryville after the incorporation of the county in 1821.[4] The county reflected broader American and border state divisions in its political tendencies.[5] During the Civil War, the local newspaper favored preservation of the Union and, while generally absent of real warfare, nearby troop

---

2. Carey, *Catholics in America*, 27.
3. Ibid.
4. According to US Census figures, Perry County grew from a total population of 5,760 (including 778 slaves) in 1840 to 13,237 in 1890. The population of the city of Perryville was first recorded in the census of 1850, when it numbered 182 residents (including 5 slaves). By 1890, the town included 875 people. "Perry County Population Figures, 1830–1990," 76–78.
5. Slawson, "Vincentian Experience of the Civil War in Missouri," 34. Slawson described Perry County as "a microcosm of the state" with its 8 percent slave population and 13 percent slaveholding households. Like Missouri as a whole, most Perry Countians avoided sectional candidates in the election of 1860, so that the county "like the state at large . . . overwhelmingly favored preservation of the Union and no agitation over slavery."

movements and the activities of small guerilla bands aroused popular fear and anxiety in Perryville.

Meanwhile, St. Mary's of the Barrens continued to grow and develop from its humble origins. However, differences within the Vincentian community and the move toward greater consolidation in the broader American Catholic Church deeply affected the fortunes of the Barrens, which lost various functions until by 1866 the old seminary was virtually abandoned. Sectional divisions were also played out at the site, with Southern sympathizers among the students clashing with Unionist faculty, and all colliding with the Vincentian norms against involvement in domestic politics. All in all, growth and fragmentation marked the history of the Barrens from the departure of John Timon for Buffalo in 1847, through the Civil War and its aftermath, up to the return of the seminary and the division of the American Vincentian province in 1888.

Growth and Differentiation

The Barrens maintained a solid population of students and faculty throughout the first half of the nineteenth century. Census figures record a total of 119 residents (including 17 slaves) at the seminary in 1840 under Timon's leadership, declining slightly to 102 residents (including 5 slaves) in 1850 before growing to a total of 138 in 1860.[6] After the removal of the lay college in the 1860s, numbers floundered until *Sadlier's Catholic Directory* listed only four Vincentians resident at the site in 1883, and they only in their capacity as parish priests, for the *Directory* no longer counted the Barrens as an educational/religious institution within the St. Louis archdiocese.[7]

As for physical growth, sources are somewhat unclear about the various buildings dotting the Barrens landscape up to 1886.[8] The

6. Mills, "Introduction to the Civil War at St. Mary's of the Barrens," 22–23. The number of residents counted at the seminary included Vincentian priests and brothers, students, and staff (including laborers, farmers, cooks, gardeners, and female servants).
7. *Sadlier's Catholic Directory 1883*, 196.
8. The problem is complicated by the tendency to rename buildings under the direction of new superiors and the lack of early building records, perhaps due to the college building fire of 1866. See Sanders and Bryant, *Our Dear Brother Joseph*, 72–73.

grand Church of the Assumption was completed in 1837, with the first permanent seminary building (1820) just to its east and the "college building" described by Rosati in 1828 some one hundred feet farther east.[9] Other log and small frame buildings served various functions, including the temporary structures erected during the earliest years of the Barrens foundation.

Barrens superior John Lynch reported a "marvelous" undertaking in an 1850 letter to Vincentian authorities in Paris:

> Now I want to tell you one of our exploits, the moving of the old seminary. Picture an old house 60 feet long and about as wide, well! all this, including galleries, being transported about 200 feet up a roadway, to make a place for a new building made of bricks. My French is not good enough to describe to you all the details of this wonderful operation; the moving over 3 or 4 weeks because the house moved only a few feet per day, the house now at its new place as if it had always been there.[10]

The building in question could only have been the original three-story frame "seminary building" constructed in 1820 to replace the temporary log cabins that housed the original Barrens missionaries, as its dimensions match those described in Rosati's memoirs and moving it two hundred feet to a location south of its original site makes sense given Lynch's description and the engineering abilities of the period.[11] The old building was moved to make way for a grander brick structure, known variously as the New House, the Priest's Building, "A" Building, and Rosati Hall over subsequent years. Designed by local architect-contractor Joseph Lansman, the

---

9. Rosati recounted the construction of a two-story brick house "exclusively for the use of the college" measuring thirty feet by forty feet and including a study hall, classrooms, and living quarters. "The location was set at a distance of 100 feet from the seminary but on the same line as the seminary and the church." Rosati, "Recollections," pt. 6, 133–34.

10. John Lynch, CM, to M. P. Martin, CM (Paris), in *Annales de la Congregation de la Mission* 15 (1850).

11. Rosati, "Recollections," pt. 4, 111; and Sanders and Bryant, *Our Dear Brother Joseph*, 72–75.

substantial new building (supply contracts include an 1848 order for 300,000 bricks[12]) included three stories built on a limestone foundation, with porches and French-style exterior stairs and topped by a cupola housing an impressive "strap" clock. Estimates for the new building top $12,000, with Lynch informing Vincentian superiors that "we shall be obliged to contract a debt" to pay for the "loudly called for" new structure.[13]

Just off the seminary campus, the old "Bishop's Mill" on the Saline Creek, bought by DuBourg in 1819, continued to serve an important economic function for the seminary and surrounding community, supplying flour and feed to areas as far away as Ste. Genevieve.[14] A larger structure was erected at the mill site in 1853, described as a "massive building" that added a steam engine to the waterwheel "and even then the capacity of the mill could not keep up with the patronage" of local residents. The mill was operated by Vincentian Brother Dan Corboy until its abandonment in 1910.[15]

Fluctuations in population and physical facilities reflected the shifting fortunes of the Barrens in this era. From its beginnings, the Barrens filled multiple roles but by the middle of the nineteenth century American Catholicism was changing both demographically and structurally. Bishops looked to regularize and differentiate the institutions in their dioceses. Turmoil over the issue of lay trusteeism reflected episcopal efforts to retain control over parishes, and the flowering of local seminaries grew from the desire to keep potential clerics within diocesan boundaries (and outside the sway of religious orders).

As a result, seminary operations began to change at the Barrens. The novitiate was moved, initially to a new establishment in nearby Cape Girardeau, then to St. Louis, before returning briefly to the Barrens in 1853. The St. Louis diocesan seminarians moved to St. Louis in 1842, leaving only a few clerical candidates for other far-flung dioceses at St. Mary's for the next twenty years. In 1862,

---

12. Personnel Files, DRMA—Lynch—"Building Supply Contract" (1848).
13. Sanders and Bryant, *Our Dear Brother Joseph*, 70–81; Personnel Files, DRMA—Souvay—Joseph Lynch to Unnamed Recipient, 2 August 1850. The 1850 building still stands on the campus of St. Mary's of the Barrens.
14. *Centennial History of Perry County, Missouri, 1821–1921*, 76.
15. Ibid.

Vincentian visitor Stephen V. Ryan moved all phases of seminary formation for the community from the Barrens to St. Louis (and, eventually, to Germantown, Pennsylvania, in 1868), effectively ending the Barrens' tenure as headquarters for the American Vincentians.

Ryan acknowledged the potential dislocation wrought by leaving the Barrens in a letter to a confrere in 1862:

We have finally executed our proposed movement transferring the central house of the Province from the Barrens to St. Louis . . . [and] I see you have your misgivings as to its expediency and results. Well, my very dear confrere,

10. STEPHEN VINCENT RYAN
The Canadian-born Ryan (1825–96) studied and taught at the Barrens before becoming visitor of the American province in 1857. He guided the community through the divisive Civil War era and was responsible for moving most of the seminary operations out of the Barrens. Ryan succeeded Timon as bishop of Buffalo in 1868.

I have had my own, yet it is not a step taken rashly, precipitously or unadvisedly, it has the well-nigh unanimous approval of the Province and of our most honored Father [Superior General Jean-Baptiste Etienne], it has been facilitated and I may say brought about by circumstances and I cannot but look upon it as the will of Heaven. It cost much to sunder the ties of affectionate attachment and hallowed recollection that bound us to the old homestead, the cradle and nursery of our community in this country, the final step was long deferred. I at least and I believe the others had no human views, we leave the issue to God and hope and pray no action of ours may prejudice his holy work, or be detrimental to our little congregation.[16]

In his later reminiscences, Ryan specified the reasons for the move, including his assessment of the inaccessible and "backward inland" location of the Barrens and the lack of "population and enterprise" in the surrounding area that he considered disproportionate to the energies expended by the Barrens missionaries.[17]

The lay college aroused suspicions among Vincentian superiors from its founding in 1823, but it continued to play an important role in financing the entire house as well as offering opportunities to serve the broader secular community. In 1843, the operations of the college were transferred to St. Vincent's College at Cape Girardeau.[18] A few collegians remained at the Barrens, however, and by 1850 the revived college

11. Abram Ryan
A young Abram Ryan (1838–86) around the time of his ordination in 1860, when he was stationed at the Barrens and gaining attention for his vocal pro-Southern sympathies. Vincentian norms forbade such partisan politicking, straining Ryan's relations with his religious superiors and contributing to his departure from the Vincentian community in 1862. Ryan moved to Tennessee and gained a reputation as the "Poet-Priest of the Confederacy" for his patriotic verses lauding the Southern cause.

16. Provincial Files, DRMA—Ryan Papers—Stephen V. Ryan, CM, to Mariano Maller, CM, 17 May 1862.
17. Ryan, "Early Lazarist Missions and Missionaries," 111–13.
18. Rybolt, "St. Vincent College and Theological Education," 292–93.

was a growing enterprise, drawing Catholic students from as far away as the state of Louisiana. Ads for the college touted its academic rigor and breadth of offerings, and the old college building filled rapidly with upwards of one hundred students in a given year. The students experienced all the emotional tensions of the Civil War, which physically separated numbers of them from their parents and deprived the Barrens of much-needed tuition revenue.

The Barrens survived the war, but in 1866 a devastating fire effectively closed educational operations at the site. The student diary entry for February 15, 1866, vividly described the conflagration:

> This morning at 8 o'clock the alma mater of so many generations of pious priests caught fire and was entirely consumed within the span of three hours. The fire started in a room of the third story usually occupied by Brother Fleuriel.[19] It being a cold morning, the old man made probably a good fire; he left his room about 6—heard Mass, and then went to the infirmary where he was occupied the whole morning, never thinking of his fire. A burning log must have rolled out on the floor and thus ignited the room before anyone could perceive it. Only at 8 o'clock an unusual thick smoke arose from the Seminary, this was the first signal; immediately after, the cry of "fire, fire" reechoed through the halls and classrooms; all rushed out, and perceived the sad reality by smoke appearing from under the roof. The boys in great consternation hastened to save their study books, trunks, etc. etc. . . . but the most valuable, alas, the valuable library of the boys became a prey to its flames; the fire had entered that room before anything could be saved. Fortunately [sic] that the wind came from northwest—otherwise the whole establishment would have been in danger. At 11 the fire subsided gradually, and the walls commenced to crumble

19. Charles Fleuriel, CM (1809–73), a French-born brother who entered the Congregation in 1851 and took vows in 1853.

down. Now the <u>dear old Home</u> of many a one is only a heap of ruins!!![20]

Within a day of the fire, classes recommenced in the hall of "New House" but the fate of the Barrens college was sealed by the disaster. Lay students were moved to Cape Girardeau, reducing the Barrens to the status of a day school and beginning a twenty-year period of malaise at the Barrens.

Even the old parish maintained by the Vincentians on the seminary campus saw its role change after midcentury. Father Aloysius Meyer, a German immigrant who joined the American Vincentian community at the Barrens in 1858, championed the religious needs of his fellow German Americans in the county.[21] In 1865, while a faculty member at the Barrens college, he was instrumental in the founding of a new parish for local German immigrants. A new church, soon taken over by diocesan priest-pastors, was erected south of the Barrens in 1868 for St. Boniface Parish, with its own school (staffed first by Precious Blood, then Ursuline Sisters after 1887) founded in 1870. The parish thrived for the next hundred years.[22]

In addition to Meyer's work in encouraging St. Boniface, Vincentians from the Barrens continued to reach out to area missions and establish new parishes. According to John Rybolt,

> The period 1830 to 1888 marked an era of expansion in the United States Vincentian mission. Many vocations came to the Community, chiefly from Europe, and as a result, more priests and brothers became available to staff the parishes that developed in view of rapidly increasing immigration. The missionaries had so many parishes that Father John Timon, the first provincial, wanted to restrict them in favor of seminaries. Father Jean-Baptiste Nozo, the superior general, urged Timon

20. SMOB Records, DRMA—Students: Diaries—Record of Principle Events, 15 February 1866.
21. Poole, "Notable Vincentians (8): Aloysius Meyer (1839–1868)."
22. Vincentians returned to the pastorate of St. Boniface in 1947. In 1963, St. Boniface merged with the old seminary Church of the Assumption to found a new St. Vincent de Paul Parish off the seminary grounds.

to do so only after mature reflection since a province having seminaries alone might excessively restrict the talents of some confreres.[23]

Among the area mission churches served from the Barrens after midcentury were Biehle, St. Mary's Landing, Crosstown, Claryville, and Silver Lake. Other older parishes were left to the ministrations of diocesan priests. "As secular priests multiplied," Ryan wrote in 1887, "the Lazarist missionaries were withdrawn from the numerous missions they had founded and zealously attended in Missouri, Illinois, and Texas."[24]

Ryan noted several reasons for the shifting parochial responsibilities of the Barrens priests—the assumption of new, more far-flung apostolates that drew Vincentians away from the Barrens to places like Niagara, New York (Our Lady of the Angels Seminary, founded in Timon's diocese in 1856) and Los Angeles, California (St. Vincent's College, founded in Thaddeus Amat's diocese in 1865); Vincentian convictions regarding the importance of community, which encouraged the establishment of central houses over individual parish assignments; and the overcommitments made in Timon's tenure as visitor during the "age of boundlessness."[25]

In general, Ryan attributed the retrenchment of the community to the loss "in a few years [of] many of its best and most experienced subjects, on whom it relied in the government and administration of its various houses; and it can be no surprise that it was thrown back for years, until it could build up and form a new generation; that it had to abandon many of its important works, to the great regret of many of its own members, and many of the bishops of the country."[26] When it came to the Vincentian seminary commitments, however, the Vincentian historian Stafford Poole attributed withdrawals from diocesan seminaries to issues of governance. "It

---

23. Rybolt, *American Vincentians*, 235.
24. Ryan, "Early Lazarist Missions and Missionaries," 96.
25. Ibid.
26. Ryan was referring to the loss of several influential American Vincentian leaders (including Mariano Maller, Anthony Penco, James Rolando, and John Masnou) who in the 1850s left the United States to return to Europe and to the loss of leaders like Thaddeus Amat, John Lynch, and Michael Domenec to American bishoprics. Ibid., 110.

is clear," according to Poole, "the principal reason for the Vincentians leaving . . . seminaries was disagreement with the bishops," especially over issues like the mixing of lay collegians and seminarians and concerns that the Vincentians might lure seminarians away from their diocesan commitments.[27]

What best explains the many changes that drew works away from the Barrens in the middle of the nineteenth century? Among the most often articulated reasons was the perceived isolation of the region. Ryan acknowledged his own belief that "if a tithe of the energy expended, of the men and the means deployed in Perry County, Missouri, had been utilized in some growing center of population and enterprise, better results would have been obtained, and hence I am partly responsible for the removal of the novitiate and mother-house to St. Louis and, afterwards, in the spring of 1867, to Germantown."[28] Ryan echoed sentiments voiced since almost the founding of the Barrens regarding "the backward inland situation, so difficult of access, its bad and at times impassable roads, making travel on horseback the only possible means of locomotion."[29] Indeed, other Vincentians complained that the lack of railroad connections at Perryville, which necessitated river travel from the nearby St. Mary's or Claryville landings to larger population centers, made it harder to travel from the Barrens to St. Louis than from St. Louis to major rail cities on the eastern seaboard.

Other complications militated against the Barrens, including Poole's recognition of the antagonisms between bishops and Vincentian superiors, the growth of new apostolates in other areas of the country, and divisions within the Barrens community (priests-brothers, Irish-Italian, southern-northern, etc.). Yet movement away from the Barrens was not taken lightly, as Ryan indicated. Even Ryan waxed nostalgic on leaving the Barrens in May 1862. His circular letter to the houses of the American province described the emotions of leaving "the old homestead, the cradle and nursery of our little Community during so many years, a place associated

27. Poole, "Ad Cleri Disciplinam," 126.
28. Ryan, "Early Lazarist Missions and Missionaries," 112.
29. Ibid.

in our minds with so many hallowed recollections."[30] Of course, the lingering question hanging over the Barrens from 1866 to the return of seminary operations in 1886, also voiced by Ryan, was if the "interests of the little Seminary, still to remain at the Barrens, be prejudiced, or its prospects blighted by our separation?"[31]

Leadership

The superiors of the Barrens and the American Vincentian community in the period from 1847 to 1886 were, for the most part, solid and highly esteemed, if unimaginative, men adapted to the circumstances of an expanding and increasingly complex religious situation. At least one contemporary observer longed for the "heroic" leadership of the earlier American Catholic Church.[32] Philip Gleason noted that mid-nineteenth-century leaders effectively closed ranks in efforts to formalize the habits and institutions of a growing church.[33] The days of Rosati and Timon, when rough-and-ready circumstances required creative and often expansive responses, had ended. New problems of growth and differentiation were met by different, often more cautious and measured, leaders determined to preserve and regularize Catholic institutions. Many of these clerical leaders continued to hail from Europe; some talented and experienced émigrés fleeing revolutionary conditions were advanced despite their own protestations and misgivings.

One such impressive newcomer was Mariano Maller. Born in Selgua, Spain in 1817, Maller joined the Vincentians in 1833 just as the Carlist Wars began and the Congregation, along with other Catholic religious orders, was suppressed.[34] The young Catalonian was transferred first to Paris and then, in 1839, to the United States to pursue his theological training. He was ordained in Louisiana in

---

30. Provincial Files, DRMA—Ryan Papers—Ryan, "Circular Letter to All Houses of the Province" (May 22, 1862).
31. Ibid.
32. Cummings, "Our Future Clergy."
33. Gleason, "Boundlessness, Consolidation and Discontinuity Between Generations."
34. For a brief biographical background on Mariano Maller, see Rybolt, "American Vincentians in 1877–78: Maller Visitation Report (1)."

1840 and assigned briefly to the Barrens before becoming rector of St. Charles Borromeo Seminary in Philadelphia in 1841 at the age of twenty-four. Even at an early age regarded as "one of the most respected priests in the United States,"[35] Maller was appointed vicar-general of the diocese of Philadelphia under Bishop Francis Kenrick in 1845. Shortly afterward, Maller was moved by the Vincentians to the newly founded St. Vincent's College in Cape Girardeau and, on the elevation of John Timon to the bishopric of Buffalo, was appointed visitor of the American Vincentians in 1847. As visitor, he "continued the high level of leadership set by Timon" and, as titular director of the Daughters of Charity in the United States, negotiated their union with Elizabeth Ann Seton's growing community of Sisters of Charity at Emmitsburg, Maryland in 1850.[36]

As visitor, Maller was concerned about the problems that had vexed the American Vincentians since their foundation at the Barrens thirty years previously. His 1849 report to the superior general focused on the problem of attracting high-quality new members to the Congregation, the need to discriminate wisely among the apostolates, and the continual (if necessary) debt incurred by the community. Maller's talents and leadership skills drew the attention of numerous church leaders, and in 1850 he was nominated for the bishopric of Monterey, California. The Spaniard had only accepted appointment as provincial visitor reluctantly and, determined to avoid an episcopal appointment, he requested a transfer away from the United States. In 1851, he was relieved of his American provincial duties and assigned to the province of Brazil in 1853. By 1861, he was moved once more back to Paris, where he corresponded often with his former confreres at the Barrens. In 1862, he was named superior of the Congregation's Spanish province, where for the next forty years he weathered the vagaries of Spanish politics and traveled widely on behalf of the international Vincentian community, including official visitations in Ireland and, in 1877/78, back to the United States.

Maller was highly prized by his Vincentian confreres. S. V. Ryan, who became visitor of the American province in 1857,

35. Editorial Staff, "Survey of American Vincentian History," 44.
36. Ibid.

12. BARRENS CAMPUS PRE-1913

Despite its humble beginnings and a period of inactivity following the Civil War, the Barrens campus grew steadily in its first century. This photo shows the Church of the Assumption (dedicated in 1837) and log cabins in the foreground, with the brick administrative/priests' building (1850) behind the church and the original white-frame seminary building to the right.

wrote of Maller's exodus from the American province in 1853, "The departure of Mr. Maller I regarded as almost an irreparable loss to myself and our Province. He was a man of talent, learning, good judgment, and a genuine religious spirit. On him I relied, perhaps too much, for the future direction of myself and the important works of the community. He was called away partly, at least, because the Superior General [Etienne] had an inkling that he was to be made a bishop, and thereby entirely lost to the community."[37] According to Ryan, Bishop Kenrick later confided that he would have squelched any episcopal appointment for Maller if doing so would have kept him in the country.[38] Maller's immense popularity, talents, and sensitivity to the unique needs of the many institutions in which he worked were revealed in the friendly correspondence he maintained with numerous Vincentians, including those at the Barrens. His 1877 American visitation included a trip to the Barrens, and his subsequent report (see below) reflected a sensitive spirit attuned to the symbolic importance of the old motherhouse.

Maller was succeeded as visitor by Anthony Penco, scion of a wealthy Genoese family who worked under Maller in Philadelphia before briefly taking over leadership of St. Joseph Seminary at Fordham (New York) in 1844.[39] Penco reflected the new spirit of differentiation and consolidation in his leadership at St. Joseph, advising the Congregation to leave that apostolate given its over-reliance on seminarians as teaching faculty at the college. He was named president of St. Vincent's College in Cape Girardeau in 1846 and pastor of St. Vincent's Parish in St. Louis in 1852, duties that continued into his tenure as American visitor from 1850 to 1855. As provincial superior, he confronted the problem of over-commitment to far-flung apostolates, withdrawing from the Philadelphia seminary and threatening to "retrench the province to

---

37. Ryan, "Early Lazarist Missions and Missionaries," 105–6.
38. Ibid., 106.
39. For brief notices on Penco's American activities, see Messmer, "Two Interesting Communications from the Most Reverend Archbishop of Milwaukee," 182–83. The Vincentians staffed the Fordham seminary from 1842 to 1844.

two or three houses."[40] Penco returned to Italy in 1855 to revive the declining fortunes of his extended family (driven to near bankruptcy by the "extravagant speculations" of his brother) and to lead the missionary college of Brignole-Sale, from which he continued to contribute to the American mission.[41]

During the period of Maller and Penco's leadership of the American province, the Barrens was led by the tireless Irishman John Joseph Lynch.[42] Born in 1816 in County Fermanagh, Lynch enrolled in the Vincentian-run Castleknock College, Dublin in 1835 and entered the Congregation of the Mission in 1839. He completed his novitiate and initial studies in Paris before returning to Dublin for ordination in 1843. Jean-Marie Odin recruited Lynch for the Texas missions in 1846, but a bout of typhoid fever removed the young missionary from Texas to New Orleans and eventually to the Barrens, where he taught and served as superior from 1848 to 1856. In 1856, he answered Bishop Timon's call to found a new seminary near Niagara Falls and led Our Lady of the Angels Seminary (the forerunner of the present-day Niagara University) until his appointment as coadjutor bishop of Toronto in 1850. In 1860, Lynch assumed the bishopric and over the next quarter century worked to counter the influence of widespread anti-Catholicism and to serve a growing influx of Irish immigrants. Lynch died in Toronto in 1888.

As Barrens superior, Lynch established a "new regime," replacing the traditional system in which discipline and moral fervor were maintained through the appointment of prefects by the implementation of an institutional honor code. Indeed, Lynch's biographer notes that, while attending the General Assembly of the Congregation in Paris in 1849, Lynch visited Rome and entertained Pope Pius IX with stories of the moral probity of the Barrens seminary.[43] Despite his own sometimes fragile health, due perhaps to the vestigial effects of typhoid, Lynch threw himself into the task of seminary leadership. He oversaw the construction of new buildings,

40. Editorial Staff, "Survey of American Vincentian History," 46.
41. Ryan, "Early Lazarist Missions and Missionaries," 107.
42. For background on Lynch, see McKeown, *Life and Labors of Most Reverend John Joseph Lynch*; and Kehoe, "Becoming a Bishop and Remaining a Vincentian."
43. McKeown, *Life and Labors of Most Reverend John Joseph Lynch*, 71.

including the large brick priests' residence begun in 1850, recruited new students (an estimated fifty new students entered the Barrens during his tenure), encouraged student recreational activities, including swimming on the Saline Creek, and embarked on "occasional missions in the surrounding country."[44] Problems remained at the Barrens, including concerns for the long-term stability of the lay college and for Lynch's own health. "While at St. Mary's," Lynch's biographer reported, "imprudent exposure and overfatigue resulted in paralysis of one side," but in general the superior brought a new spirit of energy and vitality to the campus.[45]

That spirit initially continued under the charismatic leadership of Stephen Vincent Ryan.[46] Like Timon, the son of Irish immigrant parents (born in 1825 in Ontario), Ryan entered St. Charles Borromeo Seminary in Philadelphia in 1838 during the time it was directed by Vincentian clerics. Ryan entered the Congregation in 1844, was ordained in 1849, and taught at the Barrens from 1849 to 1851 before moving to St. Vincent's in Cape Girardeau. In 1857, he succeeded Penco as American visitor and in 1868 following the death of Timon was named bishop of Buffalo, where he established a reputation as a "liberal and farsighted bishop" until his death in 1896.[47]

Remarkable for both his physical appearance—contemporaries commented on his thin, fragile form and his "mortified and ascetic . . . appearance"—and his energy and commitment to work, Ryan earned an impressive reputation as teacher and spiritual director at the Barrens. "Father Ryan came very near to filling the highest ideal of even the most exacting of what a prefect ought to be," one of his pupils later recalled. "Unsparing of himself, attentive to the needs of those entrusted to his charge, he was vigilant in guarding the exact observance of rules, prompt in correcting anything that leaned toward a relaxation of discipline." As a teacher, he was supremely confident in his own knowledge, "conscientious in his preparation," and "always kind and considerate to such a degree

44. Ibid., 73.
45. Ibid., 74.
46. On Ryan, see Cronin, *Memorial of the Life and Labors of Rt. Rev. Stephen Vincent Ryan*.
47. Editorial Staff, "Survey of American Vincentian History," 51.

that it was the student's own fault if he retired from class without a good mastery of the subject matter."[48]

Ryan's strength of character and opinion continued into his tenure as visitor. Still only thirty-two years old and a relatively inexperienced priest, Ryan proved a hardworking administrator with firm opinions on how to modernize the American Vincentian community. His communications with Abram Ryan (see below) reflected his willingness to tackle delicate or difficult subjects, as did his firm direction of the community during the crisis of the Civil War. As visitor, Ryan maintained his residence in St. Louis and traveled constantly to visit Vincentian works and preach missions. He became convinced that the Barrens had outlived its usefulness as a central house of the Congregation, and under his leadership the Vincentian formation programs were removed from the Barrens to St. Louis in 1862 and, ultimately, to Germantown, Pennsylvania, in 1867. New works, like the supervision of the Sisters of Charity and newly established institutions as distant as St. Vincent's College in Los Angeles and Our Lady of Angels in Buffalo demanded the attentions of the community in this era of consolidation.

On his elevation to the episcopacy in 1868, Ryan was succeeded as visitor by John Hayden, a native son of the Barrens who as a young boy was educated at the parish day school (contrary to later legend, Hayden was not related to the early benefactress who surrendered her home to the pioneer Vincentians in 1818). Hayden entered the Congregation in 1849, was ordained a priest in 1853, and spent many years as pastor of St. Joseph's Church in New Orleans. In 1867, he attended the General Assembly of the Congregation in Paris and served for a short time as English-language secretary to the superior general. Named visitor in 1868, his brief tenure, ended by his unexpected death in 1872, was noted mainly for his efforts to affect a division of the American province and return of programs to the Barrens, a project unrealized in his lifetime.

Father James Rolando succeeded Hayden as American visitor. Born southwest of Genoa in Armo, Italy in 1816, Rolando entered the Congregation in 1833 and migrated to the American mission

---

48. Cronin, *Memorial of the Life and Labors of Rt. Rev. Stephen Vincent Ryan*, 10.

in 1840. He was ordained to the priesthood a year later in Donald-sonville, Louisiana, and taught variously over the next few years at St. Charles Seminary (Philadelphia), St. Vincent's College (Cape Girardeau), and the Barrens before serving Vincentian parishes in St. Louis and Germantown. By the time he came to the Barrens in the role of master of novices, Rolando was already regarded as a "ven-erable and most highly respected" figure in the Vincentian com-munity.[49] Rolando returned briefly to Italy in 1863 to serve at the missionary college of Brignole-Sale, but returned a year later and was stationed at St. Vincent Parish in St. Louis on being named visitor in 1873. At fifty-seven years of age and with over thirty years of ser-vice in educational institutions and parishes, Rolando was the most experienced American superior since the inception of the province.

Rolando's tenure as visitor has been overshadowed by the prob-lems facing the Vincentian community that led Superior General Eugene Boré to send Mariano Maller to America for a general visita-tion of Vincentian houses in 1877. Maller's report to Boré criticized Rolando's regime. The Spanish provincial superior reviewed the personnel and works of the American province, noting recurring problems of division, low morale, laxity in following Vincentian norms, and (everywhere) the mounting pressure of debt.[50] Maller also commented on the idiosyncrasies of each house, including the personalities of assigned Vincentian priests and brothers. Of Roland, Maller reported that the visitor's confreres at Germantown (now the provincial headquarters of the Congregation) perceived him as "loving his office too much." While Maller thought Rolando was pious and well-intentioned, he also regarded him as hesitant and indecisive—"he tries to do good, but he is incapable of a firm resolution."[51] Although Maller recognized that Rolando failed to command the respect of his peers, he questioned the wisdom of replacing him as superior, vowing to complete his visitation of all the American houses before making judgment. After completing his

49. Personnel Files, DRMA—Rolando—Ryan, "Brief Biographical Notes: James Rolan-do," 23.
50. See Rybolt, "American Vincentians in 1877–78: Maller Visitation Report (1)"; and Rybolt, "American Vincentians in 1877–78: Maller Visitation Report (2)."
51. Rybolt, "American Vincentians in 1877–78: Maller Visitation Report (1)," 68.

review, Maller returned to his criticism of Rolando and reluctantly advised that he should be dismissed given his ineffectiveness in dealing with the numerous problems facing the province.[52]

Rolando's replacement, as recommended by Maller, was Thomas Smith (1830–1905), an Irish-born Vincentian with twenty-five years of experience in both educational institutions and parishes. Smith came to the United States in 1850, joined the Congregation at the Barrens in 1853, and was ordained a priest in 1858. Regarded as a "fine Latin and Greek scholar" and a "profound theologian," he served as president of St. Vincent's College (Cape Girardeau) and Our Lady of the Angels (Buffalo) as well as pastor of St. Joseph's in New Orleans.[53] While Maller noted that Smith's colleagues in New Orleans found him occasionally arrogant and inflexible, his intelligence and administrative skills were indispensable at a critical time in the history of the American province.[54] The growth of the Vincentian community and its array of far-flung apostolates created major administrative problems, especially given the primitive state of transportation in isolated houses like the Barrens. Just before his appointment as visitor, Smith noted these problems in a letter from New Orleans regarding assignments among the Vincentian community. "We were not posted about it at all," Smith wrote. "What is the matter? I thought Father X was the superior. Father Y an 'interim'!! I think we will have to petition to have a catalogue published every month if we wish to keep track of the movements of the Confreres."[55]

Smith's response to the challenges of leading his growing community was to petition the superior general for the division of the province. The division into eastern and western provinces was formalized in 1888, by which time an apostolic school had already been reestablished at the Barrens. As superior of the western province, Smith presided over a period of growth at the Barrens, and his long leadership became the stuff of legend in the Congregation.[56]

52. Rybolt, "American Vincentians in 1877–78: Maller Visitation Report (2)," 246.
53. Obituary, *St. Louis Times-Democrat*, 24 September 1905.
54. Rybolt, "American Vincentians in 1877–78: Maller Visitation Report (2)," 266.
55. "Father Smith, Pioneer Provincial," *DeAndrein* (October 1963): 11.
56. Ibid.

Chapter Six

CIVIL WAR AND AFTERMATH

> Our rules require us to take no part in civil dissensions
> and not make them the topic of conversation with each
> other or strangers.
>
> —S. V. Ryan (1862)

The various challenges faced by the American Vincentian community, exacerbated at the Barrens by divisions between priests and
brothers and those attached to the house and those who increasingly clamored for a move to more populous and accessible locales,
became (like all else in the American republic) overshadowed by
the threat of civil war at midcentury. While the roots of regional
discord and eventual armed conflict lay in complicated political,
economic, and cultural circumstances, perceptions of the event
were often filtered through the lens of religious faith. Americans
saw themselves as divinely blessed and guided by a benevolent
Providence, what George C. Rabble recently described as "God's
Almost Chosen Peoples."[1] The Civil War challenged that perception as deeply religious Americans on both sides of the conflict
sought justification for their cause. The war proved particularly
troubling to American Catholics, whose members looked beyond
national borders to a universal church. Many of those members

---

1. Rabble, *God's Almost Chosen Peoples*.

were recent immigrants to the United States and were often per-
plexed by regional differences. Catholic leaders were loath to draw
attention to their fledgling communities through political entanglements, and "the Catholic hierarchy—North and South—strove
to avoid divisions that would weaken the Church when it was both
prospering and facing ever more intense Protestant hostility."[2] As
a result, most Catholic priests remained deliberately apolitical,
choosing "not [to] petition Congress or deliver political sermons;
nor did they declare God's hand at work in all the bitter disputes
over slavery." This was especially true in border states like Missouri.[3]

Even the moral dimensions of the slavery issue failed to
unify Catholics politically. In the absence of any official Catholic pronouncement on slavery, Catholic leaders differed in their
approaches. Many accepted the practice, provided that slaves were
offered opportunities for religious instruction and the sacraments.
Others detested the "peculiar institution" and a few Catholic institutions divested themselves of their slaveholdings. While the moral
dimensions of slavery were pressed on churchmen by abolitionists,
most Catholic leaders persisted in their reluctance to denounce the
practice, driven by fears of social disorder, economic self-interest, a
desire to fit in with their slaveholding neighbors, and unwillingness
to associate with the perceived radicalism and anti-Catholicism of
the abolitionist movement.[4] A few more liberal Catholic spokes-
men, like Orestes Brownson, eventually embraced the abolitionist
position and called for Catholic support of the Union but, overall,
Catholics remained as divided as their fellow countrymen over the
issues that provoked the Civil War.[5]

In this as in many other trends, the Barrens reflected the typical
American Catholic experience. The seminary generally reflected its
surroundings in its economic organization and political attitudes,

2. Ibid., 28.
3. Ibid., 28, 197. Indeed, the apolitical attitudes of Catholic priests in Missouri occasioned problems over issues like opposition to loyalty oaths and willingness to minister to both armies.
4. McGreevy, *Catholicism and American Freedom*, 52–53. Some American Protestant abolitionists, like Elijah Lovejoy, depicted Catholicism as a form of slavery.
5. Ibid., 67.

although its ecclesiastical foundations, largely foreign-born priests, and student body recruited from various locales set it apart from the surrounding culture. Stafford Poole and Douglas Slawson offered a solid profile of antebellum Perry County in their 1986 book *Church and Slave in Perry County, Missouri, 1818–1865*. According to Poole and Slawson, Perry Countians remained an agricultural people for whom "life was taken slowly with intermittent bouts of hard work."[6] Some of the larger farmers of the county utilized slave labor (13 percent of households were described as slaveholding), but only 8 percent of the total population of the county was comprised of slaves.[7] The original Anglo-Catholic population of the Barrens was swelled by other immigrant groups in the first half of the nineteenth century, and especially by Germans, including Catholics from Baden and Bavaria beginning in the 1830s.[8] While the population grew, the county remained "in most ways typical of backwoods America," characterized by a patchwork of immigrant groups largely occupied with farming, a "rough and tumble" society typified by occasional outbursts of violence, politically inclined to support Democratic politics and the preservation of the Union, with only its particular religious composition to separate it from other frontier settlements.[9]

St. Mary's Seminary assimilated into this border state culture, serving the largely Catholic community through its parish church and participating fully in the agricultural economy of the county. Assimilation included slaveholding. The first slaves were sent to the seminary by Bishop DuBourg himself shortly after the establishment of the institution. While the introduction of black slaves aroused some brief consternation among the Italian superiors of the Vincentian community, the practice of slavery soon settled into seminary life. Indeed, Poole and Slawson noted the paternalistic and hierarchical nature of the Congregation of the Mission, including the traditional presence of religious brothers in Old World Vincentian houses to perform manual labor. Over time, the Roman

6. Poole and Slawson, *Church and Slave in Perry County*, 15.
7. Slawson, "Vincentian Experience of the Civil War in Missouri," 34.
8. Poole and Slawson, *Church and Slave in Perry County*, 6–7.
9. Ibid., 17–18.

superiors of the Barrens expressed more concern over the gender of slaves than the actual practice of slave labor.[10] While the slave population of the Barrens seminary fluctuated in the antebellum period, given occasional purchases, exchanges, and loans to other houses, the number of slaves grew from two in 1820 to a high of twenty-seven in 1830 (by which time the seminary was counted the largest slaveholding institution in Perry County), only to begin a gradual decline thereafter (fifteen in 1840) reflecting the anti-slavery stance of John Timon.[11] Separate quarters were constructed and policies were adopted for the more humane treatment of the seminary's slaves, including restricting any sale of slaves to other clergymen or "trusted and practicing Catholics," relatively lax discipline, attention to Catholic religious instruction and provision of the sacraments for the Barrens slaves, and efforts to maintain and/or reunite slave families.[12]

Under the leadership of the American-born John Timon in the 1830s and '40s, the number of slaves declined at the old seminary. Timon was deeply influenced by the increasingly vocal antislavery sentiment in the country, including arguments by some prominent Jesuits, and proposed the sell-off of the Barrens slaves so that by 1860 only two senior black slaves remained in the Barrens community.[13] Poole and Slawson note that Timon's position, opposed by other Barrens clerics, was based largely on pragmatic rather than moral grounds. "In summary," the authors maintained, "it can be said that the Vincentians in America were conditioned by theological teaching, the religious life as they had known it, and economic necessity to accept the peculiar institution for more than thirty years."[14]

The experience of the Civil War in Perry County reflected its border state mentality and combination of slaveholding patterns and Unionist political sympathies. In the presidential election of 1860, Perry Countians avoided extremist candidates, voting overwhelmingly for either the Democrat Stephen A. Douglas or the

10. Ibid., 150.
11. Ibid., 158.
12. Ibid., 171–78.
13. Ibid., 180–82.
14. Ibid., 189.

Constitutional Unionist John Bell. The county was largely spared direct military confrontation during the war given its perception as a nonstrategic and "out of the mainstream" locale.[15]

The county was, of course, affected by larger political and military events in Missouri. The 1861 state convention, chaired by the lawyer/politician Sterling Price, rejected secession but sought compromise with Southern states. Governor Claiborne Jackson ignored President Lincoln's call for Union enlistments in the state, and a pro-Southern Missouri State Guard was formed. A dramatic clash between the State Guard and Union troops in St. Louis on May 10, 1861, elicited shock in Perry County and at the Barrens seminary, as did the establishment of the Union Camp Grayson along Apple Creek in October 1861. Troop movements in areas surrounding Perry County occasioned rumors of imminent invasion, especially during Confederate General John Marmaduke's advance northward from Arkansas in 1863 (halted at the Battle of Cape Girardeau) and Price's 1864 advance toward St. Louis (diverted westward after the Battle of Pilot Knob).[16] A series of "bushwacking" activities ensued in the county, leading Unionists to compile a list of 194 names suspected of harboring Southern sympathies.[17] The local newspaper, the *Weekly Perryville Union*, established in 1862 as a pro-slavery but Unionist organ, remained stoutly Unionist and even embraced emancipation during the course of the war.[18] While emancipation at the cessation of hostilities decreased the personal wealth claimed by slaveholding households in Perry County (the black population in the county dropped from 762—including 739 slaves—in 1860 to 400 in 1870), the subsequent growth in overall population and in both agricultural production and manufacturing after the war eased the painful memories of Civil War divisions in the area.[19]

At the seminary, while the war strained already existing divisions and tensions, operations continued and numbers increased despite the surrounding clamor and some internal division. Letters from

---

15. Hubrick, "Perry County Through the Civil War," 5.
16. Ibid., 13–14.
17. Ibid., 17.
18. Ibid., 13.
19. Ibid., 20.

Barrens leaders to Vincentian superiors and friends in Europe attest to the growing number of students—from forty in 1861 to sixty-four in 1862, over seventy in 1863, and eighty in 1864. This growth reflected several factors, including the greater wartime disruption suffered by other institutions, including the Vincentian college and seminary in Cape Girardeau, scene of major troop movements and battles, and the inability of Southern students to travel safely back to their homes. These same letters describe the general normalcy at the Barrens, where educational and spiritual routines, including mission trips to surrounding settlements, remained relatively constant. "Everything is quiet around us," John Quigley reported to Mariano Maller in July 1861. "We are quiet here as we ever were," the provincial superior Stephen Ryan wrote to Maller in November 1862, "and we can scarcely realize the fact that our [country] is a prey to civil war, and that combats are nearby . . . and camps almost in view." "In the midst of the troubles that deluge the nation with blood, we enjoy the greatest quiet," Barrens rector Patrick McMenamy wrote, also to Maller, in July 1863. And Ryan reiterated in January 1864, "I am happy to inform you that kind Providence continues to favor us at St. Mary's with his benediction. Our little seminary continues to flourish in the midst of all the troubles and devastation that surround us."[20]

Not everything, of course, was so positive at the Barrens. While McMenamy described the house as "in a prosperous state" and without debt, in actuality, finances remained problematic.[21] Despite the growing number of students, tuition revenue lagged. Stephen V. Ryan noted that "several of those [students] we are supporting" and still others were from the South "and consequently we can receive neither communication nor remittance from their parents."[22] Even when communication was restored via relays from other Vincentian houses, payments lagged given the inconvertibility of Confeder-

20. Personnel Files, DRMA—Souvay—John Quigley to Mariano Maller, 18 July 1861; S. V. Ryan to Mariano Maller, 25 November 1861; Patrick McMenamy to Mariano Maller, 26 September 1862; Patrick McMenamy to Mariano Maller, 8 July 1863; Patrick McMenamy to Mariano Maller, 10 January 1864.
21. Personnel Files, DRMA—Souvay—McMenamy to Maller, 8 July 1863.
22. Personnel Files, DRMA—Souvay—Ryan to Maller, 11 November 1861.

ate currency to American dollars. Other concerns were also noted, including the lack of seminarians from American dioceses. Seminarians from the St. Louis diocese had been withdrawn from the Barrens as in the early 1840s and were now being educated at St. Vincent's College in Cape Girardeau. When internal Vincentian candidates were removed in 1862, the Barrens depended on far-flung American dioceses for clerical students in addition to the growing number of lay collegians. But, as McMenamy detailed in 1864, when only "three or four" seminarians remained at the Barrens:

> Bishops do not like to send us their seminarians, for they think they might leave them and enter the Congregation. Another obstacle that prevents many young men from coming here now, is that there are many such institutions established in places more accessible. Railroads are now everyplace, but none near the Barrens. It frequently takes a longer time to go from here to St. Louis than from St. Louis to New York. If we had a place like this in the state of Illinois or any other place, where there are many railroads, we would have a very large number of seminarians. We cannot however complain, for the Barrens has done well up to the present.[23]

Students and priests at the Barrens were generally "content and happy" and their conduct "as a body . . . exemplary."[24] However, a growing spirit of individualism, reflecting perhaps the increasingly American identity of the Barrens, drew attention and threatened to detract from communal norms. "There were about six young men ordained a couple of years ago," McMenamy observed, "and they appeared to have imbibed a spirit of self-will and independence, a spirit of ambition that always desires to be employed among externs and is never content in the solitude of community life. We had two or three of them here and it is sometimes difficult to get along

23. Personnel Files, DRMA—Souvay—McMenamy to Maller, 10 January 1864.
24. Personnel Files, DRMA—Souvay—McMenamy to Maller, 26 September 1862; McMenamy to Maller, 8 July 1863.

with them."[25] These men undoubtedly included the strong-minded Abram Ryan and his companions, men whose partisan spirit drew rebuke from their Vincentian superiors during the tensions over sectional politics just before and during the early stages of the war. Some older Vincentians also objected when the departure of internal seminarians led to the moving of collegians into the house formerly preserved for Vincentians, especially when these lay students were recruited to assist in community prayers.[26]

Of course, the departure of the Vincentian formation program in May 1862 dealt a blow to the historic motherhouse. McMenamy made the most of the situation, noting that "although the novitiate has been moved from St. Mary's Seminary, it has not ceased to supply the greatest number of postulants" (i.e., prospective candidates for the Vincentian community).[27] Indeed, the departing students may have fared worse in the bargain, as John Quigley noted complaints of "inconveniences not to be experienced at the Barrens" in their new St. Louis quarters, including the lack of adequate recreational space (such as the "ball alley available at the Barrens") and, more seriously, the high prices for food and fuel in St. Louis.[28] In general, the Civil War years, while exacerbating problems of debt, raising new questions regarding assimilation into American culture, and prompting the departure of the internal seminary to St. Louis, were weathered well at the Barrens, which enjoyed a growing college enrollment and relative peace compared to other area institutions.

But the war did intrude on the Barrens, sometimes in very troubling ways that tested the mettle of the institution. Perhaps the most significant of the war's effects at the Barrens was the partisanship displayed by some faculty and students in defiance of Vincentian rules. In a recent article, Douglas Slawson suggested, "At the heart of the matter was the rule of the Vincentian community which forbade members to speak or write 'deprecatingly about other countries or provinces' or to 'reveal a preference for either side in a war.' . . .

---

25. Personnel Files, DRMA—Souvay—McMenamy to Maller, 8 July 1863.
26. Personnel Files, DRMA—Souvay—McMenamy to Maller, 26 September 1862.
27. Personnel Files, DRMA—Souvay—McMenamy to Maller, 8 July 1863.
28. Personnel Files, DRMA—Souvay—Quigley to Maller, 12 January 1863.

In essence, they were expected to be apolitical. The injunction was to ensure that there would be no dissension within the community and that its members would be able to minister to all people, especially in time of war."[29] For Slawson, the difficulty over maintaining this rule at the Barrens during the Civil War reflected important concerns about citizenship "on two levels," raising questions about what it meant to be a member of the Vincentian community as well as what it meant to be a Missourian and an American.[30] In that regard, the war accentuated existing tensions regarding Americanization in a community still composed of numerous immigrants and cemented by the Old World regulations of a universal church. The Civil War tested the extent to which the Vincentian clerics at the Barrens cold reconcile the demands of Catholic community life with the emotional ties of American citizenship.

The rules of the Congregation and the relatively remote location of the Barrens did not prevent priests and students from knowledge and discussion of national affairs. Indeed, even older community members entered into political discourse. The Barrens house diary for February 19, 1861, noted somewhat bemusedly that "Father Barbier [Francis Barbier, born in France] and Tornatore [John Baptiste Tornatore, the former Vincentian visitor, born in Italy] hold many a solemn session in discussing the evils of secession. They both seem to understand thoroughly American politics but they sometimes make grave mistakes in geography, thinking some of the states only big towns."[31] While individual Vincentians might be knowledgeable and engaged citizens, community rules prohibited political partisanship. Those rules were challenged at the Barrens given the heightened emotions of the era, and especially given the mixed nature of the community (northern and southern, immigrants and native-born, priests and students).

Perhaps the clearest example of political tension among the Vincentians was reflected in the experience of Abram J. Ryan.[32] Born in

29. Slawson, "Vincentian Experience of the Civil War in Missouri," 32.
30. Ibid.
31. SMOB Records, DRMA—Students: Diaries—Record of Principle Events, 19 February 1861.
32. See O'Connell, *Furl That Banner.*

Maryland in 1838, Ryan moved to Missouri in 1840, entered the preparatory school at the Barrens in 1851, joined the Vincentian community in 1857, and, after theological study at Our Lady of Angels Seminary in Niagara, NY, was ordained a priest at the Barrens in 1860. Ryan gained a reputation for independence and political engagement early on, contributing articles to New York journals on sectional issues that reflected his pro-Southern perspectives.[33] At the Barrens from 1859 to 1861, that tendency grew. While he demonstrated a talent for preaching missions undertaken from the Barrens, Ryan came increasingly into conflict with the Vincentian visitor Stephen V. Ryan (no relation), who considered the younger man immodest and too independent for community life.[34] The superior's estimation only grew given the escalating politics of the day. In May 1861, both Ryans witnessed the tragic events at Camp Jackson in St. Louis when federal troops, attempting to secure military stores in the divided city, fired on the pro-Southern State Guard, wounding several civilians in the process.[35] Abram Ryan was moved from the Barrens shortly afterward but by 1862 he had had enough of community life and obligations. He wrote from Illinois to Mariano Maller in Paris, expressing his unhappiness in the Congregation and the lack of sympathy extended by his superiors (primarily Stephen Ryan). "Reprimands and rebuffs have been my daily bread," he complained. "I cannot live in peace in the Congregation."[36] His release from the community has been attributed variously to his overt political activities and to his anti-authoritarian behaviors.[37] Ryan later gained fame as chaplain to Confederate forces and poet for the Southern cause.

During his tenure at the Barrens, Abram Ryan was briefly responsible for the maintenance of the house diary. His entries betray his political sentiments, as in a January 1861 entry lamenting the tragedy of American sectionalism that ended, "It [the

33. Ibid., 10–11.
34. Ibid., 13.
35. Ibid., 14.
36. Personnel Files, DRMA—Souvay—Abram Ryan to Mariano Maller, 10 April 1862.
37. Slawson, "Ordeal of Abram J. Ryan," 678–719. Slawson argued that Ryan's problem accepting authority was fundamental in his relations with the Vincentians.

Union] finished its glorious career in 1861 and met its death at the hands of James Buchanan the traitor and the North."[38] While his early diary notes reflect a pronounced sympathy for the South, Ryan upheld the sanctity of the Union—"May Missouri, the western star, glitter in the spangled banner as long as the banner waves."[39] Political events, however, including the establishment of the Confederate government in February, led Ryan to a more radical pronouncement in late February: "Missouri convention meets today in the capital of the state. May we secede! Amen!"[40] The news of the battle at Fort Sumter prompted this entry: "The Union is gone. The spirit of liberty is flying away. Peace is vanquished. Commerce's paralyzed. The grave is dug. Dug by the North."[41] Following his return with Stephen V. Ryan from St. Louis, where their mission was curtailed by the Camp Jackson affair, Ryan blamed events on "the inhuman conduct of the Dutch in the seizure of Camp Jackson—where with heartless cruelty they fired into a defenseless crowd of spectators—killing and wounding men—women and children. May this brutal deed be eternalized."[42] In one of his last entries in the record, Ryan reflected on the growing conflict and the South's "firm and solemn resolve [in] girding herself for the conflict and preparing to meet the vandal hordes of Abe Lincoln and to vindicate at the sword point and the cannon's mouth Southern heroism and Southern prowess— Hurrah! for Jeff. Davis and A. Stephens."[43]

Ryan's perspective, and his willingness to publicly display his sentiments, found a ready audience among some Barrens students. By the end of 1861, partisan politics had gotten to a point that the provincial superior was forced to intervene. After a Christmas program marred by chants and demonstrations among the students, Stephen V. Ryan lectured the Barrens community. A new

38. SMOB Records, DRMA—Students: Diaries—Record of Principle Events, 4 January 1861.
39. Ibid., 19 February 1861.
40. Ibid., 28 February 1861.
41. Ibid., 21 April 1861.
42. Ibid., 15 May 1861.
43. Ibid., 29 May 1861.

house diarist noted Ryan's prohibition of activities "calculated to keep alive in our midst the party strife of North or South which now so unhappily distracts and irritates our country." The diarist's summary continued, "We have nothing whatsoever to do with politics. We can only bewail the evils to which our whole country is so sadly subjected, and must be prepared to discharge our duties hereafter either at this side or that and in any state of affairs which the Almighty will be pleased to draw out of the lamentable chaos that surrounds us."[44] While the diarist hoped "that the foolish party spirit which some boys have been fostering though perhaps unwittingly, is now at an end forever in our little seminary," Ryan returned to the theme in his report to the Barrens on completion of his official visitation in 1863. "Our rule forbidding any meddling with affairs of state," Ryan intoned, "or [siding] with political factions or making such matters the topic of our conversations, at home or with strangers is under the present sad circumstances of our poor country of the highest moment, as in the present state of distracted and divided feelings we may easily compromise ourselves and the house to the detriment of the best interests of religion."[45]

Meanwhile, the course of the war occasioned concern by Barrens residents. Any battle or skirmish in the state triggered rumors that troops were advancing on Perryville, even though the area ultimately escaped significant conflict. "Reports are so contradictory and newspapers so little to be relied upon that it is hard to arrive at a true knowledge of things," Father John Quigley observed before adding, "The signs of the times are certainly bad."[46] In a remote house where any news could ignite fears, the actual presence of federal troops aroused special notice.

> September 14, 1861—A day rendered forever memorable in the annals of the Barrens, by the martial entry into the great square of Perryville of a posse of Uncle Sam's warriors. Many an old housewife who never saw the face

44. Ibid., 26 December 1861.
45. Ibid.; and SMOB Records, DRMA—Governance: Visitations—S. V. Ryan, "House Visitation, 12 June 1863."
46. Personnel Files, DRMA—Souvay Files—Quigley to Maller, 18 July 1861.

of a soldier was on the occasion startled into the conviction that the day of Judgment had come upon her. Lackaday!! groaned the crestfallen dames, the powers of Eternity are right here!!! Well indeed the poor people, unaccustomed as they were to military maneuvering, had more than apparent cause for alarm, for the soldiers were no sooner come to town than they deployed and marched and countermarched through all the highways and byways of the Village; and the consternations of the inhabitants was such that before consciousness was reestablished nearly half the citizens and denizens were securely quartered in the courthouse as prisoners of the State. A little reflection taught them that the presence of the soldiers was for the purpose of quelling the spirit of Secession. Well, on the whole you would imagine that they succeeded tolerably in suppressing secessionary demonstrations on the part of the rational animals of this quarter; but among the irrational animals we are forced to confess the Spirit was only to an unheard of degree excited; for fat cattle walked off unceremoniously from the pasture to grease the mess-pots of the soldiery, and fast horses flew over every road in the vicinity in a way anything at all but palatable to their owners, and in a manner, forsooth, which proclaimed that the riders were United States Volunteers who had taken it into their heads to become equestrians at the expense of every quadruped in the Barrens.[47]

The troops raided the seminary orchard the next day, although some of them (perhaps in atonement) were seen at Mass that same day before moving out of the Perryville area on September 17.[48] Meanwhile, the establishment of Camp Grayson along Apple Creek in southern Perry County may have contributed to

47. SMOB Records, DRMA—Students: Diaries—Record of Principle Events, 14 September 1861.
48. Ibid., 15 September 1861 and 17 September 1861.

the fearful departure of two students from the Barrens, especially when soldiers paid an evening visit to the seminary "to wet their whistle."[49] S. V. Ryan noted recent conflict in nearby Fredericktown as well as the Apple Creek encampment of "Home Guards, federal troops numbering about a thousand," although he admitted that conditions in heavily fortified Cape Girardeau were much more severe, so that on a recent visit to the Vincentian house in that city he "was stopped by the pickets and made to show my papers five times."[50]

In April 1863, Confederate general and native Missourian John Marmaduke launched an attack on southern Missouri out of Arkansas, hoping to capture important military stores from Union outposts in Bloomfield and Pilot Knob. "There was a great scare all day about the report that Marmaduke was about to attack Perryville," the house diary reported. "He had reached Fredericktown and was on his way to Cape Girardeau, where he had a slight skirmish and then took to his heels."[51]

Perhaps the most serious panic in Perryville occurred in September 1864 in response to Sterling Price's invasion of the state. Price, a noted Missouri politician, lawyer, and soldier before the war, hoped to capture the important Union arsenal in St. Louis. Price's expedition stalled at the Battle of Pilot Knob, turning Price westward, but the Barrens diarist noted rumors of a Confederate advance on Perryville with 30,000 troops, causing stores to close and merchants to ship goods across the river to Chester for protection.[52] Most of the violence in and around Perryville took the shape of bushwacking raids and efforts to identify Confederate sympathizers, as when "some soldiers together with some men from Perryville visited our orchard and garden this evening. A man was shot in the above named town for no particular reason."[53]

49. Ibid., 10 October 1861.
50. Personnel Files, DRMA—Souvay—S. V. Ryan to Mariano Maller, 25 November 1861.
51. SMOB Records, DRMA—Students: Diaries—Record of Principle Events, 26 April 1863.
52. Ibid., 25 September 1864.
53. Ibid., 20 July 1864. The *Weekly Perryville Union* identified the man as Rufus Cox, a notorious Copperhead shot by a Union soldier.

More pertinent for the Barrens were tighter conscription laws and efforts to impose loyalty oaths during and immediately after the war. While a leading scholar suggested, "If Catholic priests during the Civil War bore arms, little evidence of it has turned up," the March 1863 conscription act passed by Congress made no exceptions for clergymen beyond the $300 commutation fee offered all affected American men.[54] Indeed, some American Catholic Church leaders differed in their reading of canon law on the matter.[55] Stephen Ryan reported to Vincentian superiors in Paris on the law, which he felt would have little real impact on American churchmen initially.[56] However, by June 1864 two Vincentians in the eastern United States were drafted, "with little likelihood of ever seeing duty," according to Ryan, and in July 1864 the commutation fee was abolished, making it more likely that conscripted men would see action.[57] A new wave of conscriptions was held in St. Louis in late 1864 with no effect on the Barrens. However, Father Daniel McCarthy of the Barrens faculty was drafted in April 1865 and reported to the Union camp at Ironton, but the war ended before he could be pressed into service.[58]

Meanwhile, the turbulent border state politics of Missouri raised new concerns for the Barrens priests. While the constitutional convention called in 1861 voted overwhelmingly against secession, Governor Claiborne Fox Jackson proved an ardent Confederate sympathizer. When federal troops occupied the state capital, the still-sitting convention assumed de facto legislative powers. Influenced by the Confederate Partisan Ranger Act of 1862, which encouraged guerilla action in Missouri, the convention passed an

---

54. Duggan, *Armsbearing and the Clergy in the History and Canon Law of Western Christianity*, 172. Duggan did cite the possible exception of the St. Louis priest Joseph Bannon (1829–1913), who served with the First Missouri Confederate Brigade as chaplain and was commended by General Sterling Price for his actions under fire. For Bannon, see Gallen, "John Bannon: Chaplain, Soldier and Diplomat"; and Tucker, *Confederacy's Fighting Chaplain*.
55. Duggan, *Armsbearing and the Clergy in the History and Canon Law of Western Christianity*, 172.
56. Slawson, "Vincentian Experience of the Civil War in Missouri," 53.
57. Ibid., 57.
58. Ibid.

ordinance in June of that year to strengthen pro-Union forces, especially in advance of the 1864 federal elections. That law required prospective voters, and anyone engaged in activities regulated or licensed by the state, to take an oath of loyalty to the Union or face legal punishment. As a legally chartered educational institution, seminary leaders were potentially exposed given the law's explicit mention of "all officers of all incorporated companies in the state" as well as clergymen who performed legally recognized marriages in the state.[59]

Stephen Ryan took advantage of the occasion to instruct the Barrens faculty on proper attitudes toward civil authority. In a September 1862 letter, Ryan advised Barrens rector Patrick McMenamy to initiate no action regarding the ordinance "unless officially notified by proper authority that you were required to conform to the enactment." In that event, Ryan counseled McMenamy that "there should be no difficulty in subscribing to the oath presented to the convention unless forms were required to which one cannot conscientiously subscribe." Allegiance to constituted political authority and "submission to the powers that be" were fundamental Catholic and Vincentian principles, according to Ryan, if accompanied by an avoidance of "party spirit or partisan politics," for "we have quite enough to do to keep to our official duties in the sacred ministry and no other employs." Of course, the Barrens, under the influence of Abram Ryan in 1861, had already evidenced a partisan spirit, and Ryan was quick to admonish the Barrens community.

> This I fear some of you forget, the gentleman who brought your letter asked some of us here on what side we were, and I told him we had no side, that we do not meddle in political matters; he told us that those of the Barrens made no secret of their sympathies and party practices, especially maintaining that everyone knew Mr. Gleeson's and Mr. Shaw's politics. All that is wrong, if you must preoccupy yourselves, engage your thoughts

59. Anderson, "The Missouri Oath of Loyalty of 1865."

and attentions on such matters, why at least not have prudence and why blab everything in the presence of strangers. Our rules require us to take no part in civil dissensions and not make them the topic of our conversation with each other or strangers.[60]

The matter did not rest there, however, for shortly after the war a newly established state convention, dominated by Radical Republicans intent on expediting emancipation of Missouri's slaves and rooting out closet Confederates, drafted a new constitution that was narrowly endorsed by the state electorate in June 1865. The so-called Drake Constitution, named for the St. Louis lawyer and prominent Radical Republican Charles Drake, included a much more restrictive loyalty oath. This "ironclad oath" detailed eighty-six acts of disloyalty against Missouri and the Union and required an oath asserting innocence of these violations.[61] This time, all clergymen were required to take the oath by September 1865, with Republican Governor Thomas Fletcher (himself a Union officer during the war) suggesting that clergy had no constitutional right to preach at all without government approval.[62] Catholic clergymen felt particularly targeted by the oath and counted among its most vocal opponents.[63] Indeed, Archbishop Peter Kenrick of St. Louis issued a pastoral letter condemning the oath and advising priests to refuse to take it.[64]

Ryan rose to the occasion in a letter to Vincentian authorities in Paris.

> Today the new constitution of the state of Missouri goes into force in which it is prescribed that all ministers of the Gospel, Priests, Bishops, etc. cannot preach, teach, marry, etc. with[out] taking a certain oath of loyalty declaring they never aided by word or act or

---

60. Provincial Files, DRMA—Ryan Papers—S. V. Ryan to Patrick McMenamy, 6 September 1862.
61. Parrish, *History of Missouri*, 3:121.
62. Ibid., 3:131.
63. Barclay, "Test Oath for Clergy in Missouri," 365.
64. Parrish, *History of Missouri*, 3:130.

sympathy the late rebellion, under penalty of five hundred dollar fine or six months imprisonment in county jail or both. The Catholic clergy will take no notice of it and continue to discharge their ministerial duties, believing it an infringement of the liberty of worship guaranteed by the constitution of the U.S. The civil power has no right to impose conditions on the exercise of our Priestly functions as long as we confine ourselves to our priestly duties and meddle not with civil or secular affairs and violate no constitutional law of the land. We know not yet what may be the consequences or how far or in what manner the authorities of the state or the radical authors of this radical constitution may see fit to enforce this clause. We will have our chance of being indicted and brought before the civil court and then the Supreme Court will have to decide on its constitutionality. We are evidently in the right and shall stand firm and eventually come out victorious.[65]

As it turned out, the oath was unevenly enforced, especially in the more Catholic and German areas of the state. The majority of clergymen refused the oath, with an estimated 600 to 1,000 nonjurors still preaching seven months after the September 1865 deadline.[66] Almost forty priests were indicted for failure to take the oath, six in Cape Girardeau County, including St. Vincent College faculty members, most prominently "the venerable and worthy" seventy-three-year-old Father John Francis McGerry, whose indictment even Governor Fletcher lamented, but none from Perry County or the Barrens.[67] The dramatic story of the "ironclad oath" culminated with the trial of Father John Cummings, an archdiocesan priest whose case was ultimately brought to the United States Supreme

65. Provincial Files, DRMA—Ryan Papers—S. V. Ryan to Mariano Maller, 3 September 1865.
66. Barclay, "Test Oath for Clergy in Missouri," 365.
67. Ibid., 372–73.

Court, which found the law unconstitutional in January 1867.[68] While "a great majority of the cases were never brought to trial, and the proportion of convictions to indictments was absurdly small," the oath reflected the depth of wartime tension in Missouri, and the consequences of that tension on the American Catholic community, including the Barrens.[69]

Postwar Desolation

Like many areas of the expanding American Republic, Perryville grew impressively during and after the Civil War.[70] The local economy prospered, with a reported 800 percent increase in manufactured goods produced from 1860 to 1870 and an accompanying rise in cultivated farm acreage.[71]

The Barrens seminary, however, did not share in the growth of the surrounding region and the country as a whole. Indeed, waves of immigration and the expansion of industrial manufacturing fixed the attention of Catholic leaders on service and provision of clergy for growing American cities. Whereas on its founding, the Barrens had been one of only four operating seminaries in the United States, by 1870 practically every American bishop either maintained or considered establishing his own diocesan seminary. Many of these institutions proved fleeting, some merely appendages to established cathedral schools or academies, and others were readily turned over to religious orders for operation.[72] Whereas the Barrens was the only Vincentian-run seminary up to 1838, after that date the community accepted responsibility for diocesan seminaries across much of the United States. Acceptance of these new apostolates further diluted an already overstretched Vincentian personnel pool. Combined with other newly established seminaries, this growth detracted from the appeal of the Barrens. Of course, Civil War tensions contributed to this trend and prevented some

68. Parrish, *History of Missouri*, 3:132–35.
69. Barclay, "Test Oath for Clergy in Missouri," 380.
70. Hubrick, "Perry County Through the Civil War," 20.
71. Ibid.
72. White, *Diocesan Seminary in the United States*, xi.

bishops from shipping their precious seminarians out to an embattled border state.

Even the Vincentians themselves questioned the utility of educating their own seminarians at the Barrens. S. V. Ryan started the exodus from the Barrens with the transfer of provincial headquarters to St. Louis in May 1862, leaving only the lay college and the few diocesan seminarians still being sent by bishops to the Barrens. The catastrophic 1866 fire that consumed the college building completed the process. With lay collegians transferred to Cape Girardeau, the Barrens campus was left with only a small day academy, operated largely to maintain the terms of the state charter, in addition to the parish and farm. "Since the removal of the Seminary," Ryan wrote in an 1867 circular letter to the American province, "the [Barrens] community has been reduced in numbers and devoted more particularly to the care of the Parish . . . [and] the education of the youth of the locality. And here you find an ample field that will repay your zealous labors and to be able to reap an abundant harvest of souls for God and merits for yourselves."[73]

Less than a year later Ryan wrote another provincial letter to announce the impending move of the community's central house from St. Louis to Germantown, Pennsylvania and to review the state of the American Vincentian province. Ryan was soon to be elevated to the bishopric of Buffalo, and his letter neatly summarized the spirit of the new age of consolidation in the American Catholic Church. "Our aim," he intoned, "has been not to accept new foundations, many of which have been persistently offered, but to consolidate, strengthen, organize with all the conditions of a regular Community the already existing houses of the Province."[74] This perceived retrenchment was necessitated by the fact of overstretched resources and personnel, owing partly to the loss of "several of our very best and most experienced confreres" through

73. Provincial Files, DRMA—Ryan Papers—S. V. Ryan, "Circular Letter to Province, St. Mary's Seminary, June 7, 1867."
74. Provincial Files, DRMA—Ryan Papers—S. V. Ryan, "Circular Letter to Province, St. Vincent's Church, St. Louis, January 13, 1868."

episcopal promotions or death. In the existing "regularly consti-tuted houses" of the congregation, Ryan called for a greater *esprit de corps* and willingness to sacrifice for the overall health of the com-munity, including support of the new central house. Ryan noted that the Barrens still housed five priests and seven brothers, with a debt of over $5,000 owed to the Province.[75]

John Hayden, Ryan's successor as visitor of the American prov-ince, proved initially more solicitous of the Barrens and in 1869 tentatively proposed the removal of seminarians from St. Vincent's in Cape Girardeau, which operated "a large school" with "near 100 boys" that threatened to overwhelm its small contingent of clerical candidates, to the Barrens.[76] Within a year, however, Hayden recog-nized the impracticality of the move.

> But after thinking and consulting I am led to believe it would not succeed. In the first place we would have to go into debt to support the seminarians, as what the bishops give would not be sufficient for that purpose. Then the place is as far out of the way and is unhealthy as ever, and the bishops would not like to send the sem-inarians, and the seminarians would not like to stay there. It is too near the Cape for a little seminary, even if there were no other reasons against. So that I do not know what can be done with it. . . . After all I think the best things we can do is to sell it. I am sure it is not my own natural feelings that have led me to this conclusion, but the good, or at least what seems to me, the good of the community. Scarcely any confrere wishes to go there and after all what good is it to the community to keep the place up as it is. If sold it would help us to build up other places and that house and Donaldsonville being broken up, we might form a good band of missionaries.[77]

75. Ibid.
76. Personnel Files, DRMA—Souvay—John Hayden to Jean-Baptiste Etienne, 28 Sep-tember 1869.
77. Personnel Files, DRMA—Souvay—John Hayden to Jean-Baptiste Etienne, 22 March 1870.

Such were the gloomy prospects of the Barrens by 1877 when Mariano Maller was commissioned to undertake a general visitation of the American Vincentian community on behalf of the superior general. The well-regarded Maller had served as American visitor from 1846 to 1850 before his departure for Brazil and, ultimately, back to his native Spain and service to the Parisian headquarters of the congregation. Superior General Etienne undoubtedly saw the trusted Maller as the ideal observer of American Vincentian conditions, especially given repeated concerns about failures to conform to Vincentian ideals. Maller's report highlighted those concerns, particularly regarding debt and lack of disciplinary norms and spiritual practices.

Maller's visit to the Barrens struck a particularly poignant note. "This is the oldest house in the province and for 20 years was the only important one," he recorded, "but it has passed through a good many troubles."[78] Maller noted the old fears regarding the unhealthy climate of the Barrens, the divisions and "spirit of innovation" that developed among the Barrens confreres as early as 1840, and the removal of programs to St. Louis and Cape Girardeau that repeatedly altered the composition of the house through the Civil War era. "At that point," he concluded with less optimism than Ryan's earlier reports, "the Barrens was almost entirely abandoned. Only the parish remained and they were constrained to open a kind of school which ran for only about six months of the year for a small number of young people from the area to fulfill one of the conditions of the charter." There were reasons for some hope of revival at the Barrens. The 1850 brick house was "comfortable, well constructed and capable" of housing up to fifty residents; the church, while no longer the "marvel of the area" it had been, was spacious and accommodating to current liturgical needs; and land was abundant, with prospects for enhanced agricultural production. Despite these advantages, however, the Barrens was still saddled with a "very large debt" (which he estimated between $3,360 and $6,720 based on the ill-kept account books of the house) and, more importantly, suffered

---

78. Rybolt, "American Vincentians in 1877–78: Maller Visitation Report (2)," 250.

from a lack of capable leadership. "At length, after several years, the house is foundering because of the negligence or incapacity of its superiors and procurators. They have been changed often, but without bettering the condition. The recently named superior [Daniel McCarthy] seems to me capable of getting the house out of its problems, since resources are not lacking, and he knows how to use them well."[79]

Maller's report included a wrenching lament for the Barrens.

> To me it would seem to be impossible to depict what I experienced there last November, when I was at the Barrens again, after an absence of more than twenty-seven years. It had been thirty-seven years since I had first come here. At that time it was so happy, so populous, so lively, while now it is so desolate, so lonely, so quiet. A profound sadness came over my soul and I wondered: what sin has merited such desolation? Isolation, of course, malaria, and everything said to justify this decision did not satisfy me, and the words of Our Lord sprang unbidden to me: *omne regnum*, etc.[80]

Maller's sentiments were echoed by Thomas J. Smith on his investiture as American visitor in 1879. The often irascible Smith called his confreres to a greater adherence to Vincentian rules and a greater allegiance to the entire American Vincentian community, including respect for its historic motherhouse.

> And so it has come to pass that the place which of all others should be called and in reality should be the Alma Mater—the center of attraction for the Congregation is become like a bye word and a reproach and seemingly a place to be shunned by all. Instead of vying with each other, as one might expect, for the honor of guarding, caring for and beautifying the place sacred by so many memories and traditions, it would seem to be a sacrifice

79. Ibid., 252.
80. Ibid, 250–51.

almost too great to be borne, for anyone to accept of the position when offered by obediences.[81]

Three years later, Smith complained that "some in comparing the condition of this house with the past are in danger of ingratitude to God not being able to appreciate and subsequently undervaluing his present favors."[82] But the new visitor had both the authority and the determination to revive the Barrens, and his later report from that house struck a more optimistic note. "In spite of our many failings and shortcomings it [the Barrens] has been moving on prosperously and steadily," he wrote in 1885, "[and] if it be His Holy Will to assign to it in the future nobler and more ambitious ends we may hope it may not be wanting in its duty in that contingency either."[83]

Smith's determination paved the way for the division of the American Vincentian province and the reopening of the Barrens as the central house for the new western province by 1888. But the revived Barrens would be a very different place, and the next one hundred years would provide another cycle of triumph and decline at St. Mary's of the Barrens.

81. Provincial Files, DRMA—Smith Papers—Thomas Smith, "Circular Letter, St. Mary's of the Barrens, July 8, 1880."
82. Provincial Files, DRMA—Smith Papers—Thomas Smith, "Circular Letter, St. Mary's of the Barrens, July 19, 1883."
83. Provincial Files, DRMA—Smith Papers—Thomas J. Smith, "Circular Letter, St. Mary's of the Barrens, November 6, 1885."

Part 4

The Barrens Triumphant, 1888–1962

Chapter Seven
REVIVAL AND GROWTH

> I was actually at home, the home of my youth, "where
> beauty, power, glory, all are aisled."
>
> —T. S. Shaw, CM (1899)

The long and eventful period in the history of the American Catholic Church stretching from the Third Plenary Council of Baltimore (1884) to the beginning of the Second Vatican Council (1962) offered new challenges and opportunities that were reflected in the history of the newly revived St. Mary's of the Barrens. A growing and increasingly confident United States provided context for an American Catholic Church struggling to resolve its own problems of dynamic growth and uncertain identity. The Barrens began this period with a new lease on life occasioned by the division of the American Vincentian province; grew in numbers, programs, and confidence despite continued problems of adequate finances; and ended in a flurry of excitement and self-questioning inspired by the prospects of Catholic and community renewal. Given its humble origins and twenty-year exile, the seventy-five-year period beginning in 1888 appears as a virtual age of triumph in the history of the Barrens.

In his brief survey of the history of the American Catholic community, Patrick Carey identified key themes in the period under review, noting the shifting fortunes of the Catholic Church amid the vagaries of American social and cultural change as well as the persistence of underlying problems occasioned by demographic growth, the needs of a largely immigrant population, and efforts to engage the broader American culture. In particular, Carey cites the "crisis that publicly divided bishops and others into warring factions over how the Church should relate to the modern and changing world" in the late nineteenth century. Leo XIII's critique of "Americanism" in 1899 and Pius X's broader condemnation of "modernism" in 1907 quieted these public disputes so that American Catholic leaders focused their efforts on confronting the spirit of American Progressivism through a renewed sense of mission, both domestic and international.[1] By the 1920s and '30s, accelerated growth fueled Catholic confidence while at the same time presenting new challenges in the forms of cultural permissiveness in the Roaring Twenties, economic uncertainty in the Great Depression, and international threats in the growth of totalitarianism and the onset of World War II.[2] Finally, the twenty years after the war witnessed tremendous institutional growth and the growing influence of the American Catholic church in defining the role of religion in Cold War disputes. At the same time, divisions loomed as Catholics debated the necessity of reform to meet new cultural realities.[3] Amid these ebbs and flows, the American Catholic community increased dramatically (to a population of over forty-five million by 1965) and Catholic institutions, including seminaries, even more so.[4]

The challenges and opportunities facing the American Catholic Church were reflected in the history of Catholic seminaries in this period. In general, the often undifferentiated and impermanent institutions of the earlier nineteenth century gave way to larger "freestanding" seminaries by midcentury, which in turn transformed into the more uniform, standardized, and Roman-influenced schools of the twentieth century. Joseph M. White reviewed these changes, especially for diocesan seminaries, in his general history of American seminaries and a series of articles outlining the broad

---

1. Carey, *Catholics in America*, 55, 68–72.
2. Ibid., 79.
3. Ibid., 93.
4. Ibid., 79, 93. Carey cites growth rates for American Catholic seminary enrollments of 140 percent from 1920 to 1945 and 127 percent from 1945 to 1965.

changes that characterized seminary development.[5] While White focused primarily on seminaries that trained diocesan clergy, his insights are relevant to the experience of the Barrens and other seminaries operated by and for Catholic religious communities. As primarily an internal seminary training candidates for the Vincentian order after 1888, the Barrens focused on the inculcation of Vincentian norms and spirituality among its students, and it answered more to the European superiors of the Congregation than to local bishops, but many of the other characteristic trends of diocesan seminaries held true at St. Mary's. Indeed, some of the issues faced by diocesan seminaries regarding encroaching Roman authority had been true of the Barrens even earlier given its accountability to European superiors. The forces at work in seminary education at the end of the nineteenth century were particularly germane to the Barrens as a "new" institution, rising (as it were) from the ashes in a period of critical change for the education of Catholic clergy in the United States.

The Third Plenary Council of Baltimore was convened in 1884 at the insistence of the Vatican in response to ongoing tensions between American bishops and priests—what Roman officials identified as the problem of "discipline and debts."[6] The Vatican attributed these problems to inadequate seminary training, and suggested reforms aimed at strengthening the course of academic studies in American seminaries and reducing exposure to secular American culture. While some American bishops demurred, the Council adopted norms that lengthened seminary studies to six years for the minor seminary (in American practice, the four years of high school and first two years of general college education), with an emphasis on a broad program of humanistic education, and six years for the major seminary (two years of philosophy and four years of theology), with more attention paid to "formerly neglected" disciplines including biblical studies, church history, and homiletics.[7]

---

5. White, *Diocesan Seminary in the United States*; White, "Diocesan Seminary and the Community of Faith"; and White, "Perspectives on the Nineteenth-Century Diocesan Seminary."
6. White, "Perspectives on the Nineteenth-Century Diocesan Seminary," 31.
7. White, "Diocesan Seminary and the Community of Faith," 9.

While not all American seminaries immediately implemented these specific norms, most accepted the new focus on training priests to be well-rounded, physically able, and broadly educated gentlemen with a proper appreciation for American culture—and bishops like James Gibbons of Baltimore, Bernard McQuaid of Rochester, New York, and John Ireland of St. Paul, Minnesota, eagerly embraced that spirit.[8] The new model and mandated norms inspired a "burst of creative thought and activity" regarding seminary reforms, including the establishment of new institutions with larger student populations, more native-born American seminarians, and more rigorous academic programs.[9]

Some of the suggested new American reforms ran counter to the increasingly centralized and anti-modernist attitude of the post–Vatican Council I papacy.[10] Leo XIII's censure of "Americanism" in 1899 and Pius X's condemnation of "modernism" in 1907 accentuated a growing trend of Romanization, culminating in the 1917 revised Code of Canon Law. Even earlier, a new Sacred Congregation of Seminaries and Universities was established to oversee curriculum and standards, requiring bishops to submit reports every three years regarding the status of their schools and seminaries. The general direction set by the Vatican favored isolating seminaries from the broader world, and as late as the post–World War II era the Sacred Congregation continued to push regulations seemingly disconnected from the spirit of broader American culture and education.[11] At the same time, Pius XII's 1950 apostolic exhortation *Menti Nostrae* encouraged high-quality academic studies, inspiring many American seminaries, including the Barrens, to pursue professional accreditation for

8. Ibid., 11–13.
9. White, "Perspectives on the Nineteenth-Century Diocesan Seminary," 34.
10. See, for example, John Talbot Smith, whose 1897 work "Our Seminaries: An Essay in Clerical Training" called for a new curriculum based on more modern historical approaches and Bishop Camillus Maes of Covington, Kentucky, who authored a series of articles in *The American Ecclesiastical Review* proposing more freedom for seminarians to pursue pastoral as well as academic pursuits. White, "Diocesan Seminary and the Community of Faith," 14–15.
11. Ibid., 16–17.

their programs.[12] In general, the trend in the period from 1884 to 1962 favored more standardized seminary programs with longer and more rigorous academic curricula and, after 1899, more direction from Roman authorities. As a result, a rapidly growing American Catholic Church, faced with pressing issues regarding care for its immigrant members and conciliation with American values, trained a cadre of native-born priests according to a new model of priesthood and consistent with more uniform Roman expectations. St. Mary's of the Barrens both reflected and contradicted these norms in the late nineteenth and twentieth centuries given its adherence to Vincentian ideas and authorities and its perceived isolation from the growing centers of American Catholic activity.

New Beginnings

From its founding in 1818 until 1835, the Vincentian community in the United States operated as a mission administered directly from the European headquarters of the Congregation. In 1835, this mission community was elevated to the status of a province, with a superior (visitor) charged with leadership and general administration. In 1888, the American province was divided into two separate provinces in recognition of its growing numbers (from 1878 until 1919 the number of American Vincentians grew from 73 priests to 265)[13] and the vast distances between Vincentian houses across the American continent. The decision to split the American province was encouraged by Thomas Smith, provincial visitor since 1879 and strong advocate for the restoration of the Barrens.

The details of the division into two provinces were spelled out in instructions by Vincentian Superior General Antoine Fiat and reiterated in a directive from Smith, who now assumed leadership of the western province, and James McGill of the eastern province. The boundary between the two provinces would run from the western border of Indiana southward to the western border of Alabama,

12. Ibid., 17.
13. Rybolt, *Vincentians*, 5:554.

13. THOMAS J. SMITH

An Irish immigrant to the United States, Smith (1832–1905) studied at the Barrens and served in numerous Vincentian parishes and seminaries until his appointment as visitor in 1879. He was largely responsible for the division of the American Vincentian community into two provinces in 1888, with the new western province headquartered at the Barrens. Smith continued to serve as western provincial superior until his death in 1905.

granting to the eastern province the existing Vincentian houses in Niagara and Brooklyn (New York), Germantown (Pennsylvania), and Emmitsburg and Baltimore (Maryland) and to the western provinces the houses in Chicago and LaSalle (Illinois); St. Louis, Perryville, and Cape Girardeau (Missouri); New Orleans (Louisiana); and Los Angeles (California). All the properties and personnel of those houses would "belong to that division or province in which it was then found to be and situated."[14] Since the only internal Vincentian seminary in existence was located in Germantown, the decision was made to divide the students at Germantown evenly among the two provinces, with eight seminarians and three novices transferred to the Barrens as the nucleus of a new western seminary.[15]

14. Provincial Files, DRMA—Smith Papers—Thomas Smith, CM, and James McGill, CM Letter of 27 October 27, 1888.
15. See SMOB Records, DRMA—History: General Histories—Musson, "Historical Sketches of the Western Province (1888–1935)," 1. Musson was one of the original three novices transferred to the Barrens, and he recalled that these novices were told by McGill that they were only "on loan" to the western province. The transfer proved difficult, and "was felt all the more when a few days later, they were told that there never was any understanding between the two Visitors that they were just loaned and

In anticipation of the division of provinces, an apostolic school had been opened on the Barrens campus two years before the formal erection of the western province.[16] The apostolic school was situated in the revamped original log building at the Barrens and was directed by William J. Barnwell, a newly ordained Baltimore native who spent his entire clerical career at the Barrens. Barnwell was assisted by two other priests, four brothers, a lay oblate, and a seminarian from Germantown who taught at the school while being tutored in theology. The student body consisted initially of six students on its formal opening in December 1886, with six more students arriving from New Orleans in the spring of 1887.[17] Reminiscing almost fifty years later on the reopening of a school at the Barrens, John Faris recalled that "reality failed to live up to their expectations" as students drawn to the historical old campus confronted the "blackened foundations" of the burned college building and a once-magnificent church "now sadly in need of repair."[18] Within two years enrollment grew to forty students, the church was undergoing extensive repairs, and the grounds were being groomed to some semblance of order.[19] By 1892, a new brick building was completed for the apostolic school, and in 1910 that school was transferred to St. Vincent's College in Cape Girardeau when that institution lost its status as a major seminary for diocesan students.

Numerous challenges faced the students and faculty of the Barrens as they reestablished themselves on the old campus. The problem of physical remoteness remained, as Perryville still lacked rail connections to St. Louis. According to William Musson, the trip from St. Louis involved crossing the river into Illinois, in the

---

would return East in the spring after making their vows"; ibid., 2–3.

16. An apostolic school was essentially a preparatory/high school for prospective candidates to the Congregation. Apostolic schools were first started in nineteenth-century France to train recruits for the foreign mission. By the later part of the century several religious communities were establishing apostolic schools to provide a pool of ready recruits for their own communities.

17. SMOB Records, DRMA—Students: Diaries—Record of Principle Events, 8 December 1886.

18. SMOB Records, DRMA—History: Anniversaries—Faris, "In Retrospect."

19. SMOB Records, DRMA—History: General Histories—Musson, "Historical Sketches of the Western Province (1888–1935)," 3–4.

process switching trains at Percy, Illinois, crossing back into Missouri via ferryboat at Claryville, and riding a surrey the remaining fifteen miles to the Barrens. "Thus," Musson recalled, "it took almost a whole day to travel from St. Louis to Perryville.[20] Once arrived at the Barrens, students found makeshift quarters in the existing buildings, the novices housed "over the present recreation room of the priests [in a room] divided by curtains."[21] Musson described the campus in 1888:

> Besides the seminary building at this time, there were two other buildings, one known as the Brothers' Building, and another which was parallel to the path running down to the statue. This was a two story building. The first floor was used as a study hall and the second as a dormitory. The old Brothers' Building had a third story with dormer windows, north and south. The older boys used this part of the building while the smaller boys used the other. Then after a year or two, a study hall was built where the present [1935] students' building now stands. It was just one story and was later used as a laundry. Then both floors of the building along the path were used for the small and medium boys as dormitories.[22]

Barrens students were expected to aid the brothers in cutting wood and repairing buildings and grounds, rewarded by meals described by Musson as "nothing to brag about."[23]

Finances remained, as always, a chronic problem at the Barrens, so much so that a special levy was laid on the other houses of the western province in 1894. "The circumstances of this Central House of your Province require your special attention and solicitude," wrote Father Malachy O'Callaghan, commissioned to visit and report on conditions in the province by the superior general.

20. Ibid., 3.
21. Ibid., 4.
22. Ibid., 6.
23. Ibid., 5.

14. Barrens Campus Before 1913
A view of the Barrens campus from the south, showing the newly constructed Apostolic School (1892) in the foreground along an axis with the administrative/priests' building (1850) and the church (1837) in the background. The original seminary building remains on the left side of the photo.

"The amount of the tax on the resources of each house on the list of those in a state to contribute has been found quite inadequate to meet the expenses of this Central House which amount to annually $12000 [for a house of] . . . 118 including 57 in the Apostolic School."[24] The problem continued through the early years of the twentieth century, so that a gift of $12,000 made to Thomas Smith on the golden jubilee of his ordination in 1903 must have seemed a windfall for the visitor, who used the money to build a new water system at the Barrens.[25]

While location, facilities, and finances remained problematic, numbers grew at the Barrens. From 1886, when the reopening of the apostolic school brought the population of the Barrens to a total of fifteen (including priests, brothers, and students), the house

24. Provincial Files, DRMA—Smith Papers—Malachy O'Callaghan, CM, Letter of 13 November 1894.
25. SMOB Records, DRMA—Buildings and Grounds—Hoernig, "Birth of a Water System," 2.

grew to sixty-one (six priests, four brothers, three novices, eight seminarians, and forty apostolic school students) only two years later.[26] By 1893, when growth led to the construction of a separate building for the apostolic school, the Barrens superior reported a total of 104 students (18 novices, 14 scholastics, and 62 apostolic school boys); by 1896 a population of 123 students; by 1897 a total of 111 students; and by 1903, according to the visitation report of Constance Demion, the Barrens community numbered ten priests, six brothers, eleven seminarians, thirty-two scholastics, and sixty-five apostolic school students.[27] Shortly thereafter the student population "leveled off," at the same time that the modernization of facilities (including the introduction of electricity) and the transfer of the apostolic school to Cape Girardeau contributed to a "quieter and more restrained air" at the Barrens.[28]

Amid the chronic financial problems and rapid growth, the overriding issue facing the restored seminary was an academic one. How would the Barrens adjust to new demands—from its own Congregation, from the Vatican, and from American bishops—for a lengthened and more rigorous academic formation program for seminarians?

Historically, Catholic seminaries in the modern era were not renowned for their intellectualism. Clerical formation emphasized the cultivation of virtue over intellect, and academic demands often focused on rote memory of standard Catholic formulae. This was true even of the French seminaries operated by the Sulpicians and Vincentians, who operated most of the seminaries in France before the Revolution. While St. Vincent had devised the division of clerical formation into major and minor phases, "the seminaries of France had neither a fixed curriculum nor a determined length of time for their training."[29] The trend was, perhaps, accentuated after the

26. SMOB Records, DRMA—History: General Histories—Musson, "Historical Sketches of the Western Province (1888–1935)," 2–3.
27. Thomas Weldon to Antoine Fiat, 5 May 1893, GCUSA, DRMA, Series A, roll #2, item 360; William Barnwell to Antoine Fiat, 20 October 1896, GCUSA, DRMA, Series A, roll #2, item 399; Barnwell to Fiat, 1 August 1897, CGUSA, DRMA, Series A, roll #2, item 360; William Barnwell to Antoine Fiat, 20 October 1896, GCUSA, DRMA, Series A, roll #2, item 411; and Constance Demion, CM, "House Visitation Report 1903."
28. Grace, "Growth and Development of St. Mary's of the Barrens."
29. Poole, *Seminaries in Crisis*, 37.

turmoil of the revolutionary age. "The clergy trained in nineteenth-century France," according to Sergius Wroblewski, "knew little or nothing of the intellectual and moral currents infusing the secular milieu."[30] By the late nineteenth century, many seminaries were "unable to accept new directions, even when they came from Pope Leo XIII."[31] When those seminaries were transplanted into American soil, where vast distances and a growing Catholic immigrant population demanded immediate accommodation, academic formation often gave way to practical needs and circumstances.

By the late nineteenth century, however, the social and cultural context of American seminaries was changing. As noted above, American bishops, partly in response to increasing Roman demands, passed new norms for American seminaries at the Third Plenary Council of Baltimore in 1884. Even before the council, however, Vincentian superiors had decreed changes for their own seminaries. The determined Antoine Fiat, longest serving superior general in the history of the Congregation (1878–1914), was known for his interest in expanding and improving Vincentian seminary education. Fiat oversaw the establishment of apostolic schools, founded a Vincentian house of studies in Rome, and encouraged priests to pursue advanced degrees there. In an 1882 circular letter to Vincentian houses worldwide, Fiat recommended a major seminary program that included a full two years of novitiate as well as two years of philosophy studies and four years of theology.[32]

As with other Vincentian seminaries, the Barrens was slow to implement the new reforms. The lack of resources to support an extended period of formation combined with the natural reluctance of Thomas Smith, who hesitated to send his men for advanced studies and proved indifferent to the demands for quality seminary education.[33] In letter after letter to Fiat, Smith temporized on directives to implement the new norms and to send Vincentians from his

---

30. Wroblewski, "Intellectual Climate in Seminary Life," 234.
31. Ibid.
32. Rybolt, *Vincentians*, 5:35.
33. Poole, "Ad Cleri Disciplinam," 140. Poole characterized Smith's view as "any Vincentian could be a seminary professor."

province to Rome for study.[34] Smith's own confreres grew frustrated with his attitude. Peter V. Byrne, superior at St. Vincent's College in Cape Girardeau and later the first president of DePaul University, along with his assistant rector Francis Nugent, were known critics of the quality of American Vincentian academic formation.[35] Byrne and Nugent were involved in raising funds for the new Kenrick Seminary in St. Louis (established in 1893), pushing Smith to appoint his best men to the faculty of the new seminary given its high visibility in the American Catholic church and complaining to Fiat of their superior's intransigence.

At the same time, William Musson recalled a routine at the Barrens that included a demanding schedule of classes and study throughout the day.[36] While Smith eventually implemented the more academically rigorous norms, some remembered the Roman degrees as less than demanding and John Faris's reminiscences of education at the Barrens condemned the "virus of rationalism" that characterized "learned" men and threatened to work itself "down to the very life of the common people."[37]

As the formation program changed and modernized, the Barrens became the home for generations of American Vincentians. From 1888 to 1985, nearly every Vincentian ordained for the western province spent at least part of his seminary years at the Barrens. The apostolic school educated high school–age students from 1886 until it was moved to Cape Girardeau in 1910. The novitiate, whether of one or two years' duration, was spent at the Barrens until its move to Santa Barbara in 1964. The "college" seminary, including the final two years of the minor seminary and the two years of philosophy attached to the major seminary, operated at St. Mary's until its closure in 1985. The "theologate," or four years of theological studies for Vincentian candidates,

---

34. As late as 1896, Barrens superior William Barnwell wrote Fiat regarding implementation of the new regulations and requesting copies of the *Directory for Major Seminaries*. William Barnwell to Antoine Fiat, 12 December 1896, GCUSA, DRMA, Series A, roll #2, item 403.
35. Poole, "Ad Cleri Disciplinam," 139.
36. SMOB Records, DRMA—History: General Histories—Musson, "Historical Sketches of the Western Province (1888–1935)," 6.
37. SMOB Records, DRMA—History: Anniversaries—Faris, "In Retrospect," 3.

was located at the Barrens until its transfer to Lemont, Illinois in 1965.

This was true even after the resignation of Thomas Smith, the avowed champion of the Barrens, in 1905. He was succeeded briefly by William Barnwell, who died of a stroke suddenly in January 1906 only four months after assuming the visitorship. After Barnwell's death, the office passed to Thomas O'Neil Finney, a native of New Orleans who entered the Vincentian community in 1892, was ordained in 1898, received doctorates in Rome in 1901, and served as director of novices at the Barrens before his appointment as provincial superior. By all accounts, Finney's tenure proved a trying period for the province, as he "proved to be an inept administrator all through his twenty years in office"—avoiding major decisions, deferring to house superiors, rarely meeting his provincial council, and amassing large debts that drove the province to "the brink of bankruptcy" by 1918.[38] Conditions in the western province and its central house only improved under the leadership of William P. Barr, another New Orleans native and graduate of the Roman house of studies who showed "energy and decisiveness" in his years as visitor from 1926 to 1938.[39]

Under Smith and his immediate successors, the Barrens remained the largest house of the new western province. Although it continued to suffer from some of the same problems that contributed to the closure of the seminary program in 1862, including complaints about its physical remoteness and chronic financial woes, the Barrens was described as a "bustling historical house" replete with growing seminary programs, parish, and mission band.[40] While the seminary seemed poised for a more secure future, the vexing issues of physical expansion, growth of both internal and outreach programs, academic, rigor and adherence to standards imposed by the superiors of the Congregation, Vatican officials, and the American episcopacy reflected broader trends in the American Catholic community.

---

38. Rybolt, *Vincentians*, 5:558; Editorial Staff, "Survey of American Vincentian History," 61.
39. Editorial Staff, "Survey of American Vincentian History," 61.
40. Rybolt, *Vincentians*, 5:558.

Bricks and Mortar

Summarizing the history of the buildings of St. Mary's of the Barrens is a difficult task. Many of the earliest structures on the Barrens campus were rough, makeshift buildings with sparse existing documentation regarding construction and precise location. Complicating the task is the frustrating practice among community members of referring to buildings by various names given their changing functions over time. From the earliest log cabins built by the pioneers of the Barrens to the most recent construction of a graduated community residence and retirement center, building at the Barrens often entailed a process of demolition of the old to welcome new structures more suited to the changing needs of the house and its works. In the process, what few strategic plans for the physical layout of the campus emerged usually gave way to short-term expedients or the constant pressure of scarce resources. The period from 1888 to 1962, however, represented the height of the Barrens' building history and the clearest reflection of the institution's "years of triumph."

The physical appearance of the Barrens at the beginning of this period was clearly, if somewhat romantically, described by a senior Vincentian returning to the campus in 1899 after an absence of some years. Thomas Shaw's letter guides the reader through a tour of the site, entering from the southeast by buggy through a double-gated entrance lined by "an avenue of stately pines" before coming upon the large and impressive new building housing the apostolic school (built in 1892) that represented the "Renaissance of this Central House."[41] Shaw comments on this "magnificent apostolic school, the most easterly of the [Barrens] buildings" that replaced the burned-out old college building. From the east, Shaw moved through the community chapel (Oliva Hall or the "brothers building," constructed in 1898) to the student's dormitory and the "Community and boys' refectories" to the "Missionaries house" (the red-brick Rosati Hall or priests' building constructed in 1850) before coming to the Church of the Assumption, "in the rear [of which] still stands the great oaken log house put together by the

---

41. Shaw's letter is reprinted in the *De Andrein* 3, no. 4 (January 1933).

15. CHURCH FAÇADE
Workers pose during the construction of the remodeling of the Church of the Assumption around 1913. The renovation removed the twin towers from the sides of the church and added a large rose window to the façade.

Timons and Odins, a little modernized but substantially the same as it was." Coming out of the church, Shaw notes the community cemetery (dating from the 1840s, replacing the older Barrens Settlement cemetery on present-day Sycamore Lane to the north of Rosati Hall) and, nearby, the "little log cabin in which the illustrious Bishop Rosati lived and which he made his sacristy." Along the way, Shaw admired the well-kept grounds, with their quarter-mile "avenue which opens in the rear of the buildings and runs its way through the old orchard where it ends, forming a circle around which arise lofty pines [estimated in the 1950s to be almost a century old] and in the center of which a mound is raised on which the great Mother of God under the figure of the Immaculate Conception stands as our Protectress."[42]

42. Ibid.

The first new building constructed after the reopening of the Barrens seminary was designed to house the apostolic school and was completed in 1892 near the site of the lay college building that was destroyed by fire in 1866. Known variously over the ensuing decades as the Apostolic School, Thomas Smith Hall, and "C" Building, the three-story, red-brick late Gothic revival structure was located east of Rosati Hall and was built under the direction of Joseph Lansman, the same Cape Girardeau Catholic who constructed Rosati Hall over forty years earlier. After the transfer of the apostolic school to St. Vincent's College, Cape Girardeau in 1910, Smith Hall served a variety of functions, including library and classroom building, residence hall for the brothers, kitchen, dining hall, and (after a major remodeling project in 1973) infirmary and retirement center.

Unusually, a matching red-brick building was built between Smith and Rosati Halls in 1898 and christened Oliva Hall after Vincentian Brother Angelo Oliva, architect of the Church of the Assumption who died in 1835. Also known as the Brothers Building, the community chapel, and "B" Building, the three-story structure interestingly lacked a central staircase, depending on an external fire escape to connect the second and third floors. Tradition has it that Oliva Hall was designed by Nicholas Steines, a Barrens student born in Luxembourg with previous training in architecture who was ordained a priest in 1902 and also worked on plans for St. Thomas Seminary in Denver.[43] Oliva Hall included a dining room (originally divided by a wall to separate priests and students), a community chapel, and residences. Smith, Oliva, and Rosati Halls were distinguished from later campus buildings by their red-brick construction and, stretching westward to the church, formed an impressive east-west array of buildings on the northern side of the Barrens campus.

Sometime in the early twentieth century, the old log cabins south of the church were demolished (with the exception of Rosati's old log sacristy, which was moved closer to the community cemetery) to make room for modern construction. A cottage-like building used as a recreation center for Vincentian novices, who lived in the priests' building but could not take recreation in that

43. "National Register of Historic Places Registration Form," 5.

building, was torn down to make room for a three-story blonde brick building in 1927. Dedicated exclusively to the needs of novices, this Novitiate Building included dormitories, classrooms, and a chapel. When the novitiate was moved from the Barrens in 1965, the building was used for a variety of purposes, including a visitors' center maintained by the Miraculous Medal Association.

By 1925, the century-old, white clapboard seminary building—the two-and-a-half-story structure on which the original Barrens settlers and students labored in the early 1820s, the building that John Lynch described as being physically moved in 1850 to make room for Rosati Hall, the multipurpose building with a long history of various usages (classrooms, library, science labs, student and brothers residence)—was demolished, along with a separate dormitory building and study hall to its south. In their place, a new scholasticate building arose in 1931. This large four-story blonde brick building included 102 rooms (mainly residences for seminarians), an impressive chapel with a white marble altar and hand-carved wooden Stations of the Cross, and an auditorium. The building was formally christened Kulage Hall in honor of the well-known St. Louis Catholic patroness Maria Theresa Kulage, who donated a large sum toward its construction and took special interest in the details of its chapel interior.[44] Kulage Hall was designed by St. Louis architect Henry P. Hess, whose many works included Cardinal Glennon College and Rosati-Kain High School in St. Louis. Hess brought to the building several interesting design features, including art deco–style brick details between the upper floor windows, exterior brick buttressing, and Gothic arch windows and doors on the first floor.[45]

44. Maria Theresa Kulage (1862–1934) was the daughter of St. Louis millionaire flour-mill owner Mathias Backer and wife of German immigrant and brick manufacturer Joseph Kulage. She was noted for her generosity to Catholic causes and her devotion to the Catholic Eucharist. In 1927, she donated $250,000 to the Sisters of the Holy Ghost of Perpetual Adoration (Pink Sisters) in St. Louis for their convent and chapel. She devoted a similar sum to the Vincentians for the student building and a smaller sum for the St. Louis Preparatory Seminary operated by the Vincentians. In 1908 she was named a Lady of the Holy Sepulcher by Pius X in recognition of her services to Catholic institutions. It was said that she left $1.9 million of her $2 million estate to Catholic organizations. See *De Andrein* 4, no. 9 (June 1934) for an obituary of Kulage.
45. "National Register of Historical Places Form," 6.

The novitiate and student buildings enclosed a new quadrangle to the rear of Rosati Hall, with sidewalks leading to the old Mound of Our Lady (ca. 1850) and, farther south, to a grotto dedicated to Our Lady of the Miraculous Medal, built by Barrens students beginning in 1917 and dedicated by St. Louis Archbishop John J. Glennon in 1919. The grotto became the site of a large annual May procession attended by large crowds of Perryville Catholic school children and parents.

The growth of the postwar period inspired what may have been the first strategic plan for the physical growth of the Barrens campus. Perhaps as early as 1945, the vision emerged of a new quadrangle to the east of Kulage Hall, framed by a library/academic building, recreation center with gymnasium, central administration building, and new chapel. The ambitious new plan was outlined in the provincial newspaper in 1952 as ground was broken for the first of the proposed new buildings, the Joseph A. Finney Library.[46] The new library was intended as the first building on the Barrens campus dedicated exclusively to academic purposes. A memo from the visitors' office noted, "This building should be restricted strictly to library classroom purposes. The museum and exhibit rooms do not clash with this purpose; but other facilities in conflict with this purpose should be eliminated. These latter demands will be provided in later constructions."[47] Careful plans were laid out for a library consistent with a population of 160 students, including a stack area for over 100,000 volumes; the Bishop Sheehan Museum, housing artifacts from the Vincentian Chinese missions; a rare book depository, librarians' offices, textbook room, archives vault, bindery, audiovisual labs, ten classrooms, two science laboratories, auxiliary student services (including a barber shop in the basement), and an imposing main reading room of over 2,000 square feet.[48] The resulting three-story blonde brick and stone structure, begun in 1952 and dedicated in May 1954,

---

46. *De Andrein* 22, no. 8 (May 1952).

47. SMOB Records, DRMA—Buildings and Grounds—"Perryville Library-Classroom Building."

48. Ibid.; and SMOB Records, DRMA—Buildings and Grounds—"Space Recommendations for St. Mary's Seminary Library and Classroom Buildings."

featured a modern Gothic design with rock surfacing, upper-level projecting oriel windows, and a patio extending from the front entrance with soft flagstone and gray granite border.[49] The impressive reading room of the library included stone interior walls with inlaid and freestanding wooden bookshelves and large windows featuring the seals of Vincentian institutions. All in all, the new building, designed by the St. Louis architectural firm of Maquolo and Quicke, represented the most carefully planned and decorated structure on the Barrens campus.[50] The funds for this new building, and the accompanying new structures to follow, were raised by the Miraculous Medal Association and Carrie Estelle Doheny, renowned patron of Vincentian causes.[51]

Of the other proposed components of the new quadrangle plan, only the student recreation center came to fruition. Completed in 1956, the blonde-brick recreation center was located just southwest of the library, with an enclosed walkway connecting it to both the library and the scholasticate building. The center featured a full-size gymnasium, swimming pool, locker rooms, shower and locker facilities, and basement bowling lanes and workout room. By the late 1950s and early 1960s, the ambitious plans for additional growth at the Barrens were sidelined by discussions regarding the future of American Vincentian formation programs.

---

49. "National Register of Historic Places Form," 7.

50. George J. Maquolo studied at the Ecole des Beaux Arts in Paris and designed buildings in New York City and Paris as well as the Midwest; "National Register of Historic Places Form," 7.

51. Carrie Estelle Doheny (1875–1958) was the daughter of German immigrants who moved to Los Angeles in 1890. She married Irish immigrant and millionaire oilman Edward Doheny in 1900. After her conversion to Catholicism, Mrs. Doheny became devoted to Catholic causes and particularly to the Congregation of the Mission and Daughters of Charity. She was a noted collector of rare books, including a Guttenberg Bible, and was a generous benefactor of Catholic institutions in the United States, China, and Mexico. Her gifts to the Vincentian community included the Vincentian House of Studies on the campus of the Catholic University of America and buildings on the campuses of St. Vincent's Minor Seminary in Montebello and St. John's Seminary in Camarillo, California. Doheny's gifts to St. Mary's of the Barrens included large contributions to the library building fund and the Estelle Doheny Museum with first edition American classics, rare paperweights, and jade and porcelain art objects. Mrs. Doheny was made a Lady of the Holy Sepulchre in 1931 and a Papal Countess by Pius XII in 1939. See the website for the Carrie Estelle Doheny Foundation (www.dohenyfoundation.com) and De Andrein 29, no. 3 (December 1958).

In the meantime, other auxiliary buildings were raised on the campus throughout the twentieth century. The growth of the Miraculous Medal Association inspired plans for a national shrine dedicated to Our Lady of the Miraculous Medal within the Church of the Assumption. The shrine was added to the southern side of the church in 1928 and was dedicated in January 1930, the centennial of the Marian apparitions to St. Catherine Labouré in Paris that inspired the devotion. The shrine features a dome over a white marble altar with a statue of Mary in a niche inlaid with gold mosaics, wall panels of rosatto marble, and floors of green and white terrazzo.[52] The addition of the shrine necessitated additional remodeling in the old church and the construction of a new sacristy joining the church to the priests' building in 1929. In 1932, the only log cabin still existing from the original seminary, usually referred to as "Rosati's Sacristy," was moved for the second time. Originally located near the front entrance of the seminary grounds, Rosati's cabin was first moved to the center of the novitiate grounds, but construction of the new novitiate building necessitated another transfer, this time "to a new location in the center of the novices' old tennis court, near the community cemetery." As part of its transfer, the cabin underwent an extensive renovation, including the replacement of deteriorating logs, new shingles and caulking, a new concrete foundation floor, and a covering "large arched stone pavilion" surmounted by a copper cross.[53]

Service buildings to support the growing seminary followed, including a garage on the eastern edge of the campus in 1940, a new power house adjacent to the garage in 1941, and a central workshop for the brothers just north of the priests' building in 1950 with outbuildings to support the community farm (barn and farrowing sheds). By 1963, a wooded area to the west of the campus was cleared and excavated to build a dam and create a small lake with a cabin and picnic area connected by a gravel road leading from the seminary to the site.[54] In 1972, the offices of the Miraculous Medal

52. "National Register of Historic Places Form," 4.
53. *De Andrein* 3, no. 8 (May 1933).
54. Derbes, e-mail to D. Steele, 11 November 2002: "St. Mary's of the Barrens/The Lake."

Association, originally located on the seminary campus but moved to a building on St. Joseph Road in Perryville, returned to the seminary grounds at a site just west of the community cemetery. Over the course of the twentieth century, the Barrens transformed physically into an impressive small college campus.

Building a Modern Community

Like American Catholic institutions everywhere in this era of growth, the Barrens developed a host of auxiliary enterprises and activities in its efforts to build an authentic and satisfying community. The increasing prosperity of many Americans led to rising expectations and a demand for a variety of educational and social activities. American Catholic institutions, accustomed to providing a social support system for their immigrant congregations, became increasingly Americanized in the twentieth century as their members assimilated into the broader culture. For many Catholic institutions, this meant pressure to conform, both to American expectations and to the demands of Roman officials who were often concerned about rampant Catholic assimilation into a largely Protestant and increasingly secular American culture. For American Catholic seminaries, the resulting tensions often drove developments. At St. Mary's of the Barrens, these tensions were combined with a long-expressed concern with the isolated locale of Perryville. Building a community at the Barrens with all the attendant activities demanded by authorities and enjoyed by the broader American culture also created a more hospitable environment for students and faculty, many of whom hailed from larger urban centers throughout the midwestern and western United States.

The numerous activities and enterprises developed at the Barrens, therefore, often grew in response to varied stimuli. Some were inspired by the distinctive nature of Vincentian spirituality and the Vincentian charism; others by the demands of external authorities; a few as more formalized outgrowths of the historical culture of the Barrens; and some simply as expressions of a growing and vibrant community of mostly young men seeking outlets for their interests and energies. The history and ongoing activities of these enterprises were faithfully recorded in the *De Andrein*, originally an in-house newsletter for the Barrens community that grew into a province-wide small newspaper circulated among alumni, family, and friends of the Barrens, from 1930 until 1965.

Among the twentieth-century activities inspired directly by Vincentian history and spirituality were a variety of foreign and domestic mission enterprises (see below) and a formal association and shrine dedicated to Our Lady of the Miraculous Medal.[55] Devotion to the Miraculous Medal grew shortly after the apparitions of Our Lady to Catherine Labouré at the motherhouse of the Daughters of Charity in Paris in 1830. By 1832, a medal engraved with the image of Mary as she appeared to St. Catherine spread throughout Europe, where it came to the attention of Jean-Marie Odin of the Barrens during his 1833 European sojourn. The Miraculous Medal reaffirmed the traditional Vincentian devotion to the Virgin Mary and the practice spread internationally over the course of the nineteenth century thanks to the work of Odin and others. The Vatican approved a special liturgy and prayers around the devotion in 1894, and in 1909 Pope Pius X approved statutes for the establishment of the Association of the Miraculous Medal to be headed by the superior general of the Vincentians.

The American Vincentian community recognized the potential for formal associations to both spread devotion to Mary among the Catholic population and to support the work of the Congregation's internal seminaries. The eastern province of the American Vincentian community founded a Central Association of the Miraculous Medal in 1915 with great success, followed in 1926 by the construction of a Central Shrine Chapel at the Vincentian church in Germantown, Pennsylvania. In the western province, an Association of the Miraculous Medal was approved in 1918, with offices in the library of the Barrens, under the direction of the Barrens superior with the assistance of student workers. By 1926, Father Joseph Fin-

---

55. On the Association of the Miraculous Medal and National Shrine of Our Lady of the Miraculous Medal, see Rybolt, "Works of Devotion, Evangelization and Service," 401–8; and articles in the *De Andrein* 13, no. 4 (January 1943); 19, nos. 8–9 (May–June 1949); and 28, no. 7 (May 1959).

ney became the first full-time director of the association and under his leadership a shrine to Our Lady of the Miraculous Medal was built around an altar on the southern wall of the old Assumption Church in 1928, dedicated in 1930 during centennial observances of the original Marian apparitions. In the meantime, the offices of the association were moved off the Barrens campus to the local Knights of Columbus building in 1924 and a two-story office building was constructed in Perryville in 1930 dedicated solely to the work of the association, which housed a staff of thirteen by 1943 and, after a 1949 addition doubled the space of the original building, a staff of forty by 1959.

As the association grew, it became more and more important to the operations of the western province. In 1939, Father Finney reported that the association realized a net profit of almost $8,000 through its annual and perpetual memberships (with total memberships of almost 55,000 individuals), and the sale of votive lights and religious items.[56] The association donated directly to the 1930s building program at the Barrens, providing generous amounts for the construction of the scholastic and novitiate buildings. By the 1940s, the Miraculous Medal Association provided over $40,000 annually to the operations and building funds of the western province, and Finney reported a net profit for 1947 of over $108,000.[57]

The size and scope of the association grew throughout the middle decades of the twentieth century. With the introduction of a novena dedicated to Our Lady of the Miraculous Medal, special novena bands were established in both the eastern (1937) and western (1946) provinces. The novena banks were active at the Barrens, although some Vincentians in the western province criticized the practice as an interference with traditional Vincentian parish missions and questioned its theological focus in the increasingly progressive climate leading to the Second Vatican Council.[58] During World War II, the association promoted prayers for American

56. Provincial Files, DRMA—Winne Papers—"Annual Financial and Statistical Statements (December 31, 1939)."
57. Provincial Files, DRMA—Winne Papers, J. A. Finney, CM to Marshall Winne, CM, 5 February 1948.
58. Rybolt, "Works of Devotion, Evangelization and Service," 407–408.

troops through its Victory Club of Prayer that placed the names of soldiers on the shrine altar. Finney led the growth of the association throughout its initial decades until his replacement by Father Charles Rice in 1962. Subsequent directors included Charles Shelby (1983–2004), Henry Grodecki (2005–9), James Garcia Ward (2009–12), Oscar Lukefahr (2012–15), and Kevin McCracken (2016). The Miraculous Medal Association (MMA) offices returned to the Barrens campus with a new building completed in 1972, reached a peak in its membership and staff in the early 1990s, and currently still operates at the Barrens with a staff of fifty-six full-time workers.[59]

The roots of other Barrens traditions may be linked to the concerns of external authorities. The activities of American Catholic seminarians during the long summer academic break became a source of concern for some Roman officials in the late nineteenth century. Indeed, a report compiled by the Jesuit curial official Giovanni Franzelin prior to an 1883 meeting of American Catholic Church leaders in Rome highlighted the problem of seminarians returning to the "outside" world where they might be "so much in contact with the spirited company of friends, among petty politicians and other such types, that they are made to lose the love of study that they had and all idea of ecclesiastical spirit."[60] The 1883 meeting set an agenda for the forthcoming plenary council in Baltimore, and included the recommendation that each seminary erect "summer villas" to house students during the summer vacation months. Although accepted by the American bishops at the 1883 meeting, the "villas" proposal was not supported at the Third Plenary Council the following year, given disagreements over the expense and purpose of such European practices.[61] The issue remained, however, and expectations were set for the proper conduct of seminarians during the summer months.

For religious communities like the Vincentians, the summer break offered an additional opportunity to socialize students and

59. According to data supplied by the MMA, the association employed a staff of 62 people in 1971, 113 in 1980, and 147 in 1990 before contracting to 115 in 2000, 78 in 2010, and 56 in 2015; Sandy Paulus, e-mail to author, 4 November 2015.
60. White, *Diocesan Seminary in the United States*, 152.
61. Ibid., 154–58.

build an *esprit de corps* among its fledgling members. A number of efforts were made at the Barrens in the late nineteenth century to keep seminarians together in some sort of community-building summer activity. Trips to the Barrens' sister seminary in Cape Girardeau and occasional picnics are mentioned by student diarists at this time.[62] In the early twentieth century, properties were procured for a regular summer camp experience, including sites on the nearby Saline Creek and a more distant locale in Arlington, Missouri, near present-day Rolla on the Gasconade River. By 1910, a regular summer camp was being held at Saco, Missouri, near Fredericktown on the St. Francis River, soon interrupted by the Great War, when students worked to build a Grotto of Our Lady of the Miraculous Medal on the Barrens campus from stones quarried near the site. By the late 1920s, a few permanent huts, especially for a refectory and a priests' residence with altar and sacristy, supplemented the tents that housed the majority of seminarians, until the owner of the Saco property sold the land in 1934 to what one source called a "native . . . who had no use for the 'catlicks.'"[63] A nearby location was scouted and in 1935 Camp St. Vincent was established at a site near French Mills where Cedar Bottom Creek meets the St. Francis River. A forty-acre lot was purchased (reportedly for $500) and summer camp at the "Cedar Bottoms" location became a fixture among Vincentians for the next half century.

Camp rules made it clear that "Camp St. Vincent is part of St. Mary's Seminary, and is under the leadership of the superior of St. Mary's Seminary" with officers and a camp council delegated to administer the Barrens community at the site.[64] The purpose of the camp encompassed both socialization and vacation for students at various points in their formation program and for students from other community seminaries, including De Andreis's theological school in Lemont when parts of the formation program began to

---

62. SMOB Records, DRMA—Student Activities—Rybolt, "Camp St. Vincent."
63. SMOB Records, DRMA—Student Activities—John F. Zimmerman, CM, to Jim Osendorf, CM, 9 November 1973.
64. SMOB Records, DRMA—Student Activities—"Camp St. Vincent, January 1983."

spin off from the Barrens in the 1960s. "Socialization involves getting to know other members of the community, building, renewing and strengthening friendships," a 1983 document stated. "In addition," the document continued, "the camp season also offers a time for students to develop their own programs for camp and to carry them out."[65] Most Vincentian students and faculty, however, remembered Camp St. Vincent as a time for fun and relaxation and stories abound of adventures experienced at camp. Hiking, swimming, sports, recreational reading and study, and a more informal spiritual regimen characterized life at Camp St. Vincent. Permanent huts, including a full chapel, and well-laid-out grounds dotted the property. The site continued to fulfill its purpose of providing socialization for Catholic students after the closing of the Barrens seminary—to this day the diocese of Springfield–Cape Girardeau operates a youth summer camp there known as "Camp Renew-All."

External Vincentian authorities directly influenced the establishment of another enterprise on the Barrens campus. In 1939, responding to the query of interested Barrens seminarians, provincial superior Marshall Winne authorized the founding of an official provincial archive at the old seminary. In recognition of its rich historical heritage, Winne designated the Barrens as the site for a depository "to gather, preserve and make available for research work" all the documents and sources compiled since the founding of St. Mary's. Those items included sources transcribed and collected by scholars like Charles Souvay, superior general of the Congregation of the Mission from 1933 to 1939 but previously a prolific historian, librarian, and administrator at Kenrick Seminary in St. Louis. Christening the new collection the De Andreis–Rosati Memorial Archives (DRMA), Winne further charged students with preserving "such matter pertaining to current Community activities and contemporary confreres as those in charge may deem useful to subsequent generations," including artifacts from the early days of the seminary and articles belonging to Vincentians moved from the Barrens to establish missionary outposts throughout the region.[66]

65. Ibid.
66. *De Andrein* 9, no. 7 (April 1939).

The DRMA collected copies of documents from other archives in the United States and Europe relating to American Vincentian history and grew to become an important collection of materials related to American Catholic history. It became a central source for the work of the Vincentian Studies Institute, itself initially housed on the Barrens campus after its founding in 1979.

Many other Barrens activities grew naturally out of the historical culture of the old seminary and the social needs of a growing and energetic community. Music played a large role, in accordance with the traditional interests of Italian Vincentians, and chant classes were introduced early in the Barrens curriculum. The Barrens archives contain numerous examples of titles and hymnals employed at liturgical celebrations from the late nineteenth century onward. One special example of Vincentian liturgical music was the well-known Christmas novena, a nine-evening observance with prayers, antiphons, and collects celebrated among European Vincentians since the founding of the Congregation.[67] The earliest Vincentian Christmas novena was composed by Carlo Antonio Vacchetta for a patroness of the order in 1720. Vacchetta's novena spread throughout Italy and through Vincentian missionaries to other parts of the globe. The novena is thought to have been celebrated as early as 1816 or 1818 in the United States, and the Barrens church became home to an annual celebration of the Christmas Novena, which was revised and translated by twentieth-century Vincentians.

Musical performances were featured at Christmas and other holidays celebrated at the Barrens through a series of programs, banquets, and activities recorded in the pages of the *De Andrein*. Theatrical plays and musical productions also dotted the Barrens calendar from the nineteenth century to the closing of the old seminary. Founder's Day (commemorating the return of the seminary to the Barrens campus in 1886), commencement, ordinations and vows, the visits of bishops and dignitaries, the initiation ceremonies and works of student organizations—all were celebrated at the Barrens with special liturgies, music, speeches, and banquets.

---

67. See Rybolt, "Christmas Novena."

Academic competitions and recitations also abounded at the seminary. The feasts of St. Catherine of Siena and St. Thomas Aquinas were celebrated with formal programs, featuring solemn Masses, the presentation of student papers, Scholastic-style disputations, and Latin allocutions, often against stage sets with designs honoring the lives and works of these Doctors of the Church. These observances highlighted the academic work of Barrens students while affirming the Church's insistence on the central role of Thomistic studies in the seminary curriculum.

News of sporting events and athletic competitions, from baseball and basketball to handball, tennis, and golf, often filled the pages of the *De Andrein*. Students competed against novices, philosophers against theologians, Barrenites against preparatory seminary teams from Cape Girardeau and the local Perryville Catholic high school. One Barrens sports apologist lauded the value of athletics as a tool of evangelization as well as an outlet for energy, distraction from studies, and guarantor of good physical health. "By taking a moderate interest in sports," a high-minded Barrens journalist wrote, "he [the priest] can make himself agreeable, popular, and well-liked. . . . From a baseball session the priest can guide to a spiritual session. His presence as a priest will naturally remind the people of real and lasting things—the salvation of their souls. He will be as a pebble dropped into a pool, causing untold ripples to flow out in an unceasing circle."[68]

Clubs, summer camp, the seminary lake, musical performances, holiday celebrations, academic and athletic competitions, and numerous other activities contributed to the growth of community at the Barrens and reflected the vitality of a growing twentieth-century Catholic institution.

Reaching Out

The "modern community" at the Barrens proved increasingly willing to connect to broader developments in the world outside the

68. *De Andrein* 22, no. 4 (January 1952).

seminary, both the surrounding area in rural southern Missouri and the far-flung mission fields of the universal Catholic Church. St. Vincent de Paul established his little community as a band of missioners, initially among the spiritually impoverished Catholics of post-Tridentine France. As such, it seemed natural for the sons of St. Vincent to seek new outlets for their missionary impulse, even in their years of formation at an isolated midwestern American house. The Vincentians at the Barrens participated fully, and increasingly confidently, in this missionary impulse in the twentieth century through innovations like the Motor Missions, Catholic correspondence courses, and Student Mission Crusade. These activities reflected the connections of the Barrens (despite its location) to broader movements outside the seminary and reflect the relative stability of the community in the middle years of the twentieth century.

St. Mary's of the Barrens Seminary contributed directly to the development of what one historian called a "novel and uncharacteristic method of evangelization" in the form of Catholic motor missions to relatively non-Catholic areas.[69] The motor missions were inspired both by a renewed American Catholic focus on rural, agrarian interests (note the establishment of the National Catholic Rural Life Conference in 1923) and a new wave of anti-Catholic agitation following World War I and the failed 1928 presidential campaign of Alfred Smith.[70] As early as 1927, three St. Mary's seminarians resolved to combat the growing anti-Catholic bigotry in southern Missouri. Lester Fallon, Joseph Phoenix, and Joseph McIntyre went so far as to draft a contract "to the effect that [they] would go down into the towns of southern Missouri . . . and there ask for the privilege of talking in public."[71] After their ordinations, Fallon, by now a faculty member at Kenrick Seminary in St. Louis, made a connection with the Oklahoma priest Stephen Leven, a former student at the Louvain University in Belgium who had spent

69. Slawson, "Thirty Years of Street Preaching," 81.
70. For a review of the Motor Missions in the context of the NCLRC, see Marlett, *Saving the Heartland*.
71. McKenna, "Catholic Motor Missions in Missouri," 103.

summers preaching on London streets in conjunction with the
Catholic Evidence Guild established in 1918 to counter English
anti-Catholicism. Fallon spent the summer of 1934 working with
Leven in Oklahoma, and the following year Fallon recruited fellow
Vincentians to adapt Leven's methods for use in hotbeds of anti-
Catholic bigotry in Missouri.[72]

The resulting Vincentian Motor Missions was headquartered
out of St. Louis but drew on Vincentian personnel and resources
from other houses, including the Barrens, where advanced seminarians eventually formed an important part of the missionary
teams. Motor missionaries traveled throughout southern Missouri and, under the encouragement of the diocese of Kansas City,
Missouri, also in some northwestern Missouri towns during the
summers from 1935 to 1965. The Motor Missions developed a
well-defined program, scouting towns and distributing pamphlets
to draw crowds, offering presentations and question-and-answer
sessions under the theme "If it is a question about the Catholic
Church, ASK A CATHOLIC," and working to dispel misconcep-
tions about the Catholic faith and Catholic practices. Back at
the Barrens, the *De Andrein* tracked the activities of the summer
preachers, mapping their progress and indicating the numbers of
people reached in Missouri towns with little or no Catholic presence. The Motor Missions thrived, despite the reluctance of Vincentian superiors to commit resources to the task, up to the point
of American entry into World War II, when gas rationing made it
difficult to sustain the summer road trips. The missions enjoyed a
resurgence after 1948, until the influence of television and home
air-conditioning made attendance at street-preaching events less
attractive and numbers dwindled. By 1965, Vincentian superiors
surrendered the apostolate to the clergy of the southern Missouri
diocese of Springfield–Cape Girardeau.

Over a thirty-year period, however, the Motor Missions
attracted widespread interest and participation among the Barrens
community and led to additional programs to stimulate interest in
the Catholic faith. As a follow-up to the summer Motor Mission

72. Slawson, "Thirty Years of Street Preaching," 64.

trips, correspondence courses were begun to maintain contact with interested attendees. Some Barrens students, including members of the Stephen Vincent Ryan Unit of the Catholic Students Mission Crusade (see below) were inspired by the so-called Narberth Movement to distribute pamphlets on the Catholic faith to interested correspondents beginning in 1935.[73] In February 1938, Barrens seminarians began a more organized series of "Crusade Correspondence Courses." Operating out of a room in the recently completed Kulage Hall, Barrens seminarians answered letters and distributed materials on the Catholic faith to a growing list of "non-Catholics, converts under instruction and Catholics" in states "as far removed as California, New York, Michigan and Louisiana," supported financially by sponsors who became "personal patrons" of the corresponding students.[74] By 1940, 829 students were enrolled in the Crusade Courses, with a quarter of those enrollees attaining "graduate" status and twenty-five converting to Catholicism as a result of the courses.[75] The progress of the courses was tracked proudly in the *De Andrein*, including sample letters from enrolled students and statistics on the origins and status of those students.[76]

The Crusade Courses fed into what became the Confraternity Home Service (CHS), headed by Lester Fallon and headquartered in St. Louis with Barrens seminarians again forming a crucial part of the teaching team. As the CHS grew, with large numbers of soldiers joining the mailing list during World War II, it gathered increasing attention, and by 1944 the Knights of Columbus joined their Religious Information Bureau and its resources to the movement. By 1947, over six million people had responded to the ads of the Confraternity, and its home office in St. Louis handled over 10,000 pieces of mail a week. The Knights moved their operations to New Haven, Connecticut, in 1971 but the Confraternity remained in St.

73. *De Andrein* 6, no. 4 (January 1936). The Narberth Movement, or Narbeth Plan, was named for the parish in Narberth, Pennsylvania, that developed the concept of distributing pamphlets on Catholic issues to combat anti-Catholicism and subsequently published a number of such pamphlets.
74. *De Andrein* 8, no. 7 (April 1938).
75. *De Andrein* 10, no. 5 (February 1940).
76. Ibid.

Louis, still affiliated with the Missouri councils of the Knights of Columbus, until its move back to the Barrens as the Catholic Home Study Service in 1991.

The Motor Missions and its spinoffs were significant to the history of the Barrens in several ways. They helped counter the persistent prejudice against the isolation of the Barrens by making a virtue out of its rural locale, they provided an innovative approach to the traditional Vincentian work of parish missions, and they linked the Barrens to broader movements in the American and universal Catholic Church. Indeed, the activities of the Vincentians in Missouri were tracked in the pages of *The Homiletic and Pastoral Review* for several years after 1938 in a series of articles by the Benedictine Edgar Schmiedler and others.[77] The follow-up catechetical movements of the Motor Missions, culminating in the establishment of the Confraternity Home Study Service under Lester Fallon, owed much to the efforts of the Barrens seminarians, who in turn profited from the experience of practical catechesis and contact with a broader audience through widespread correspondence courses.

The Barrens community cast an even wider net with its growing interest in the foreign missions of the Congregation beginning in the 1920s. The Vincentians had engaged in missionary activity outside of Europe, especially in northern Africa, Madagascar, and China, since the seventeenth century, and the establishment of missions in the eastern part of the Kiangsi (Jiangxi) province of southeastern China in the 1920s stimulated interest in foreign missionary activity.[78] This interest reflected a broader movement in the American Catholic community. Considered mission territory itself until the early twentieth century, the maturing American Catholic Church "founded a multitude of national organizations and networks to more effectively serve Church and society, including

---

77. Marlett, *Saving the Heartland*, 135–36.
78. The eastern American province began sending missionaries to China in 1921 at the behest of assistant general Patrick McHale in order to relieve pressure on the post–World War I French province of the Congregation. After a brief period of demurral, the western American province followed suit shortly thereafter and began to send missionaries to the vicariate of Yukiang in eastern Jiangxi. See Udovic, "Go Out to All the Nations!"

a strong thrust for Americans to serve the Church internationally and to assert their significance within a global body."[79]

This interest was shared by young American Catholics, leading to the establishment in 1919 of the Catholic Students Mission Crusade (CSMC) by students at the seminary of the Divine Word Missionaries in Illinois. Described by one historian as a somewhat naive effort by young Catholics to combine fervor for both faith and country at a time of growing tension between the Catholic Church and American culture, the CSMC grew to incorporate eventually over one million members drawn from American colleges and seminaries.[80] The Crusaders engaged in a variety of activities to raise awareness of the world mission movement, including rallies and conferences featuring symbols evoking the medieval Crusade movement and a national magazine entitled *The Shield*.[81]

The CSMC drew much of its early strength from American seminaries, which in itself indicated "a shift in priestly training, an increasing emphasis on the seminarians' participation in the life of the local Church beyond the seminary."[82] This was certainly true of the Barrens, which established an early chapter of the CSMC named the Stephen Vincent Ryan Unit. The Ryan Unit was active in the early decade of the Crusade, sending representatives to its national conference and in 1935 electing a Barrens seminarian (Thomas Mahoney) to the executive board of the organization. The Ryan Unit became an umbrella organization under which other student activities were organized, reflecting the broad interest in the foreign missions among the Barrens seminarians. In 1923, the western provincial superior Thomas Finney, recognizing the energy behind the Barrens missionary unit, asked it to focus its attention on the particular missionary activities of the Vincentian community, and specifically its Chinese missions. The result was the establishment of the Vincentian Foreign Mission Society (VFMS) as "a work separate but affiliated to the [S. V. Ryan] Unit" to encourage prayer

79. Endres, *American Crusade*, xii.
80. Ibid., xi.
81. Ibid., 43.
82. Ibid., 46–47.

and fund-raising for the missionary efforts of the Congregation and the Daughters of Charity.[83] The student-operated VFMS engaged in a variety of activities, sponsoring fund-raising activities like the "Baby Ransom League" to support Chinese orphanages run by the Daughters of Charity, holding essay competitions to promote mission awareness, advertising the sale of religious goods, collecting stamps, and publishing news items on the Chinese missions in the popular magazine *The Vincentian*.[84]

Another affiliate of the Barrens CSMC unit, the Clet Correspondence Guild, was established in 1932 as a reorganization of earlier efforts to encourage exchange of letters with Vincentian missionaries in China. The Clet Guild featured regular letters written by students to designated confreres in China (450 letters in a four-year period, according to the *De Andrein* in 1937). This systematic correspondence program was intended to provide the missionaries with news from their confreres in the United States, and to educate Barrens seminarians on conditions in the missions "regardless of whether they answer—and, more often than not, answering is impossible." As with the other mission awareness activities of the Barrens, the students acknowledged that "it is only a remote assistance; but it is a true cooperation in the mission work."[85]

The work of the VFMS spread beyond the Barrens student body as it enlisted the support and aid of the entire American Vincentian community and generous lay patrons. As a matter of fact, the work of the VFMS eclipsed that of the S. V. Ryan Unit until the Depression threatened the existence of both student organizations. By 1936, the *De Andrein* noted that "the Society is moribund but not yet dead," while the S. V. Ryan Unit enjoyed a renaissance through its adoption of two new initiatives—the Narberth Plan to distribute Catholic pamphlets and the establishment of the Edward T. Shee-

83. *De Andrein* 6, no. 4 (January 1936).
84. *The Vincentian* was a popular Catholic magazine dedicated to promotions of Vincentian apostolates, including the support of seminaries, the Miraculous Medal Association, and the Chinese missions. The magazine began publication in 1923 and was taken over by the VFMS in 1952 until its demise in 1963. See Rybolt, "Works of Devotion, Evangelization and Service," 412–15.
85. *De Andrein* 7, no. 4 (January 1937).

han Museum to commemorate the work of the Vincentian missionary bishop to China and Barrens graduate who died in 1933.[86] By 1938, the VFMS was reorganized and its operations taken over full-time by Vincentian priests in recognition of its importance to the work of the community. In 1941, the operations of the Mission Society were centralized in St. Louis under the direction of Father Paul Lloyd, with Barrens students maintaining the "stamp department" to raise funds and the publication of a mimeographed newsletter, "China Clippings," directed at school-aged children.[87]

In the 1950s, the work of the S. V. Ryan Unit and that of its affiliate, the VFMS on the Barrens campus often merged in the *De Andrein's* notices of student activities. An article in the December 1958 issue of the paper, for instance, noted that the Mission society was being "renovated" with a closer adherence to the original focus of the Catholic Students Mission Crusade, from which it had strayed in recent years. The Society pledged to recapture its initial focus on the foreign missions, and especially the Chinese (by now Taiwanese) missions of the Congregation through educational programs and material aid.[88] Of course, the communist takeover of China in 1949 (necessitating the transfer of the Vincentian missions to Taiwan) and changing Catholic approaches to the foreign missions in the 1960s curtailed student activities. News of the foreign missions and the activities of the Ryan Unit and the VFMS after 1960 faded from the pages of the *De Andrein* after dominating its issues for over twenty years.

In the meantime, however, the S. V. Ryan Unit had actively promoted the establishment of the Sheehan Museum, announcing in 1935 its intent to commemorate the late missionary bishop on the Barrens campus through displays including his personal effects, official documents, biographical information, letters, testimonials, and "anything that will help to preserve the memory of Bishop Sheehan or serve to perpetuate his spirit."[89] Plans for the museum were met

86. *De Andrein* 6, no. 4 (January 1936).
87. *De Andrein* 12, no. 2 (November 1941).
88. *De Andrein* 29, no. 3 (December 1958).
89. *De Andrein* 6, no. 2 (November 1935).

enthusiastically by the Barrens and the entire Vincentian community, and the *De Andrein* ran a series of articles about the progress
of its operations, including dedicated space in the new scholasticate building, curators appointed by the director of students, and
donations of items from Sheehan's family, friends, and missionary
confreres streaming into the Barrens. The museum was dedicated
on May 23, 1936, with a special ceremony presided over by provincial superior Timothy Flavin, Barrens superior William Brennan,
and members of the VFMS.[90] The Sheehan Museum moved to the
new academic building in 1954 and outlived both the CSMC and
the seminary. With the closure of the seminary and disposition of
Barrens property after 1985, the museum holdings became more
difficult to maintain. In 2001, many of the artifacts and Chinese art
objects from the museum were auctioned by Christie's, while the
personal effects of Sheehan and other Chinese Vincentian bishops
were transferred to DePaul University along with the rest of the De
Andreis–Rosati Memorial Archives.[91]

   While the Barrens community reached out to the surrounding
region through its Motor Missions and the universal Catholic Church
by its various foreign mission guilds, the outside world sometimes
intruded more directly on the otherwise isolated seminary community. In January 1924, for example, the student diary reported
the curious incident of "a large yellow airplane [that] circled the
seminary and landed in the field in back of the mound this after-
noon."[92] The owner of the airplane, the St. Louis auto dealer Leon
Klink, was a friend of "Brother Walters" of the seminary community.[93] The local newspaper reported that Klink was accompanied by
his friend Charles Lindbergh, "an experienced aviator [who] for the
last three years has been employed by the government as a pilot.[94]
Klink and Lindbergh were barnstorming throughout the Midwest

---

90. *De Andrein* 6, no. 7 (May 1936).
91. For more on the Bishop Sheehan Memorial Museum, see Harney, "Enshrining the
Mission."
92. SMOB Records, DRMA—Students: Diaries—Scholasticate Diary, 25 January 1924.
93. Possibly Brother Walter Eckery (1888–1959), a legendary Vincentian brother with
ties to various American Vincentian houses.
94. *Perry County Republican*, 31 January 1924.

before Lindbergh was called for further training with the Army Air Service in San Antonio. Their Perryville stop drew large crowds and offered trial flights to some bystanders, including Brother Walter and Barrens superior William Barr who, after his flight, "forbade any Vincentian to go up in the air in an airplane."[95]

More tragic events influenced the Barrens as well. A student editorial in the *De Andrein* offered a glimpse of student attitudes at the Barrens in 1931, noting the rise of tyrannical regimes throughout Europe and Asia and signs of "unrest and disorderliness" in the United States as the Depression created "hordes of jobless workers in the midst of undreamed-of physical riches."[96] A year later, the student paper noted continued economic distress, even while at the Barrens "the long procession goes on, each student daily drawing closer to his goal. Everyone is happy and well content to be back at work. There is no lack of employment. Though the stocks in Wall Street may reach new lows; though the blight of depression may calm the hum of La Salle Street; though the world of politics may seethe and rock come November and March [the 1932 presidential election and inauguration], yet the procession will go on."[97]

News of the Spanish Civil War directly touched the Barrens, as the community followed the plight of their Spanish confreres (Vincentian priests and brothers as well as Daughters of Charity) who were "actually engaged in a great Catholic war against the Red menace."[98] The young writers at the Barrens student newspaper followed the conflict closely, noting its outbreak on July 19, 1936, during the feast of St. Vincent while many Spanish Vincentians celebrated in Majorca; tracking the fortunes of Vincentian houses and members of the Vincentian "Double Family"; receiving updates from Benito Romero, the Spanish vice-provincial superior residing in Puerto Rico who eventually visited the Barrens in 1938; noting the special series of lectures on Franco's army presented by Vincentian Father Ulpiano Arano, staying at the Barrens for a two-year intensive English

---

95. SMOB Records, DRMA—Students: Diaries—Scholasticate Diary, 27 January 1924.
96. *De Andrein* 2, no. 1 (October 1931).
97. *De Andrein* 3, no. 1 (October 1932).
98. *De Andrein* 7, no. 4 (January 1937).

language study; cheering the eventual victory of Franco and the rebels; and mourning the final tally of Vincentian losses.[99]

The Japanese invasion of China (which triggered the Second Sino-Japanese War in 1937) drew special attention given the persecution of Chinese Catholics and the physical presence of Vincentian missionaries. The Barrens Mission Crusade focused its intentions on the war as it neared the site of Vincentian missions. A campus lecture (with motion picture reels) by William McClinnot of the eastern province focused on "Communist terrorism and the heroic resistance of Chinese Catholics to deprive them of their faith." A special class on the Chinese language was added to the Barrens curriculum in anticipation of the need for additional missionaries to rebuild the Vincentian missions after the war, especially as it broadened into the larger world war.[100]

The beginning of World War II in Europe brought early news of Vincentian losses in Poland (five houses lost, eighteen Daughters of Charity killed, priests imprisoned, the seminary at Bydogzcz confiscated, a church in Warsaw destroyed in early 1940).[101] American entry into the war occasioned a moment of reflection on the part of Barrens seminarians, raising the question, "where does the Seminarian fit into this scheme of concerted action? How is he helping his country in this present crisis?" While seminarians were exempted from military service, the student editorial writer determined that the students "can and will by [their] prayers go a long way toward establishing a just and lasting peace."[102] St. Mary's students and faculty did more than pray, however. The Confraternity Home Study Service on the Barrens campus enrolled 900 soldiers in their apol-

99. *De Andrein* 7, no. 4 (January 1937); 7, no. 6 (March 1937); 7, no. 8 (May 1937); 8, no. 1 (October 1937); 8, no. 4 (January 1938); and 9, no. 8 (May 1939). The Spanish Congregation lost twenty-five priests, twenty-five brothers, and six houses, while the Daughters of Charity undoubtedly lost more. Pope Francis I beatified eleven Vincentian priests and three Vincentian brothers killed in the Spanish Civil War as martyrs for the faith on 13 October 2013.
100. *De Andrein* 8, no. 3 (December 1937); and 14, no. 2 (November 1943). By 1943, Chinese language courses were taught at the Barrens by a former Vincentian missionary recently returned to the United States.
101. *De Andrein* 10, nos. 4 and 6 (January and March 1940).
102. *De Andrein* 12, no. 5 (February 1942).

ogetics courses and the Barrens chapter of the Catholic Student's Mission Crusade maintained contact with additional soldiers.[103] In 1944, the Barrens campus briefly provided campgrounds for 2,000 soldiers and Italian prisoners of war from the nearby Weingarten POW camp who came to assist with the flooding waters of the Mississippi River in eastern Perry County.[104] The Barrens community celebrated the end of the war in Europe in grand liturgical style, with solemn liturgies, a procession to the Perryville town square, and songs by the seminary choir, but the community continued to assist war-torn Europe after the conflict through participation in the Cooperative for American Remittances for Europe (CARE).[105]

From the reopening of the Barrens seminary in 1888 through much of the twentieth century, the old campus grew in facilities and programs, reflecting the broader expansion of the American Catholic community. Growth inspired confidence and the isolated Barrens community reached out to other Vincentians, Catholics, and non-Catholics in the surrounding communities and throughout the globe. Programs were developed to encourage this outreach. By the middle of the twentieth century, Barrens programs would undergo a process of standardization in response to outside authorities and demands for greater quality.

103. *De Andrein* 12, no. 7 (April 1942).
104. *De Andrein* 14, no. 8 (May 1944).
105. *De Andrein* 15, no. 9 (June 1945).

16. Barrens Campus Post-1913

A view of the front of the Church of the Assumption after its 1913 renovation.

Chapter Eight
CONFORMING TO NEW DEMANDS

> It seemed that since the common element in the lives
> of all the members of the Community was their years
> of formation at Perryville . . . these days should be the
> rallying point of community loyalty.
>
> —Cyril LeFevre, CM (1941)

Standardization

As the Barrens developed and responded to broader developments
in the Catholic Church and the world, it sought legitimization of
its status in line with its growing size and relative stability. The
pursuit of a more standard and professional status was reflected in
the programs of the Barrens, in efforts to gain academic accreditation, and in the accomplishments of its alumni and faculty.

The letters of Barrens superior Cyril LeFevre offer a glimpse of
events at the Barrens in the middle years of the twentieth century.
LeFevre, a native Iowan who graduated from the Barrens before his
ordination in 1934, spent most of his priestly career in Vincentian
seminaries and provincial administrative posts. Described as an
intense-looking and serious young scholar with a distinguished
student record, LeFevre was appointed superior of the Barrens
in 1939, having spent the five years since his ordination on the
faculties of St. Thomas College in Denver and Kenrick Seminary
in St. Louis. After his six-year tenure at the Barrens, he returned
briefly to Kenrick as treasurer and dean of students before beginning a twenty-five-year stint (1946–71) as provincial treasurer.

"Cy" LeFevre, whose brother was also a Vincentian priest and sister a Daughter of Charity, was in every way a "Barrens man" and model of a twentieth-century Vincentian.

LeFevre's letters to provincial visitor Marshall Winne, a native Californian and energetic Vincentian administrator in his own right, show something of his serious attention to duty and details at the Barrens. He was interested in many things—the quality of the Barrens faculty, the discipline of the students, the physical and financial needs of the house, the place of the Barrens in the future of the western province, and the effects of World War II on the motherhouse. A March 1940 letter provides insight regarding LeFevre's purpose:

17. Cyril LeFevre
"Cy" LeFevre studied at the Barrens and worked at seminaries in Denver and St. Louis before returning as superior in 1939. LeFevre proved an energetic and conscientious administrator who worked to modernize operations at the old seminary. After leaving the Barrens, LeFevre became treasurer of the western American Vincentian province for twenty-five years.

According to my knowledge, there has never been prepared a report that would indicate all of the work that the Provincial Superior must provide for. As our training here [at the Barrens] ought to be geared to the present and future needs of the Province and designed to have on hand adequate replacements in case of retirement and death of the present teachers, we should know what is being taught and how such work is divided among the various faculties. If we had such a report from the various houses we could make intelligent plans for specialization at this central supply station.[1]

LeFevre's business-like attitude and efforts at strategic planning were new to the Barrens, and were very much a product of the middle twentieth century. He never hesitated to assert the needs of the Barrens community as central to the welfare of the entire province. To that end he forwarded numerous recommendations to Winne. LeFevre complained about the number and quality of the Barrens faculty, at one point reminding the visitor that St. Mary's had "just 12 teaching members on this faculty" to deliver eight years of education, with LeFevre himself forced to teach three subjects in addition to running the seminary.[2] He apparently felt that Winne slighted the Barrens in favor of the diocesan seminaries run by the Vincentians, and threatened to resign on that account in 1941.[3] He encouraged Winne to send as many Vincentians as possible, including faculty already teaching at the Barrens, to the Catholic University of America for advanced degrees so as to improve the pool of professors for St. Mary's.[4] He insisted that "no professor should be assigned who has not already celebrated the third anniversary of his ordination, preferably the fifth" (so as to avoid conflicts with students who had been his younger classmates), "no professor should be assigned who has not been regular in the fulfillment of his Community obligations, both spiritual and temporal" (to insure a good role model for Barrens students), and "no professor should be assigned who has not been successful in his teaching elsewhere."[5]

LeFevre also obsessed over discipline at the Barrens, expressing concern in 1940 over rumors that a troublesome priest was being

---

1. Provincial Files, DRMA—Winne Papers—Cyril LeFevre to Marshall Winne, 1 March 1940.
2. Provincial Files, DRMA—Winne Papers—LeFevre to Winne, 16 September 1939.
3. Provincial Files, DRMA—Winne Papers—LeFevre to Winne, 15 September 1941.
4. Provincial Files, DRMA—Winne Papers—LeFevre to Winne, 15 September 1942. LeFevre sang the praises of Father Joseph Lilly, professor of scripture on the Barrens faculty, when Lilly was recruited to join the faculty of CUA; Provincial Files, DRMA—Winne Papers—LeFevre to Winne, 5 May 1942.
5. Provincial Files, DRMA—Winne Papers—LeFevre to Winne, 1 March 1940.

sent to St. Mary's. The Barrens, he felt, should not be a "house of penance" for wayward confreres but a place for the best in the community to set role models for prospective new Vincentians.[6] He was a stickler for maintenance of community rules, seeking permission for a student to go to New York for his grandmother's funeral, which was technically against disciplinary norms, and to enroll a potential recruit to the brotherhood who was "illegitimate" (also against the rules).[7] LeFevre preferred to eliminate movies entirely from student recreational activities, "except . . . on rare occasions [when] some extraordinarily fine production comes along."[8] Other letters suggested denying permission for a novice to attend his brother's first Mass and not allowing alcoholic drinks at post-ordination celebrations. He brought the same attention to detail to the Barrens' finances, complaining about the lack of communication from a California parish acting as agent for property owned by the Barrens that contributed $3,000 in annual income.[9] He looked for ways to improve the Barrens, at one point wondering whether Japanese American detainees might be secured "to assist us here," and rejoicing over receipt of eight boxes of books (containing almost 800 volumes of first edition American classics) from the collection of California benefactor Estelle Doheny.[10] Near the end of World War II, LeFevre noted the increasing problem of dealing with draft boards and the need to "appeal cases to Washington, and that as an outcome of this appeal, there is a great probability of future difficulties."[11]

LeFevre's focus on planning and attention to detail characterized the modern bureaucratic academy. He compiled lists of courses, indicating their weekly hours and rotation in the curriculum, and a roster of "Duties Assigned to the Personnel of Saint Mary's Seminary" indicating courses taught, including hours per

6. Provincial Files, DRMA—Winne Papers—LeFevre to Winne, 7 January 1940.
7. Provincial Files, DRMA—Winne Papers—LeFevre to Winne, 25 September 1939.
8. Provincial Files, DRMA—Winne Papers—LeFevre to Winne, 12 March 1940.
9. Provincial Files, DRMA—Winne Papers—LeFevre to Winne, 29 December 1939.
10. Provincial Files, DRMA—Winne Papers—LeFevre to Winne, 11 September 1943 and 29 August 1944.
11. Provincial Files, DRMA—Winne Papers—LeFevre to Winne, 9 July 1945.

week in the classroom, as well as other administrative and pastoral assignments.[12]

LeFevre's constant theme was the improvement of the Barrens seminary. "It seemed that since the common element in the lives of all the members of the Community was their years of formation at Perryville, that these years should be the rallying point of community loyalty. That such loyalty should make them look on the Motherhouse as their real Community 'home' in which they would maintain a constant interest and to which they would always be glad to return." The problems of the Barrens and the entire American Vincentian community were "problems that need not be. . . . That in the Community were all the elements of a magnificent organization, if only these were put together correctly and allowed to function smoothly." He realized the physical and financial challenges of operating the motherhouse, but hoped those challenges could be countered by cultivation of "unselfish, loyal and learned priests." But he often felt that organization and discipline dampened his hopes. When that happened, he could despair, lamenting that "I now realize that failure was inevitable. Perryville is best characterized by the French proverb 'Le plus ca change, le plus c'est le meme chose.'" Such moments led him to consider resignation, as he did in a letter of September 1941.[13] But he continued on for another four years, despite himself still absorbed in the details of personnel transfers, internal discipline, and quality formation at the Barrens.

Postwar, Pre-Council (1945–62)

The era between the end of World War II and the beginning of the Second Vatican Council, although brief, represented perhaps the height of the American Catholic resurgence and the halcyon days of St. Mary's of the Barrens. Accelerated growth in numbers,

---

12. SMOB Records, DRMA—Administration: Superior's Correspondence—LeFevre: "Curriculum Saint Mary's Seminary" and "Duties Assigned to the Personnel of Saint Mary's Seminary."
13. Provincial Files, DRMA—Winne Papers—LeFevre to Winne, 10 September 1941.

programs, and facilities promised a prolonged golden age, even if persistent problems regarding the isolation of the Barrens, its standing in the province, and financial pressures combined to curtail that dream.[14] In the meantime, the Barrens reflected trends in the broader world and church, including a heightened international awareness given postwar problems and Cold War tensions and a concern for improved programs, as well as endemic problems of financial resources and growing strains on seminary leadership. These issues reflected both the promises and the problems attached to accelerated growth, and would soon result in reconsiderations among American Vincentians regarding governance and formation programs. Those reconsiderations, occurring in the context of a broader reform during the Second Vatican Council, dramatically altered the course of the Barrens' future in the 1960s.

The immediate postwar political and moral climate, characterized by heightened concern for international developments amid a growing estrangement between the capitalist and largely Christian West and the communist and atheistic East, was reflected in the attention given those tensions in the Barrens community. The student writers of the *De Andrein* doted on those issues, demonstrating the conjoining of American and Catholic sensibilities in their approach to the postwar world. In a series of articles in 1947, the paper vividly described the plight of Vincentians' suffering from the anticlerical climate of postwar Italy, ran appeals for assistance to needy confreres in Yugoslavia and China, and noted approvingly the efforts of students at Vincentian-operated colleges to adopt a pro-American line (DePaul University's condemnation of the American Youth for Democracy and St. John's University's prayer cam-

---

14. One Vincentian wrote to Marshall Winne in 1949, "Incidentally, you might like to know how I feel about the Barrens. As regards the personnel . . . I think it is peerless but, unfortunately for me, this is the most obnoxious climate I have encountered since I entered the community. . . . If only some angels would pick up St. Mary's Seminary 'body and bones'—as they did the house of the Holy Family—and transport it to some secluded spot in the Rockies! I prayed for such a miracle (or its equivalent) during our annual retreat. Maybe I didn't have enough faith . . . or may I just have to be patient!" Provincial Files, DRMA—Winne Papers—J. M. O'Sullivan, CM, to Marshall Winne, CM, 10 February 1949.

paign in opposition to international communism).[15] The plight of impoverished East German women shared headlines with letters from Vincentian missionaries in China describing their treatment at the hands of Chinese Communists.[16]

Growing international tensions were brought home to the Barrens in very direct ways. By 1949, the Barrens community counted a growing number of European Vincentians, including Italian, French, Greek, Slovenian, Polish, and German speaking confreres.[17] A family of displaced Yugoslavs found refuge on the Barrens campus. The Mejac family lived in a farmhouse on Barrens property, the grandfather and son working odd jobs for the seminary and the daughter cleaning for the Miraculous Medal Association and local residents.[18] Barrens students followed Chinese conditions closely as deteriorating conditions led to the final exile of Vincentian missionaries and their flight to Taiwan, orchestrated by VFMS director Father Paul Lloyd in 1951.[19] Desperate postwar conditions in liberated Europe as well as the expulsion of Vincentian missionaries from China led a contingent of Dutch Vincentians to the Barrens by 1951, three of whom, including Cornelius Louws, a longtime Dutch missionary from China who spent three years in a Japanese prisoner-of-war camp, joined the Barrens faculty.[20] St. Mary's Seminary must have seemed a virtual United Nations to the surrounding community. The influx of foreign-born Vincentians hearkened back to an earlier missionary age of Barrens history and reflected the increasingly interconnected fortunes of the universal Catholic Church.

Like the broader American Catholic community, St. Mary's experienced dynamic institutional growth. Within five years (from 1943 to 1948), the seminary grew from 115 members to 152, including novices and "scholastics"—major seminarians studying philosophy and theology, with anticipation of even greater

15. *De Andrein* 17, no. 7 (1947); 17, no. 8 (1947); and 18, no. 3 (1947).
16. *De Andrein* 18, no. 5 (1948); and 18, no. 6 (1948).
17. *De Andrein* 19, no. 8 (1949).
18. *De Andrein* 20, no. 2 (1949).
19. Udovic, "Go Out to All the Nations," 390; and *De Andrein* 22, no. 2 (1951).
20. *De Andrein* 22, no. 2 (1951).

growth. The number of annual ordinations throughout the decade after World War II approached twenty; the population of Vincentian brothers neared forty; a new building program (see above) was started to meet the needs of a community of between 150 and 200 members.[21] All the new programs and fund-raising machinery of the community were mobilized to meet this growth. The projected new quadrangle, virtually a new Barrens campus, that started with the construction of the Finney Library and envisioned a new administration building as well as a large freestanding chapel, was to be funded by an alliance of the Miraculous Medal Association and the Countess Estelle Doheny.[22] In the meantime, the old campus needed major repairs. In a report entitled "Projected Repairs and Improvements, St. Mary's Seminary, Perryville" dated August 30, 1954, Barrens superior Daniel Martin anticipated a spate of needed maintenance and construction projects, from the purchase of new vestments for the church to the paving of sidewalks, reconditioning of grounds, remodeling of the old community chapel, and tuckpointing of virtually every older building on campus.[23]

Growth required vigilance to maintain traditional discipline and innovation to insure academic quality in a modernizing culture. The result was a dual concern with avoidance of internal "irregularities" while simultaneously pursuing external opportunities like new summer school venues and North Central Association accreditation.[24] The pursuit of graduate degrees at the new house of studies on the campus of the Catholic University of America was encouraged.[25] A new summer school policy allowed Barrens scholastics who had already completed the required philosophy curric-

21. On the growth of the brothers, see Provincial Files, DRMA—Winne Papers—William Brennan to Marshall Winne, 27 July 1948.
22. *De Andrein* 22, no. 8 (1952).
23. SMOB Records, DRMA—Buildings and Grounds—Martin, "Projected Repairs and Improvements, St. Mary's Seminary, Perryville."
24. See Provincial Files, DRMA—Stakelum Papers—Daniel Martin to James Stakelum, 8 December 1955, regarding "irregularities" detected while students attended summer school at other institutions, including drinking, smoking, dancing, and exposure to "illicit and immoral reading materials" like *True*, *Look*, *Life*, and *Post* magazines.
25. According to the *De Andrein*, twenty-eight American Vincentians received graduate degrees at the Catholic University of America from 1941 (when the CM house of studies opened) until 1948—including fifteen doctoral degrees; *De Andrein* 19, no. 5 (1949).

ulum to pursue undergraduate programs in other subjects at places like CUA, DePaul University, St. Louis University, and even nearby Southeast Missouri State University.[26] In a report on a visitation of the house dated as early as 1943, the visitor noted the need to train seminarians for teaching opportunities in the congregation's minor and major seminaries throughout the United States, citing the recent opening of the CUA House of Studies as recognition of that need. "Consequently," the visitor concluded, "many of our dear novices and students must look forward to forming themselves in the sacred and secular sciences with more than ordinary diligence as well as acquiring that virtue and piety so necessary to lead those whom they shall form in coming years for the secular priesthood."[27] The inclusion of this reminder in an otherwise traditional litany of the spiritual condition of the house reflected the new tensions in the Vincentian community and the American Catholic Church between traditional discipline and programmatic innovation.

Greater numbers, expanded facilities, and new programs complicated the always tenuous financial situation at the Barrens. As early as 1948, Barrens superior Michael O'Connell pressed the need for additional resources to provincial superior Marshall Winne. Undoubtedly used to a different kind of financial accounting from his days as president of DePaul University, O'Connell found himself in the awkward position of approaching the provincial superior about the penurious state of Barrens finances. "I hate to be bothering you, and I hate to be put in a position where I have to bother you about money," O'Connell wrote, "but our account here is so low that we are actually living on the deposits of the various confreres and on some special funds that are on deposit."[28] O'Connell noted, and itemized, almost $10,000 in outstanding bills, "and while we can stall some of them off, it is a process that I don't approve of and cannot stomach save in rare instances." His review of the "costs of the Seminary" showed that the allowance granted the Barrens from

26. Ibid.
27. SMOB Records, DRMA—Governance: Visitations—"Visitation Report 1943."
28. Provincial Files, DRMA—Winne Papers—Michael O'Connell, CM, to Marshall Winne, CM, 27 October 1948.

provincial coffers for 1948 "was the same in 1940–41–42 when the personnel of the house averaged 117 as it [is] now with 152 in the community here." The average allotment in previous years of $460 per man would suffice even given the greater numbers at present, "but we cannot get along on an allowance of $4,500 a month." O'Connell concluded with a plea to "work out some formula which will enable us to get along a little bit more comfortably than we are at present."[29] The provincial allowance was supplemented by gifts from the Miraculous Medal Association, income from the seminary farm, and the largesse of donors like Estelle Doheny, but money remained tight throughout the history of the Barrens' operations.[30]

The financial situation at the Barrens was complicated even further by certain external developments, including a 1944 IRS probe into the status of the seminary in the context of a close vote in the Missouri constitutional convention regarding the tax exemption for the state's earliest private colleges (including St. Mary's, Washington University in St. Louis, William Jewell College, Lindenwood College, and Westminster College). The convention questioned the tax-exempt status for those institutions in light of their property holdings and auxiliary operations not used for educational purposes.

The tax-exempt status was upheld, but a few years later other controversies arose regarding the fund-raising operations of Catholic religious communities and the solicitation of Mass stipends. In 1950, Vatican pronouncements based on the Code of Canon Law seemed to raise concerns about the status of Catholic fund-raising associations.[31] In response to this direct threat to the work and finan-

29. Ibid.
30. Doheny was said to have contributed $5,000 annually to the new library after 1954 in addition to her contributions to capital campaigns and gifts of valuable books and art objects.
31. A March 1950 decree by the Sacred Congregation of Council, based on the provisions of Canon 142 outlawing commercial activities by clergymen, required Catholic religious associations that engaged in "trade or business of any kind" to secure the approval of the local bishop for such activities or be subject to severe penalties. See Okwuru, *Responsibilities and Significance of the Congregatio pro clericis*, 255–58; and Beal, Coriden, and Green, *New Commentary on the Code of Canon Law*, 378–79. As a result of the decree, a few bishops looked closely at the fund-raising activities of religious communities operating within their dioceses. MMA director Joseph Finney informed provincial superior James Stakelum that some benefactors had pulled their memberships

cial well-being of the Barrens and other Vincentian apostolates, provincial superior James Stakelum wrote directly to Archbishop Joseph Ritter of St. Louis regarding the activities of the Vincentian Press, the Christmas Card Program of the Miraculous Medal Association (MMA), and the Vincentian Foreign Mission Society—all of which raised funds through direct mail solicitations. Stakelum assured Ritter that these auxiliary activities were "initiated in good faith" to support the legitimate religious works of the Congregation, and that Vincentian canon lawyers and moral theologians found them consistent with the ethical norms and canons of the Catholic Church.[32] Ritter responded that, on the basis of the report of his Curia, "our judgment is the same as yours, namely that the activities mentioned in no way come under the prohibition of Canon 142."[33] By the 1950s, the Miraculous Medal Association was funneling between $700 and $1,000 per month into provincial coffers from the Mass intentions of donors. Some American bishops began to question that practice and some even pronounced against Mass "leagues or associations" as violations of canon law and forbade their operations within their dioceses, causing some nervousness among patrons of the Miraculous Medal Association and a stout defense of MMA operations by its director, Joseph Finney.[34]

The increasing costs of maintaining the larger and more complex operations of the Barrens, combined with concerns about the status of auxiliary sources of income, formed the context for an ongoing disagreement over the Barrens budget. In 1953, Barrens superior Daniel Martin compiled a detailed financial report of Barrens operations for provincial authorities, contending that the rising expenses of the seminary resulted from "large outlays

in the Miraculous Medal Association in response to their bishop's warnings; Provincial Files, DRMA—Stakelum Papers—Joseph Finney, CM, to James Stakelum, CM, 27 June 1951.
32. Provincial Files, DRMA—Stakelum Papers—James Stakelum, CM, to Archbishop Joseph E. Ritter, 3 August 1950.
33. Provincial Files, DRMA—Stakelum Papers—Archbishop Joseph E. Ritter to James Stakelum, CM, 14 August 1950.
34. Provincial Files, DRMA—Stakelum Papers—Joseph Finney, CM, to James Stakelum, CM, 27 June 1951. Among the bishops cited were the ordinaries of Mobile, Cincinnati, and Steubenville.

for repairs . . . [and] reconditioning of the house and properties," in addition to "expenditures which you [provincial superior James Stakelum] and I have agreed were the prudent or the just thing to do—such as medical expenses of the Novices" and "a general rise in the cost of living."[35] Subsequent letters detailed the needs of the growing Barrens community and considered prudent ways to repurpose existing space.[36] Disagreements continued, however, for in the following year Martin wrote directly to provincial treasurer Cyril LeFevre, ostensibly regarding the selection of furnishings for the new library building. Martin confessed, however, that the bigger issue in his mind was LeFevre's "deep disapproval of the administration of the Seminary as now conducted."[37] Martin continued, "In fact, for about two years now, I have been hearing from all sides . . . that Fr. Martin will soon run the Province into bankruptcy, that there isn't any money for this or that because you have had to send all you had to Fr. Martin in Perryville, that Fr. Martin hasn't a sense of appreciation or management of Community funds, etc. etc."[38] Martin's unusually frank and emotional letter reminded LeFevre that the internal administration of the seminary was his (Martin's) responsibility, not a topic for community gossip or judgment, and that "there are factors which affect my prudential judgments other than stupidity, pig-headedness, or just plain carelessness." He ended with a call for mutual respect as each discharged their difficult responsibilities in the most judicious, prudent, and collegial manner possible.[39]

The expanding profile of the seminary and the need for additional funds inspired numerous unrealized proposals for new projects in the mid-twentieth century. In the early 1940s, Father Joseph Finney of the Miraculous Medal Association briefly pursued the idea of opening a radio station at the Barrens as an evangelical tool for

35. Provincial Files, DRMA—Stakelum Papers—Daniel Martin, CM, to James Stakelum, CM, 17 March 1953.
36. Provincial Files, DRMA—Stakelum Papers—Daniel Martin, CM, to James Stakelum, CM, 3 July 1953.
37. Provincial Files, DRMA—Stakelum Papers—Daniel Martin, CM, to Cyril LeFevre, CM, 24 March 1954.
38. Ibid.
39. Ibid.

the community and a potential money-maker for the province.[40] Barrens superior Daniel Martin informed the provincial superior in 1953 of a possible scheme to lease Barrens-owned property along the Mississippi River to an oil exploration firm provided that enough landowners joined in the venture.[41] In the same year, Martin raised the possibility of starting a training school on the Barrens campus for candidates for the Vincentian brotherhood.[42] Finally, provincial superior Marshall Winne briefly entertained the idea of applying for Pontifical Seminary status for the Barrens.[43] As with other American Catholic institutions in this period, these schemes reflected the growing confidence of the Barrens and the need for creative thinking to keep up with the expanding demands and financial pressures on the seminary.

The growth of the Barrens in the post–World War II era put a particular strain on the superiors of the institution. The position of Barrens rector, always complicated given the multiple roles filled by St. Mary's, became even more complex given the demands of

40. Provincial Files, DRMA—Winne Papers—Joseph A. Finney, CM, to Marshall F. Winne, CM, 2 December 1940. Finney initially resisted the visitor's conclusion that, based on consultation with experts, opening a radio station would be a financially unwise move. Finney solicited experts of his own to make the case that a commercial radio station might be operated for an initial investment of $25,000 (to be raised by Miraculous Medal Association donations) and could easily pay for itself with a minimum of advertising spots. Provincial Files, DRMA—Winne Papers—Finney to Winne, 29 March 1941.
41. Provincial Files, DRMA—Stakelum Papers—Daniel Martin, CM, to James Stakelum, CM, 17 March 1953.
42. Provincial Files, DRMA—Stakelum Papers—Daniel Martin, CM, to James Stakelum, CM, 3 July 1953. According to Martin, Vincentian Father William McClimont of the eastern province expressed interest in the idea, proposing a visit to Perryville to explore the possibility of "a separate house, adjacent to the Seminary here, but under separate administration, where the candidates could be trained and directed in their own regime, adapted to their own needs, but with regular periods of apprentice instruction under the guidance of the older Brothers, until such a time as they would be old enough to enter the Novitiate."
43. Provincial Files, DRMA—Winne Papers—Marshall Winne, CM, to Joseph Lilly, CM, Passion Sunday, 1949. Apparently, the idea never got past the point of querying the Vincentian superior general. The only seminary granted official pontifical status in the United States is the Pontifical College Josephinum in Columbus, Ohio, established in 1888 and granted pontifical status in 1892, although St. Mary's Seminary in Baltimore (1822) and St. Mary of the Lake Seminary in Mundelein, Illinois (1929), were granted permission to award Roman degrees.

the period. The superior of the Barrens answered to Vincentian
authorities, especially the provincial superior of the American western province, but
increasingly to both Roman
authorities and to external
agencies (see the issue of
academic accreditation) as
well. The rector-superior
of the Barrens acted as
college president, business
executive, farm manager,
and religious superior at
the same time. The superior
often taught seminary courses
as well. The men who filled this
role were usually accomplished
theologians with often
broad experience as semi-
nary faculty but with little
real experience in admin-
istering complex institu-
tions.

The superiors of St.
Mary's of the Barrens Seminary in the immediate
postwar period included
William Brennan (1945–

18. JAMES A. FISCHER
Barrens student and faculty member, Fischer
was a highly regarded scripture scholar who
served as rector-president at the Barrens from
1957 to 1962 and superior of the western
American Vincentian province from 1962
to 1971. He worked hard to upgrade the
academic status of the Barrens and secure
academic accreditation, and he brought a
Vatican II spirit of *aggiornamento* ("updating")
to the leadership of the province.

48), Michael J. O'Connell (1948–51), Daniel Martin (1951–57),
and James Fischer (1957–62). Brennan was born in Marysville,
Kansas, in 1885 and ordained to the Vincentian priesthood in
1912; O'Connell was born in Chicago in 1899 and ordained in
1923; Martin was born in St. Louis in 1912 and ordained in 1939;
and Fischer was born in St. Louis and ordained in 1943. All four
men received seminary training at the Barrens seminary. All four
men received graduate degrees from Roman universities, with

19. Farm Buildings
A number of auxiliary operations grew up to support seminary operations at the Barrens, including a thriving farm worked by Vincentian brothers.

Martin and Fischer also studying at the Catholic University of America. All four taught at other Vincentian-operated seminaries before assuming leadership at the Barrens (Brennan at Kenrick and St. Thomas Seminary in Denver, O'Connell at the Barrens and Kenrick Seminary in St. Louis, Martin at St. John's-Assumption Seminary in San Antonio and Kenrick, and Fischer at St. John's-Assumption and the Barrens). Brennan had previous experience as seminary superior—at the Barrens from 1933 to 1939 and at St. Thomas. O'Connell had the most administrative experience of the lot, starting a career at DePaul University in 1932 that saw him serve as vice-president, dean of the College of Arts and Sciences, and president of the university (1935–44) as well as superior of the Chicago Vincentian community. Indeed, O'Connell gained a solid reputation as DePaul's president, leading the university through the war years and expanding its programs in the sciences to position it for postwar growth. His appointment to the Barrens probably reflected the need for someone with previous academic leadership experience to deal with the thorny issue of academic accreditation through the North Central Association.

Most of these men continued active careers after their tenure as Barrens superior. Brennan worked in St. Louis; O'Connell at the

Vincentian Foreign Mission Society and as Barrens faculty member; Fischer as visitor of the western province, superior of Kenrick Seminary, and campus minister at the University of Arkansas. Martin and Fischer were published theologians and biblical scholars. The experience of guiding the Barrens through its period of greatest growth and attendant challenges wore at these priests, as reflected in their relatively brief terms as superior. O'Connell and Martin, as noted above, chafed at the pressures of operating a growing institution on a shoestring budget. O'Connell was forced to resign in 1951 as a result of recurring health issues. Of course, the pressures on the Barrens' leaders would only increase after 1962, with shifts in the broader American culture, Catholic reform, and Vincentian reconsideration of formation programs contributing to the altered fortunes of the old seminary.

Academics and Accreditation

The story of the academic development of the Barrens reflects the tension between the long educational tradition of the Catholic Church and the emerging standards of the American school system. At the Barrens, practical circumstances interacted with the demands of both church authorities (the increasing involvement and expectations of Rome, the American bishops, and European Vincentian leaders) and institutional leadership. Much of that tension is revealed in the evolving organization of the Barrens' curriculum and the pursuit of academic accreditation over the course of the middle decades of the twentieth century.

In its early years, the rather makeshift formation program at the Barrens mirrored the general Catholic approach that left seminary formation largely to the discretion of the local bishops. The needs of a frontier church short on priests to serve a far-flung Catholic population inspired the Barrens and other early American seminaries to adapt and shorten their programs in an effort to get missionaries in the field more readily. Indeed, in nineteenth-century America it was not unusual for Catholic seminaries to offer as little as one year of college and three years of theological study to serve the needs of a growing Catholic community. By the end of the century, however,

20. Novitiate Building

The Barrens campus enjoyed a construction boom in the middle decades of the twentieth century, including impressive blonde-brick buildings housing the novitiate program (the one- to two-year period during which candidates for membership in Catholic religious communities are oriented to community life and spirituality) and the scholasticate (student residence hall) in the 1930s.

pressures mounted on seminaries to standardize both their organization and curriculum.

Among the problems facing American seminaries was the dissonance between the structure of the American educational system with its four years of high school followed by four years of college and the European model in which "high school" and early college were often combined. The church-mandated 6–6 system—six years of "minor" seminary and six years of "major" seminary—did not coincide, then, with the normal structures of American schools.[44] In addition, a growing emphasis on academic professionalization, reflected in a demand for graduate training of seminary priests and the granting of recognized degrees by American seminaries, strained the resources of institutions like the Barrens. Finally, the American move toward voluntary academic accreditation impinged on seminary academic programs. As accreditation became a recognized seal of academic quality, both institutional pride and practical requirement—seminary graduates, especially in Vincentian institutions like the Barrens, might require state licenses before embarking on teaching careers or recognized degrees before beginning graduate study—pressured seminaries to seek accredited status. All of these issues were evident in the history of the Barrens in the twentieth century.

The academic experience at St. Mary's of the Barrens Seminary in 1939/40 consisted of a total of eight years of study. The "College Department" consisted of four years, including the initial two-year novitiate (during which students took the equivalent of one year of college courses) and two years of full-time college instruction. As indicated in the seminary prospectus, "The first year of College is not offered at the Seminary" but was left to the apostolic/preparatory schools, although a total of ninety-two credit hours were taken in the four-year cycle.[45] The course of studies included astronomy, biology and chemistry (although only one hour of algebra), English and American literature, speech, American history, church history,

44. See Poole, *Seminaries in Crisis*, 50.
45. SMOB Records, DRMA—Academic Files: Curriculum—"St. Mary's Seminary, Perryville, Mo.," in "Curriculum of Studies, 1939–40."

and music (with a focus on Gregorian chant) with a heavy focus on languages (Latin, French, German, and Spanish), education, and philosophy.

The "Theology Department" included four years of study covering every aspect of Catholic theology, canon law, scriptures, church history, patrology, sociology, liturgy, chant, homiletics, catechetics, and Hebrew (for the select few destined for graduate studies in scriptures).

The curriculum was designed to inculcate the virtues of piety, discipline, study, and refinement. "The Catholic priest must possess more than sacerdotal virtue. He must be a man of learning," the prospectus intoned, as well as a gentleman habituated to "the usages of polite society" and the expectations of "intellectual culture." To promote those ends, the Barrens curriculum sought a "logical unity and sequence in the individual course, also of the relations between one course and another" so that the student, "instead of amassing an agglomeration of knowledge, achieves a vision of truth."[46]

As early as the 1940s, discussion began among Barrens officials regarding revision of the existing curriculum. Apparently, the discussion was motivated by recent concerns regarding graduate school acceptance of Barrens students and teacher certification requirements in states where the Vincentians staffed parochial schools and seminaries. Barrens superior Daniel Martin began corresponding with other seminary deans about the possibility of reorganization in order to bring the Barrens curriculum into greater alignment with other schools, including DePaul University. In a 1945 letter to Father James Richardson, superior at St. John's Seminary in Camarillo, California, Martin indicated that he had initiated contact with J. D. Russell, secretary of the North Central Association of Colleges and Secondary Schools and had reason to believe that "we are not too far from a successful candidacy for admission into North Central if the proper backing is given by the authorities."[47]

46. Ibid.
47. SMOB Records, DRMA—Academic Files: Faculty—Correspondence, Dean of Studies: Daniel Martin, CM, to James W. Richardson, CM, 30 January 1945.

Voluntary academic accreditation was a uniquely American phenomenon that had developed since the early twentieth century as an effort to standardize academic performance, recognize academic accomplishment, and facilitate student admission to leading American colleges and graduate schools. The pursuit of accreditation by Catholic schools reflected many important issues in the history of American Catholic education. Catholic seminaries faced particular challenges in their pursuit of accreditation, including the broad tension between acceptance of evolving American norms and loyalty to Catholic tradition and authority as well as more practical considerations of size, organization, and governance.[48] The North Central Association became the largest and most influential of the regional accrediting agencies, and its relationship to American Catholic schools and seminaries developed gradually over the course of the century. By the 1950s, papal directives on the educational quality of seminary programs (*Menti Nostrae* in 1950 decreed that the education of seminarians "be at least not inferior to that of laymen who take similar courses of study" and *Sedes Sapientiae* reiterated this theme in 1956) encouraged seminaries to reform curricula and seek academic accreditation. The first seminaries to be accredited by North Central on the collegiate level did so in the mid-1950s.

In June 1946, a young James Fischer visited with North Central Association officials in Chicago about the prospects of Barrens accreditation. In meetings with Pius Barth, OFM, and J. D. Russell, Fischer sought advice regarding necessary academic changes at the Barrens and the accreditation process. Fischer admitted to obstacles, preventing the Barrens application for North Central Association membership. "We discussed the attitude among many older men that the North Central was a dictator of educational policy," he noted; they also discussed the long educational tradition of the community—"I remarked that we had been teaching for 300 years and weren't going to fall over our heels getting into the North

---

48. For a thorough review of the history of seminary accreditation and the problems encountered in the process, see Baer, "Development of Accreditation in American Catholic Seminaries, 1890–1961."

Central in a couple of months"—and the lack of "degreed professors" at the Barrens. Fischer nevertheless left with the impression that NCA officials would be well disposed toward a Barrens application for membership.[49]

In response to these overtures, Father Pius Barth visited the Barrens in November 1946 and left a report on his findings.[50] Barth made recommendations regarding several areas of the seminary program, including administrative structures, finances, college curriculum, theologate, faculty, library, entrance requirements, records, and physical plant. In general, he encouraged more systematic and well-articulated structures and policies in accordance with North Central expectations. Regarding curriculum, he emphasized the need for "a clear statement of Objectives of the College," including "1. General and advanced education for future priests and teachers. 2. Professional education for Catholic priesthood in the Vincentian order." He noted the present degree programs in which all college seminarians received A.B. degrees with a double major—philosophy and either English or Latin—with a total of 145 credit hours. He also delineated the course of studies, reflecting the changes since the 1940 prospectus with the addition of another year of college studies, so that the Barrens program now consisted of two years of novitiate, one year of "scholasticate," and two years of philosophy allowing the entire undergraduate program to be completed at the Barrens. Barth had little to say about the theology program, which he defined as "Professional Education" about which North Central "will have

49. SMOB Records, DRMA—Academic Files: NCA Accreditation—Correspondence and Notes, 1942–47: "By Father Fischer on trip to Chicago, June 8, 1946."

50. Pius Barth (1908–90) was a Franciscan priest and educator. Born and raised in Chicago with a doctorate from the University of Chicago, Barth taught at Quincy College and DePaul University before becoming superior of the Midwest Province of the Order of Friars Minor in 1954. He served on the Accrediting Committee for Institutions of Higher Learning of the North Central Association while chairing the education department at DePaul and was an early leader in the seminary accreditation movement. Barth encouraged seminaries to seek accreditation as liberal arts colleges rather than as professional schools. He was a key speaker at an important 1960 meeting of Midwest seminary leaders in Chicago that urged a broad approach to accreditation and encouraged seminaries to incorporate modern trends and topics in their curricula. On that meeting, see Baer, "Development of Accreditation in American Catholic Seminaries, 1890–1961," 271–74.

21. ACADEMIC BUILDING

The impressive neo-Gothic Joseph A. Finney Library, dedicated in 1954, served as academic center of the Barrens seminary. The building was subsidized by donations from the Miraculous Medal Association and Vincentian benefactor Estelle Doheny. It included classrooms and a library as well as museums and a rare book depository. The building currently hosts extension classes administered by Mineral Area Community College.

nothing to say . . . as long as reason can be shown for teaching the things that are on the curriculum." He did recommend that faculty, especially in the major areas taught, hold doctoral degrees and that faculty transcripts and syllabi be closely recorded. Finally, he encouraged systematic record keeping and the use of an entrance examination "especially for students from other than Cape [the high school seminary in Cape Girardeau whose graduates supplied a number of Barrens seminarians]." In general, Barth recognized the academic quality of the Barrens program but encouraged a few changes, especially regarding more intentional and systematic delineation of programs and policies, to conform to NCA standards.[51]

Over the next few years, Barrens officials pursued changes consistent with Barth's recommendations—establishing a system of standardized testing of seminarians, constructing a new academic building, and instituting a new summer school policy to broaden the range of courses available to students at other, larger institutions.[52] Other problems remained, however. In a revealing letter to Barrens superior James Fischer by Edward Riley, superior of the St. Louis Preparatory Seminary, dated January 13, 1959, Riley enumerated his concerns about the academic program at Perryville. Riley noted that the Barrens lacked prominence, even among fellow Vincentians, and failed to solicit the ideas and recommendations of other seminary educators. He criticized the faculty of the Barrens, especially the faculty of the college department, for their lack of academic competence. Finally, he advised that the Barrens must "acquire the trappings of academic respectability, e.g. accreditation, recognition, etc." in order to enhance its profile and standing in the seminary community.[53] Riley would have occasion to address those problems when he became superior of the Barrens in 1962.

---

51. SMOB Records, DRMA—Academic Files: NCA Accreditation—"North Central Association Accrediting: Recommendations made by Fr. Pius Barth, O.F.M.," 27–28 November 1946.
52. Provincial Files, DRMA—Stakelum Papers—Daniel Martin, CM, to J. W. Stakelum, CM, 3 July 1953.
53. Provincial Files, DRMA—Fischer Papers—Edward Riley, CM, to James Fischer, CM, 13 January 1959.

In the meantime, external developments led the North Central Association to question the admission of Catholic seminaries, citing the small size of most seminaries as an impediment.[54] Interest in curricular reform and accreditation increased, however, among seminaries—partly a result of papal directives and partly due to continued practical problems regarding graduate school admissions and teacher certification. The movement gained momentum after 1958 with the appointment of Cyril Dukehart as associate director of the seminary division of the National Catholic Educational Association. Dukehart, a Sulpician priest and rector of St. Charles College Seminary in Maryland, encouraged the modernization of seminaries and seminary pursuit of regional accreditation. In an address to school superintendents in 1959, he noted that seminaries were "being challenged by low standards for assessing admissions, a lack of qualified instructors, and a failure to recognize the need for cooperation in establishing educational standards."[55] Under Dukehart's encouragement and stimulated by the broader debate over Catholic intellectual life in general, some seminaries began a process of curriculum review, and seminary leaders gathered to consider the problems attached to accreditation. Edward Riley was a participant in one of those regional meetings in Chicago in 1960.[56]

As rector of St. Mary's of the Barrens, James Fischer continued the push toward curricular reform and academic accreditation. In 1957, Fischer interviewed Paul Reinert, the well-known Jesuit president of St. Louis University and recently elected president of the North Central Association, about the NCA's attitude toward seminaries. Reinert informed Fischer that, after a period of abeyance, the association was reopening the issue of seminary accreditation and would issue a report on the matter the following year.[57] Two years later, John Richardson wrote Fischer from DePaul University that

54. Baer, "Development of Accreditation in American Catholic Seminaries, 1890–1961," 265.
55. Anello, *Hand of God at Work*, 7.
56. Baer, "Development of Accreditation in American Catholic Seminaries, 1890–1961," 265.
57. SMOB Records, DRMA—Academic Files: NCA Accreditation—Correspondence and Meeting Notes: NCA, 1957–61: James Fischer, CM, "Accreditation Talk with Father Reinert, S.J., in St. Louis, 2 October 1957."

his talk with NCA officials convinced him that the association had overcome its reluctance to accredit small institutions and, indeed, might be eager to help seminaries gain membership. "Here is the real change over the past few years," Richardson wrote, "for the central office has, at least allegedly, changed its entire philosophy. It now assumes the position of a big brother using all of its resources and experiences to assist institutions meet given standards. It wants to work <u>with</u> the school as it makes its self-study and considers changes, rather than sit in judgment of the school's qualities after the studies and reports have been made." Given that change, Richardson outlined the process that the Barrens needed to make application, though he warned that the new "friendly attitude" of the NCA did not imply a lessening of standards.[58]

Fischer responded within days to Richardson's "extremely valuable letter" by acknowledging the need for "drastic action" to improve the academic status of the Barrens. While the seminary was completing a "self-evaluation of aims" and working on a new catalog, Fischer acknowledged that "we can't self-evaluate ourselves for the rest of our lives." Indeed, the Barrens superior admitted that "it is a simple, but painful fact that we are not running a good college. *Sedes Sapientiae* doesn't think so. As a matter of fact, *Sedes Sapientiae* is about as tough as N.C.A. on professors." The crux of the problem, as identified by Fischer, was the need for more highly credentialed and experienced faculty at the Barrens. Such a commitment required the support of the provincial superior and the entire community, which agreed with the need to upgrade the college but might balk at the "meat and potatoes business of stripping the Province to establish a suitable Faculty at Perryville." Fischer was willing to push the issue in the interests of serving "the next generation of priests and Catholic laymen."[59]

Pushing the issue meant serious review and potential change at the Barrens, and Fischer determined to undertake that task. In

58. SMOB Records, DRMA—Academic Files: NCA Accreditation—Correspondence, Richardson: John Richardson, CM, to James Fischer, CM, 22 February 1959.
59. SMOB Records, DRMA—Academic Files: NCA Accreditation—Correspondence, Richardson: James Fischer, CM, to John Richardson, CM, 25 February 1959.

a response to the notes of provincial superior James Stakelum on the Barrens curriculum, Fischer resolved to publish a catalog of the course of studies at Perryville that aligned seminary courses with the prevailing semester organization of mainstream American colleges and honestly acknowledged the problems facing the Barrens. "I am not afraid of the growling I hear," Fischer noted.

> A considerable body of confreres believe, as our Faculty believed two years ago, that we do not have any educational problems. They say: we know how to teach in seminaries; the Vincentian tradition is to stick to one book, one opinion and to give practical solutions; don't try to tell the Professors how to run their business. They also believe that Perryville is dying of intellectual dry rot. To approach such men and get even a hearing I think that we must take account of their prejudices. I have tried to put some of these objections into words in the section on Aims. I have included the statement on the Program of Self-Evaluation to indicate that Perryville is waking up . . . by stating honestly our problems and the progress we have made to solve them I think we can encourage as many as will be encouraged to back a program of self-evaluation in their own seminaries.[60]

Fischer's immediate response to the need for academic review and change at the Barrens focused on the need to raise awareness in the Vincentian community, and the "self-evaluation of aims" and new academic catalog addressed that need. In essence, Fischer aimed to enhance the academic culture at Perryville by inspiring a new enthusiasm for academic quality expressed in a more professional manner, consistent with the standards and procedures of the broader American educational system.

Fischer's program, while not immediately tied to pursuit of NCA accreditation, resulted in the submission of a "Self-Study Report" to the association requesting the status of "candidate

---

60. SMOB Records, DRMA—Academic Files: Curriculum—Proposed Changes, Correspondence, 1957–65: "Notes on Father Stakelum's notes," undated copy.

for membership." The request was promptly denied by the NCA, with little indication of specific reasons for the denial. In July 1961, Fathers Fischer and Joseph Falanga met with David Madsen, the associate secretary of the North Central Association, to request clarification for the denial. The report of that interview revealed a rather sheepish Madsen noting the "very close" decision of the committee, but he was unable to volunteer any specific reasons for that decision. "Put it this way," Madsen is quoted, "an unfavorable decision usually reflects the Committee's doubts that a school has shown sufficient intellectual vigor." Insufficient vigor might mean too little emphasis on scholarly pursuits, too few doctorates among the faculty, too little scholarly publishing by the faculty—Madsen had trouble delineating which, if any of these points, applied to the Barrens. In response to specific questions by Fischer and Falanga, Madsen asserted that the documents submitted by the Barrens were "perfectly satisfactory," the self-study report was "excellent" in his opinion, the small size and rural location of the college were not factors in the decision, and any plans to move the college would not affect the NCA's deliberations. Finally, Madsen advised that the Barrens resubmit its application for the October 1961 meeting of the committee, with few revisions other than an introduction focusing on issues of faculty quality and scholarship. Fischer and Falanga agreed that Madsen "was embarrassed by this interview" and probably disagreed with the decision of the committee. While nothing specific came out of the interview, Barrens officials were convinced that the size and location of the Barrens were not factors in the NCA's decision, and that "moving to Lemont would not be very impressive by itself."[61]

An application for candidacy was resubmitted in May 1962 and the Barrens was accepted as a "Candidate for Membership," although the Association recommended that the seminary secure

---

61. SMOB Records, DRMA—Academic Files: NCA Accreditation—Correspondence and Meeting Notes: NCA, 1957–1961: "Report of Interview with Mr. Davis Madsen, Associate Secretary of the North Central Association: Chicago, July 5, 1961, Frs. Fischer and J. Falanga attending."

the services of a consultant to help address remaining problems before submitting a more detailed report for full membership. The first consultant to visit the Barrens was Dr. William H. Conley, director of the Center for the Study of Catholic Education at the University of Notre Dame, and former president of the National Catholic Educational Association. Conley visited the Barrens in November 1962 and left a report of his findings, which generally commended the college for its "substantial progress . . . and excellent and experienced leadership." He found the general education program of the college to be a potential strength of the institution but recommended better sequencing of courses in fields outside philosophy and a possible reduction in minors, including the deletion of science and foreign languages. The outstanding weakness of the college remained the preparation of faculty, and Conley reiterated the need for more PhD holders in the fields for which the Barrens offered major and minor programs. The college also needed to assess the quality of its student body through administration of standardized tests, including the Graduate Record Examination, and the compilation of a record of accomplishments. Finally, he noted the "imminent" move of the institution to Illinois and recommended that the period of candidacy (to expire in 1966) be extended to allow a more thorough and "drastically revised" self-study report after the final transfer.[62]

By the March 1964 visit of the next consultant to the Barrens, the decision had been made to maintain the college at Perryville and seek accreditation independently of DePaul University by the end of the candidacy period. John P. Raynor, Jesuit academic vice president (and soon to be president) of Marquette University, visited the Barrens three times in 1964–65 and offered pointed advice on the college's prospects for accreditation. Raynor's March 1964 report focused on the need for an appropriately credentialed and distinct college faculty—"Either St. Mary's obtain the promised

---

62. SMOB Records, DRMA—Academic Files: NCA Accreditation—Report of Visit: Conley, "Report on Visit to St. Mary's Seminary, Perryville, Missouri, November 1962." As it turned out, the move to Lemont in 1965 ultimately involved only the theology program and the college remained on the Barrens campus.

faculty members as minimum requirements in September 1964, or they should forget about making the self-study in the 1964–65 year"—and advised that the self-study de-emphasize the matter of priestly training in favor of attention on "the autonomy of the College as a college."[63] His follow-up visit in the spring of 1965 yielded observations regarding the organizational structure of the college, reiterating his earlier point that the self-study focus less on priestly training and more on "a good liberal arts education." Raynor advised that the role of the Vincentian community, especially the provincial superior, be de-emphasized given the state charter enjoyed by the Barrens and that the Barrens as a religious community house be separated from the college as an academic institution.[64] Finally, Raynor's report of December 1965, based on his November visit to the Barrens, commended the college for its progress, although now-President Raynor wondered whether "too many students are taking too many courses from too few faculty." Regarding the small size of the student body, Raynor noted that his informal consultations with North Central Association officials convinced him that the "fundamental point is not physical size per se, but the implication of physical size on the extensiveness and effectiveness of educational offerings and programs." In other words, "The Association takes no position on size of student body, per se."[65]

The institutional self-study finally submitted to the North Central Association in May 1966 provided a comprehensive overview of the Barrens as a seminary college at that moment. The study describes a small college (just over one hundred students and thirteen "regular" faculty) in an isolated geographic location positioned in the context of a larger American Vincentian program for priestly formation, reflecting the fact that by 1965 the Barrens had embraced the usual American four [high school]-four [college]-four [graduate school] academic structure with a novitiate

63. SMOB Records, DRMA—Academic Files: NCA Accreditation—"Report of a Visit to St. Mary's Seminary, Perryville, Missouri (1964)."
64. SMOB Records, DRMA—Academic Files: NCA Accreditation—Correspondence, Raynor: John P. Raynor, SJ, to Edward F. Riley, CM, 11 June 1965.
65. SMOB Records, DRMA—Academic Files: NCA Accreditation—Correspondence, Raynor: John P. Raynor, SJ to Edward F. Riley, CM, 2 December 1965.

period intervening between high school and college. The college focused primarily on a liberal arts education consistent with Catholic Church directives for high academic quality aimed at producing "well-informed and well-formed" graduates.[66]

The 1966 self-study highlighted the relative financial stability of the college, although its conclusions admitted that given its small student body the Barrens was "basically an inefficient institution."[67] The faculty, long an issue of contention among would-be reformers, included thirteen members, seven of whom held a doctoral degree, teaching a maximum twelve credit-hour load per semester among whom "publications are not one of the strong points."[68] The relatively new academic and library building was hailed as a great advance. The curriculum was demanding and essentially classical, with all students completing a minimum of 158 credit hours (including summer sessions off the Barrens campus), that included an eighty-six-hour "general education" program (twenty-four hours in Latin and Greek, twelve hours in French, etc.), a thirty-six-hour major program in philosophy, a twenty-one-hour minor in education, and a second minor in either English, Latin, history, or mathematics of sixteen hours. The students, as measured by a variety of standardized examinations, were generally capable and high-achieving, especially in philosophy and the humanities. While student life revolved around the religious and spiritual activities of the house, opportunities for intramural athletics and a variety of other co-curricular activities (music, plays, student government, student publications, summer camp, photographic laboratory, bindery, woodworking, and more) abounded. In general, the self-study considered the greatest strengths of the college to be its "dedicated and scholarly faculty and an intelligent and zealous student body," academic program "geared to the needs of its students," solid physical facilities, strong spiritual and character formation focus, and hon-

---

66. SMOB Records, DRMA—Academic Files: NCA Accreditation—Correspondence: NCA 1962–1966: "Institutional Self-Study, Saint Mary's Seminary, Perryville, Missouri, May, 1966," 10–11.
67. Ibid., 91.
68. Ibid., 47.

esty regarding its limitations and challenges.[69] Among the acknowledged weaknesses of the institution were its physical isolation, which limited extensive cultural opportunities, tendency to favor traditional instructional and classroom methods, an underutilized library, and small student body.[70]

The visiting committee of the North Central Association's Commission on Colleges and Universities conducted an on-site review of the Barrens on December 7–8, 1966.[71] The committee's report essentially validated the Barrens self-study, noting the adequacy of college programs and structures in nearly every category, noting especially the library and the "splendid counseling system" for students. Perhaps the most notable weaknesses recognized by the committee were lack of modern teaching methods by some faculty, the need for a "clear perspective of the total educational thrust of the institution [beyond the philosophy curriculum] . . . in future academic planning and programming," the "little vital contact between the college students and the local community," and the need to improve the academic performance of the non-American (mostly Filipino) students.[72] The positive response of the visiting committee led to the acceptance of St. Mary's of the Barrens College as a full member among "Bachelor's Degree–Granting Institutions" of the North Central Association in April 1967.

The scheduled reaccreditation review by North Central in 1977 went less smoothly for the Barrens. Despite the "unusually thorough Self-Study with extensive use of standardized test instruments" compiled by the seminary and the generally satisfactory quality of the Barrens' programs and facilities, the visiting team, chaired by distinguished Notre Dame professor of philosophy Frederick J. Crosson, noted weaknesses linked to declining student

69. Ibid., 89–90.
70. Ibid., 90–91.
71. SMOB Records, DRMA—Academic Files: NCA Accreditation—Report of Visit: Horner and Pendergast, "Report of Visit to St. Mary of the Barrens Seminary, Perryville, Missouri, 7–8 December 1966 for the Commission on Colleges and Universities of the North Central Association of Colleges and Secondary Schools." The visiting committee consisted of Joseph S. Pendergast, SJ (dean of Milford College), and Dr. John E. Horner (president of Hanover College).
72. Ibid., 3, 7, 11.

enrollment.[73] Too few students and courses, too much dependence on opportunities for summer and winter classes at DePaul University and Southeast Missouri State University, meant that "St. Mary's is too little in charge of its own programs, in quality control and other aspects. The threat to the coherence of the curriculum shows up in omissions and rhythms which disregard the learning process." The team recognized that these issues stemmed from the small size of the student body, and not "ignorance or indifference" on the part of the generally solid faculty and Vincentian authorities.[74] St. Mary's urgently needed "qualitative changes as well as high cost-benefit ratios" to remedy its perceived academic ills.[75] In its conclusions, the team reiterated its concern about declining student numbers but recommended reaccreditation with a follow-up visit in five years. "Unless the sharp decline in enrollment can be reversed, it is hard to see how it [the Barrens] can remain viable as an independent college seminary."[76]

While seminary officials accepted the recommendations of the visiting team and responded with questions to guide its follow-up visit, the NCA Commission on Institutions of Higher Education reacted strongly to the visiting team's report. The Commission modified the recommendations of the team, moving the follow-up visit from five to three years and requiring the seminary to submit annual progress reports addressing the weaknesses identified in the report.[77]

As it turned out, the required follow-up visit was postponed given administrative changes—both a new rector-president and a new academic dean took office in 1978/79 at the Barrens. When the visit occurred in the spring of 1982, the team, chaired by Francis C. Brennan, SJ, academic vice president at Xavier University,

---

73. SMOB Records, DRMA—Academic Files: NCA Accreditation—NCA Accreditation Process 1975–77: "St. Mary's Seminary, Perryville, Missouri." The team noted that St. Mary's student enrollment had nearly halved in a five-year period, declining from seventy-six students in 1973/74 to thirty-seven in 1977/78. Seminary officials responded with guarded optimism regarding future enrollments.
74. Ibid., 17.
75. Ibid., 22.
76. Ibid., 23.
77. Ibid., 26–27.

found a very different academic program in place at a temporarily rejuvenated seminary college. The report of April 1982 focused on three areas identified as weaknesses in the 1977 report—student enrollment, curriculum, and faculty stability.[78] The team found that enrollment had improved, from a low of thirty-eight in 1977 back to seventy-two students in 1980/81, due to heightened recruitment efforts and the postponement of the novitiate until after the college experience.[79] The academic curriculum of the seminary had been totally redesigned with an eye toward more flexibility and innovation. Under the creative leadership of new academic dean Ralph Pansza, the traditional fifteen-week semester was replaced by five-week modules, during which students enrolled in two courses. The shorter modules allowed for "increased student activity during the shortened time available for each course subject," as the NCA report noted, in addition to a "sharpening of attention" and a greater ability to recruit visiting faculty given the shorter time obligation.[80] The organization of courses was also revamped, with the freshman and sophomore years devoted to courses on basic academic skills, including a required Human Heritage Intensive, "an exercise in intellectual history . . . in an interdisciplinary fashion" that offered a broad perspective on the historical development of western civilization as a foundation for later courses. The philosophy major was also revised. Although still essentially Thomist in perspective, a required introductory course on philosophical methods and new elective courses were added to the program. The fine arts curriculum was enhanced with the hiring of an artist-in-residence and new courses in sculpture, ceramics, painting, and photography. New courses, including introductory skills and methods courses, were introduced in the social sciences as well.[81] One result of the new curriculum noted by the NCA report was a "striking shift toward

78. SMOB Records, DRMA—Academic Files: NCA Accreditation—Report of Visit: Dr. Bannan and Brennan, 1982, "Report of a Visit to St. Mary's Seminary College, Perryville, Missouri 63775, April 25–26, 1982, for the Commission on Institutions of Higher Education of the North Central Association of Colleges and Schools."
79. Ibid., 2–3.
80. Ibid., 3–4.
81. Ibid., 5–7.

dialogue and away from the lecture method" that previously characterized instruction at the Barrens.[82] Finally, while rapid faculty
turnover remained a problem, the seminary had plans to hire three
new full-time lay faculty in addition to the thirteen nonresidential
visiting faculty employed over the course of the 1981/82 academic
year.[83] All in all, the Barrens proved its adaptability once again in the
development of its innovative undergraduate curriculum, although
imminent changes in the status of the Barrens meant that these
innovations would be short-lived.

Barrens Men All

While the Vincentians in twentieth-century America, despite their
growth and prominent role in staffing numerous seminaries, may
not have drawn the public attention as other Catholic religious
communities did, or as their own community did in the pioneer
American Catholic Church of the previous century, the Barrens
continued to produce a number of important clerical leaders. With
the growth of more American-born priests in large American dioceses, fewer Vincentians were tapped for the domestic prelacy. One
who was elevated to the American episcopacy in this period was
Joseph Glass.[84] Born in Bushnell, Illinois, in 1874, Glass hailed from
an affluent Irish American family that moved to California in 1887.
He attended St. Vincent's College in Los Angeles before entering
the Vincentian community at the Barrens in 1891. He was ordained
to the priesthood in 1897 and shortly thereafter moved to Rome,
where he earned a graduate degree in theology from the Pontifical University of St. Thomas Aquinas in 1899. For the next two
years, he served on the faculty of St. Mary's of the Barrens, teaching moral theology and directing novices, until his elevation to the
presidency of St. Vincent's College in Los Angeles at the tender age
of twenty-seven in 1901. His leadership of St. Vincent's College created some controversy given the financial difficulties and eventual

82. Ibid., 4.
83. Ibid., 8.
84. On Glass, see Poole, "An Active and Energetic Bishop."

closure of the institution in 1910, but Glass remained prominent in the Los Angeles church, enjoying the patronage of the wealthy Doheny family and the regard of Bishop Thomas Conaty.[85] Glass continued to serve as pastor of St. Vincent's Parish in Los Angeles and was instrumental in the conversion of Estelle Doheny to Catholicism in 1918.

Glass's good fortune in attracting such powerful patrons certainly contributed to his appointment as second bishop of Salt Lake City in 1915. The selection process highlighted the controversial reputation of Glass, with some of his own confreres questioning his administrative abilities as well as his "too liberal" observance of Vincentian rules.[86] As bishop, Glass continued his worldly lifestyle, purchasing a new episcopal residence, accepting gifts (including two Pierce Arrow automobiles and a generous annual allowance) from the Dohenys, hobnobbing with prominent LA celebrities, and renovating the Salt Lake City cathedral with art purchased during his European travels.[87] While he contracted huge debts and was widely belittled for his lack of administrative acumen, Bishop Glass did fulfill the expectations of those who desired an "active and energetic" leader for the vast Utah diocese, traveling widely, becoming a well-known public figure, and generally leaving the diocese "in better condition than he found it" on his death in 1926.[88] Glass was the last Vincentian to serve as bishop of a diocese in the continental United States until the appointment of David M. O'Connell to the diocese of Trenton, New Jersey, in 2010.

A number of Vincentians with connections to the Barrens were elevated to bishoprics in mission territories, however, reflecting the growing involvement of the community in missionary work in the

---

85. Ibid., 121–23. According to Poole, some fellow Vincentians questioned Glass's leadership and financial management of the institution, and a few went so far as to levy "accusations of conduct that bordered on the criminal."
86. Ibid., 150.
87. Ibid., 156–57.
88. Ibid., 162. One of Glass's harshest critics was the prominent Vincentian scholar and superior general Charles L. Souvay, who attributed Glass's success to the influence of his wealthy father and wrote in 1919 that "an attentive study of what was done there would not contribute to putting a halo on the present bishop of Salt Lake City"; ibid., 124.

twentieth century. The particular interest of the Barrens community in the Chinese missions of the western American province made it a fertile field for missionary recruits, including episcopal leaders for the Kiangsi vicariate. Edward Sheehan was born in 1888 in Farm Ridge, Illinois, and entered the apostolic school at the Barrens in 1903.[89] Sheehan spent the next thirteen years at the Barrens and was ordained to the priesthood by Bishop Glass in 1916 before assignments at the University of Dallas, New Orleans, Kenrick Seminary, and St. Vincent's College (Cape Girardeau). In 1923, he became one of the first volunteers for the Chinese missions of the western American province and was named superior of the small Vincentian missionary band as well as pastor of the church in Yukiang. In 1929, he was named successor to the Vincentian Bishop Clerc-Renaud in Yukiang, a "large and poor vicariate" of just over 34,000 Catholics in the Kiangsi province. Sheehan returned briefly for a visit to the Barrens in 1931 before his premature death by pneumonia in 1933.

Sheehan was succeeded as vicar-apostolic by Paul Misner, a native of Peoria, Illinois, who worked briefly as a stonemason before entering the Vincentian novitiate at the Barrens in 1911.[90] Ordained in 1918, Misner was sent to graduate school in Rome, earning a doctorate in theology in 1922 and almost immediately thereafter volunteering for service in the original western American provincial missionary band. He became director of the seminary established by the Vincentians in Kienchangfu, Kiangsi, but returned to the United States for health reasons in 1925. By 1930, Misner had returned to China as an advisor to Sheehan, nearly died after a bout of pneumonia in 1933, succeeded Sheehan as vicar-apostolic, and was consecrated bishop in 1935. Misner was on an American visit in 1937 but returned to China with the onset of the Sino-Japanese War. His *De Andrein* obituary noted that Misner wanted only to be a missionary but was saddled early on with administrative duties and suffered numerous bouts of sickness,

---

89. For biographical information on Sheehan, see his obituary in the *De Andrein* 4, no. 1 (1933).
90. For biographical information on Misner, see his obituary in the *De Andrein* 9, no. 3 (1938).

precipitated by local conditions, before his death in China in 1938.

Charles Quinn was a native Californian educated at the Barrens and the Angelicum in Rome before his ordination in Los Angeles in 1931.[91] He entered the Chinese missions in 1932 and succeeded Misner as vicar-apostolic of Yukiang in 1938, although the difficulties of war prevented his consecration until 1940. Quinn and his small group of Vincentian missionaries endured terrible hardships during the war, at one point moving into nearby mountains to escape a Japanese invasion of the area and uncovering evidence of Japanese atrocities against those left behind in Yukiang.[92] Quinn and his companions assisted the American survivors of the famed "Doolittle Raid" on the Japanese mainland after their aircraft crashed in the Yukiang area in 1942, prompting a massive Japanese search. By 1944, conditions led to the evacuation of most Vincentian missionaries from the province. Quinn and a larger number of American Vincentian missionaries returned after the war, and he was named first bishop of the newly elevated diocese of Yukiang in 1946. He was expelled from his diocese by Chinese Communists in 1951 and, after a brief sojourn in the United States, returned in 1955 to the Vincentian missions in Taiwan, where he was buried after his death in 1960.

Given the widespread involvement of American Vincentians in seminary education, it is perhaps not surprising that a number of prominent Catholic scholars and educators were linked to the Barrens over the course of the twentieth century. A good number of Vincentians went on to graduate schools in Rome and the United States before serving on the faculties of the various seminaries operated by the community. A few achieved scholarly distinction, especially in theology, and even more particularly in biblical studies. Indeed, four individual Vincentians, all educated at the Barrens, served as presidents of the Catholic Biblical Association of America between 1939 and 1977 (Joseph Lilly, Gilmore Guyot, Bruce Vawter, and James Fischer). Other Vincentians were noted for their contributions to various disciplines, although Vincentian historian Stafford Poole

91. For biographical information on Quinn, see Udovic, "Go Out to All the Nations," 385–86; and Rybolt, *American Vincentians*, 479.
92. Udovic, "Go Out to All the Nations," 385.

maintained that "the Vincentians themselves showed relatively little leadership on the national level in advancing seminary education or facing contemporary needs."[93] Key individuals, however, contributed much to the intellectual life of the American Catholic Church in the twentieth century.

Among the most prominent of the Barrens scholars was Joseph Donovan (1880–1958).[94] Born in Marysville, Kansas, he received an undergraduate degree at St. Vincent's College, Chicago (the present-day DePaul University) in 1902 and entered the Vincentian community at the Barrens that same year. Ordained in 1906, he spent the next three years earning a doctorate in canon law at the prestigious Pontifical Lateran University. For most of his professional life he taught on the faculty of Kenrick Seminary in St. Louis, where he also served a term as rector from 1944 to 1950. Donovan contributed numerous essays to the *American Ecclesiastical Review* and served as editor of the popular "Question and Answer" department of the *Homiletic and Pastoral Review*, in which capacity he "became widely known for his original research and forthright opinions on many controverted points of Canon Law and Theology."[95] He was a charter member of the Catholic Rural Life Conference and other prominent Catholic associations and was well-known for his role in the establishment of the Legion of Mary in the United States, whose founding he inspired through a 1931 essay in the *American Ecclesiastical Review* entitled "Is This the Long Awaited Church Society?" Donovan's career exemplifies the active role of a seminary priest in the affairs of the American Catholic Church.

Father Joseph Lilly (1893–1952) spent nearly half of his fifty-eight years on the campus of St. Mary's of the Barrens as student or faculty member.[96] Ordained in 1918, he received graduate degrees from the Angelicum in Rome (S.T.D., 1922) and the Pontifical Biblical Commission in Palestine (S.S.L., 1933). He taught at St. Thomas Seminary in Denver and, as an affirmation of his scholarly achieve-

93. Poole, "Ad Cleri Disciplinam," 160.
94. On Donovan, see his obituary in the *De Andrein* 29, no. 4 (1959).
95. Ibid.
96. On Lilly, see his obituary in the *De Andrein* 22, no. 7 (1952).

ments, at the Catholic University of America (1942–48). Lilly was an active member of the Catholic Biblical Association of America, serving as president (1939–40) and executive secretary (1942–48). He is, perhaps, best remembered for his collaboration with the Jesuit scholar James Kleist on a modern English translation of the New Testament (the *Kleist-Lilly New Testament*, published in 1954, noted for its modern idiom but superseded by officially sanctioned translations like *The New American Bible*). Lilly remained active in Vincentian activities, editing *The Vincentian*, preaching in the Motor Missions, encouraging high academic standards in his role as provincial director of studies, and serving as pastor of missions attached to the Barrens before his death at Kenrick in 1952.

Lester Fallon (1902–58), already noted as co-founder of the Motor Missions and director of the Confraternity Home Study Service, studied at the Barrens and in Rome before his ordination in Paris in 1928.[97] Fallon served on the faculty of Kenrick Seminary before becoming full-time director of the CHSS, which he administered until his relatively early death after a long illness in 1958.

Mention has already been made of James Fischer (1916–2005) in his role as superior of the Barrens from 1957 to 1962.[98] Born in St. Louis in 1916, he studied at the St. Louis Preparatory Seminary before entering the Vincentian community at the Barrens in 1936. Fischer was ordained in 1943 and received graduate degrees from the Catholic University of America (1949) and the Pontifical Biblical Institute in Rome (1951). His seminary professor Joseph Lilly encouraged him in his biblical studies and in his involvement in the Catholic Biblical Association of America, at that time dominated by seminary priest-scholars. Fischer taught at numerous Vincentian-run seminaries, including the Barrens, before becoming superior of the Barrens in 1957 and superior of the western province in 1962. He was provincial superior at a critical time in the history of the Catholic Church and led deliberations regarding

97. On Fallon, see his obituary in the *De Andrein* 29, no. 3 (1958).
98. On Fischer, see his obituary in the *Southeast Missourian* (November 27, 2005), and a typed transcript of his interview with Carolyn Osiek, RSCJ, as part of the Catholic Biblical Association Oral History Project (dated May 2, 1997) in the Personnel Files, DRMA—Fischer—Osiek, "Interview."

the future of the American Vincentian community. His "liberal" views as provincial superior were both fostered and tempered by his studies, reflecting changes in biblical scholarship in the 1960s, and his insistence that his "interest always has been pastoral," focusing on the relationship between scriptures and the people of God.[99] A recent history of Catholic higher education in the 1960s describes Fischer as "a force to be reckoned with at DePaul" given his efforts as board chair and Vincentian superior to move "the university community away from merely symbolic to a more open and action-centered approach."[100]

Fischer's pastoral approach to biblical scholarship is reflected in books, many published by the Paulist Press, aimed at a popular audience and reflecting his storytelling approach to scriptural study.[101] Fischer continued his long career after his stint as provincial superior with faculty positions at De Andreis Seminary in Lemont, Illinois, Kenrick Seminary in St. Louis, and St. Thomas Seminary in Denver. In his later career as priest-in-residence at the Barrens, Fischer worked at the Newman Centers at Southeast Missouri State University and the University of Arkansas in Fayetteville.

Fischer's student Bruce Vawter (1921–86) continued the line of American Vincentian biblical scholars.[102] Born in Fort Worth, Texas, Vawter entered the Barrens in 1942 and was ordained in 1947. He earned the doctorate in Sacred Scripture from the Pontifical Biblical Institute in Rome; studied as a Fulbright scholar at Eberhard University in Tubingen, Germany; and taught at Kenrick, St. Thomas (Denver), and the Barrens before joining the faculty of DePaul University, where he chaired the theology department from 1969 to 1985. As a well-regarded scholar, he enjoyed visiting stints at Vanderbilt University and the Pontifical Biblical Institute and was active

99. Personnel Files, DRMA—Fischer—Osiek, "Interview," 1, 9.

100. Dosen, *Catholic Higher Education in the 1960s*, 208–9.

101. Works by Fischer include *God Said, Let There Be Woman: A Study of Biblical Women* (Alba House, 1979); *How to Read the Bible* (New York: Dodd, Mead, 1987); *Interpreting the Bible: An Investigation of the Hidden Reasons Why We Draw Conclusions About Biblical Texts* (Paulist Press, 1992); *Looking for Moral Guidance: Dilemma and the Bible* (Paulist Press, 1993); *A Lighthearted View of Wisdom in the Bible: How to Read Inspired Books* (Paulist Press, 2002); and *Leaders and People in Biblical Stories* (Paulist Press, 2004).

102. On Vawter, see the obituary in the *Chicago Tribune*, December 3, 1986.

in the Catholic Biblical Association of America—editing works on behalf of the CBA, serving as president in 1961–62 and on the executive board for many years.

Like Fischer and Lilly, Vawter's scriptural scholarship incorporated a broad perspective. His obituary quotes from *Job and Jonah: Questioning the Hidden God*: "The biblical message is meant not only to console but to challenge and provoke. If one reads the Bible only to find comfort and consolation in fixed positions, the meaning of the Bible has been missed. Some Bible Christians misunderstand the Bible precisely in this way. They search it for confirmation in their prejudices rather than for a summons to re-examine their premises."[103]

Stafford Poole remains an active Vincentian scholar and historian.[104] Born in California to a family whose prominence dates to the American colonial era and educated at the Los Angeles diocesan minor seminary, Poole entered the American Vincentian community at the Barrens in 1947 and was ordained in 1956. He taught at various Vincentian seminaries, including Cardinal Glennon College in St. Louis, the Barrens, and St. John's College in Camarillo, California, where he served as president from 1980 to 1984. While at Cardinal Glennon College, he attended graduate school at St. Louis University, earning a master's degree in Spanish literature and a PhD in history in 1961. His dissertation research exposed him to a wealth of Spanish sources on the history of New Spain and redirected his scholarly focus toward Spanish colonial history. Reflecting on his teaching stint at Glennon College, Poole wrote an article for the Jesuit magazine *America* in 1964 entitled "Tomorrow's Seminaries" that garnered national attention and resulted in his book *Seminary in Crisis*, earning him national attention as an expert on seminary formation.[105]

Poole's scholarly reputation was built on a spate of books and articles on the history of New Spain. On his retirement from seminary

103. Ibid.
104. On Poole, see Schroeder, "Seminaries and Writing the History of New Spain."
105. James Fischer, Poole's provincial superior at the time of the book's publication, recalled that Egidio Vagnozzi (apostolic delegate to the United States) requested a meeting to discuss the book. Personnel Files, DRMA—Fischer—Osiek, "Interview," 4.

teaching in 1990, Poole devoted himself to the study of the Nahuatl language and wrote two important books on the cult of Our Lady of Guadalupe.[106] At the same time, Poole developed his interests in the history of the American Vincentian community, resulting in the publication of an important book on slavery and Missouri Catholic institutions—*Church and Slave in Perry County, Missouri* with Douglas Slawson, CM. Poole served as archivist for the western province of the Congregation and as editor of *The Vincentian Heritage Journal* from 1986 to 1997 and contributed prominently to *The American Vincentians: A Popular History of the Congregation of the Mission in the United States, 1815 to 1987*. He continues to research and publish articles on the history of colonial Latin America and the Vincentian community. Poole also remains a critic of seminary intellectual life, telling a recent interviewer in answer to a question about challenges in his long scholarly career, "I think the overall problem was trying to be a scholar in a seminary environment. The two are just not compatible."[107] Despite this problem, Poole has managed to publish fourteen books and over eighty book chapters and scholarly articles in his long and distinguished career.

The career of Oscar Lukefahr (1939–2015) combined many Vincentian apostolates, including seminary and parish work, missions, catechetical formation, and Marian devotion. Born in Perryville, Lukefahr attended St. Vincent's College in Cape Girardeau and entered the novitiate at the Barrens in 1957. He moved to De Andreis Seminary in Lemont when the theologate was transferred there from the Barrens in 1964 and was ordained a priest in 1966. After teaching at various Vincentian-run minor seminaries, Lukefahr entered parish work, becoming pastor of a large Vincentian parish in Denver, Colorado. Eventually, he became involved in the work of the Catholic Home Study Service, which he directed for fourteen years and for which he wrote nine books of popular catechism and apologetics published by the Liguori Press[108] as well as

---

106. Poole, *Our Lady of Guadalupe: The Origins and Sources of a Mexican National Symbol, 1531–1797* (University of Arizona Press, 1995); and Poole, *The Guadalupan Controversies in Mexico* (Stanford University Press, 2006).
107. Schroeder, "Seminaries and Writing the History of New Spain," 252.
108. Lukefahr's works include *We Believe: A Survey of the Catholic Faith* (1990); *The Priv-*

articles and essays syndicated in Catholic diocesan newspapers. In 2012, he became spiritual director of the Association of the Miraculous Medal, following in the footsteps of long-serving directors like Joseph Finney (1924–62), Charles Rice (1962–82), and Charles Shelby (1983–2005). He remained a popular mission preacher, conducting parish missions throughout the country and maintaining ties with thousands of Catholics and prospective Catholic converts through his personal ministry and CHSS courses, until his abrupt death from advanced pancreatic cancer in August 2015.

John Rybolt attended the Barrens in 1963–64 before completing his formation at De Andreis Seminary, where he was ordained in 1967. A learned and prolific scholar, Rybolt holds graduate degrees from DePaul University (MA, Latin, 1967), Harvard University (MA, Near Eastern Languages and Literature, 1968), the Catholic University of America (STL, Sacred Scripture, 1969), the Pontifical Biblical Institute (SSL, 1972) and Institute of Christian Archaeology (Diploma, 1972) in Rome, and St. Louis University (PhD, Biblical Languages and Literature, 1978). He has taught at St. Thomas Seminary in Denver (where he served as president/ rector in addition to teaching Old Testament), Kenrick Seminary (where he served as dean) in St. Louis, and De Andreis Seminary in Lemont. From 1994 to 2003 he served as director of the Saint Vincent de Paul International Formation Center at the motherhouse of the Congregation of the Mission in Paris. Rybolt's scholarly interests range from Old Testament studies to the life and legacy of Vincent de Paul and the work of the Vincentians in the United States and internationally. He was a founding member of the Vincentian Studies Institute and served as its presiding officer from 1982 to 1991. Rybolt's career connects the Barrens to the international Vincentian community through his scholarly works and his involvement in the VSI, the International Formation Center and the Secretariat International d'Études Vincentiennes. No one—

---

ilege of Being Catholic (1993); *A Catholic Guide to the Bible* (revised, 1998); *The Search for Happiness: Four Levels of Emotional and Spiritual Growth* (2002); *We Worship: A Guide to the Catholic Mass* (2004); *We Pray: Living in God's Presence* (2007); and *We Live: To Know, Love and Serve God* (2010).

scholar, academic, or member of the Vincentian family—pursues even a cursory study of the Vincentian heritage without confronting the important work of John Rybolt.

Finally, the Barrens exercised influence on the entire Congregation of the Mission and, indeed, the Universal Church, through the work of James Richardson (1909–96).[109] Born in Dallas and reared in the shadow of Vincentian institutions (Holy Trinity Parish, Dallas Academy, University of Dallas), Richardson was educated by Daughters of Charity and Vincentians. Three of his siblings joined him in consecrated religious life—a sister as an Ursuline nun, another sister as a Daughter of Charity, and a brother as a Vincentian priest (John Richardson, another son of the Barrens, prominent in his own right as president of DePaul University from 1981 to 1993). James Richardson entered the Vincentian novitiate at the Barrens in 1925 and was ordained in 1933. He earned a doctorate in canon law at Rome in 1936 and returned directly to the Barrens as faculty member for the next three years. In 1939, he became a charter faculty member of St. John's Seminary in Camarillo, California. For the next thirty years, he worked at St. John's in various capacities, including rector and vice-provincial of the western vice-province.

Richardson represented the western American vice-province at the General Assembly of the Congregation in 1968, where he was elected twentieth superior general of the community. As superior general from 1968 to 1980, Richardson reorganized the administration of the community, sanctioned the revised constitutions of the Congregation, presided over the General Assemblies of 1968 and 1974, and transferred the curial offices of the community in Rome. His great challenge was implementing these changes in the spirit of the Second Vatican Council and presiding over the Congregation in an era of tremendous complexity and transformation.

On the conclusion of his second term as superior general, Richardson spent several years helping to establish the Vincentian community in Kenya. He expressed to Superior General Richard McCullen his wish to die in Kenya, but was recalled to the United

---

109. On James Richardson, see McCullen, "Father Richardson: An Appreciation"; and (John) Richardson, "Father Richardson: Some Incidents in His Early Life."

States to work in the Midwest province in St. Louis.[110] He moved back to the Barrens when his health failed, and died there in 1996. James Richardson's life and work, like that of the other Vincentians described above, attests to the influence of the Barrens in forming talented and compassionate teachers, scholars, and pastors and in shaping the contours of twentieth-century Catholicism in the United States and the world.

Conclusion

Like the broader American Catholic Church, St. Mary's of the Barrens grew in size and complexity from 1886 to 1965. Despite its continued financial struggles and some questions about its isolated location in an increasingly urbanized American Catholic Church, the Barrens entered into a period of sustained growth in numbers, facilities, and programs in this era. That growth reflected both the fortunes of the American Catholic community and the influence of external factors. Rome, often fearful of the influence of American culture on Catholic institutions, made demands on seminaries. The pressure to conform and standardize often drove developments at the Barrens, as did the legacy of its long history and even older Vincentian customs. Despite these tensions, the Barrens seemed poised to continue its "age of triumph" into the 1960s and beyond. Events in the Catholic Church and the broader American culture conspired to change the historical trajectory of the Barrens, however. The late twentieth century proved anything but triumphant for the old seminary.

110. Richardson, "Father Richardson," 81.

Part 5

Decline and Fall of
St. Mary's of the Barrens,
1965–2016

Chapter Nine
CLOSURE AND CONTROVERSY

> A question arose as to whether the Province really
> supports any future for Perryville. It is an enormous
> plant with little going on and it will take time to
> develop something.
>
> —Midwest Provincial Council (1985)

"It looked as though Catholics, having ceased to be a People, just might become a power," Garry Wills wrote in the opening pages of his highly subjective essay on American Catholicism in the era of the Second Vatican Council.[1] The rest of Wills's book reflected on that "false promise," examining the "unfulfilled hopes" of the Council in the context of a divided American Catholic Church. A spate of studies over the past half century have followed up on Wills's assessment, finding both hope and disappointment in the story of a growing Catholic community caught between the broad trends of a rapidly secularizing American culture and more traditional Catholic beliefs and practices.[2]

Prominent among the challenges facing American Catholicism in this period were the status and fortunes of the clergy, including

---

1. Wills, *Bare Ruined Choirs*, 1.
2. See, for example, O'Toole, *Faithful*; Dolan, *In Search of an American Catholicism*; Shaw, *American Church*; Greeley, *Catholic Revolution*; Massa, *American Catholic Revolution*; McDannell, *Spirit of Vatican II*; Tentler, *Church Confronts Modernity*; Marienburg, *Catholicism Today*; Gleason, *Keeping the Faith*; D'Antonio, Dillon, and Gautien *American Catholics in Transition*; Steinfels, *A People Adrift*.

members of religious orders, and the institutions established by those orders. The overriding tension evident in the religious clergy, as documented in numerous studies, has been the conflict between corporate identity and the needs of the individual members of that corporation.[3] These issues, resulting in often acrimonious debates over the past half century, have occasioned changes in the identity of religious clergy and in the works they pursued. Declining personnel and resources have added to the pace of change until the institutional landscape of many religious orders has undergone profound alteration. Apostolates once regarded as essential have been reevaluated, commitments once thought sacrosanct have been reconsidered, and institutions once thought secure have been neglected or abandoned.

The closing of St. Mary's of the Barrens Seminary in 1985 and the subsequent disposition of seminary property by the Midwest province of the Vincentians illustrates several characteristic elements in the late twentieth-century contraction of American Catholic religious orders. Among those elements are attempts to come to grips with the new demographics of Catholic religious vocations, the new contours of American Catholic culture, and uncertain efforts to maintain a communal identity in increasingly individual-oriented organizations. The story of the Barrens over the past half century highlights important issues in the recent history of the American Catholic Church and trends in the contemporary history of Catholic religious orders.

St. Mary's of the Barrens and the American Vincentian Community

The seeming security in numbers and mind-set of the American Catholic clergy over the course of the twentieth century, interrupted only by brief concerns over Vatican condemnation of an

---

3. See Nygren and Ukeritis, *Future of Religious Orders in the United States*; Wittberg, *Rise and Decline of Catholic Religious Orders*; Schneiders, *Finding the Treasure*; and Fiand, *Refocusing the Vision*. For an interesting recent analysis of an individual religious order, see McDonough and Bianchi, *Passionate Uncertainty*.

"Americanist" heresy in the early 1900s, masked a growing tension between proponents of modernization and adherents of traditionalism in the international Catholic Church. That tension found its clearest expression in the debates of the Second Vatican Council, an event that ushered in a period of "change, questioning, turmoil, confusion, discovery and progress" for the American Vincentian community.[4] In response to the Vatican decree on the renewal of religious life (*Perfectae Caritatis*), the Congregation of the Mission established a commission "to examine the whole life of the community in the light of Vatican II and help prepare for adaptation."[5] That commission, and the call for an extraordinary General Assembly of the order in 1968/69, inspired Vincentian provinces and houses throughout the world to undertake critical self-studies of their operations. In the United States, provincial assemblies held often contentious debates over the future of the community. In the western province, a tentative preparatory document was rejected and a Committee on the Apostolate was established to review the future commitments of the community.

The General Assembly of 1968/69 contributed to the growing decentralization of authority in the international Vincentian community and revealed tensions, evident among many Catholic religious orders, over how to meet the challenges of cultural modernity. That tension was often expressed as a struggle between the demands of corporate identity/mission and the needs of individual community members. In this climate, exacerbated by a growing exodus of priests from the American Catholic Church and the western province of the Congregation, discussions regarding the apostolic commitments of the Vincentian community proceeded.

The Committee on the Apostolate (COTA) offered its final report in preparation for the 1974 Joint Provincial Assemblies.[6] The committee pursued its charge of reviewing the status of Vincentian works

---

4. Editorial Staff, "Survey of American Vincentian History," 85.
5. Ibid.
6. Provincial Assembly MW, DRMA—Provincial Assembly 1973–74: First Session—"Report on Self-Study, Joint Provincial Assemblies, 1973–74.

through a self-study involving two separate questionnaires. The surveys were designed and evaluated with assistance from consulting psychologists and St. Louis University faculty, and the tabulated results offer a revealing snapshot of the attitudes of Vincentians in the western United States in the early 1970s. Overall, two-thirds of respondents agreed that "the Province is stretched too thin with respect to manpower, and a drastic strategy must be developed to alleviate the strain."[7] The feeling that the community was approaching a critical situation in its ability to honor its apostolic commitments preceded the most precipitous decline in personnel experienced in the later 1970s. Respondents indicated some preference for reevaluating present commitments—24 percent said the province should "gradually contract or eliminate some apostolate-commitments and strengthen some remaining apostolate-commitments"; while 21 percent said the province should maintain present commitments but shift resources to address the needs of the highest-priority apostolates.[8]

The COTA report also addressed specific attitudes about Vincentian commitment to its college formation program at St. Mary's of the Barrens. While an impressive majority of Vincentians (87 percent) supported the strengthening or maintenance of "our own" college seminaries (even more among Vincentian students and novices), 52 percent foresaw major adjustments in the broader seminary commitments of the order.[9] The "CM college seminaries [i.e., St. Mary's of the Barrens]" placed third in a ranking of support for "general apostolate categories," just under "CM theology seminaries" and parishes, and second among Vincentian students and novices (just under "CM theology seminaries").[10] A significant number of students indicated a preference for future work in the province's college seminary at the Barrens.[11] The results reflected a broad feeling that the order should seriously review its present commitments but an overall satisfaction with its existing college formation program.

7. Ibid., 95.
8. Ibid., 113.
9. Ibid., 119–23, 114.
10. Ibid., 124.
11. Ibid., 133.

Among the results of the self-studies and provincial discussions of the early 1970s were the subdivision of the western province in 1975 into separate Midwest/South/West provinces and a conscious decision to return to the original Vincentian charism of concern for the poor. The reconsideration of American Vincentian organization and values led the Congregation to pull back on its seminary commitments, and the quarter century after 1975 witnessed a dramatic decline in the number of seminaries operated and staffed by the Vincentians.

The Closing of St. Mary's of the Barrens Seminary

For St. Mary's of the Barrens, the cultural, demographic, and structural changes brought on by the Second Vatican Council meant further adaptation of its always variable role and, eventually, questions about its future as a house of formation. Already in 1964 the novitiate program had been moved to Santa Barbara, California, and the theologate to Lemont, Illinois. If the Barrens was to continue as a viable house of formation, its aging facilities required expensive maintenance. At the same time, educational costs were beginning to rise dramatically. Aware of the need to update and maintain the campus, Vincentian superiors planned extensive renovations in the early 1970s. Funds were sought from the Estelle Doheny Foundation in 1971 and, in response to the Foundation's concerns about the future of St. Mary's of the Barrens, provincial superior Cecil Parres wrote to his fellow Vincentian William G. Ward, an officer of the foundation. "The Provincial and his Council now see St. Mary's Seminary at Perryville as a center of education for the students of the province and do not foresee any circumstances that will lead to its abandonment in the future," Parres noted.[12] When the Doheny Foundation agreed to fund the renovation project, eventually providing $950,000 for various improvements and renovations, Father Parres expressed his gratitude, noting that the project would make it possible to "preserve our Vincentian heritage in the western

12. Provincial Files, DRMA—Parres Papers—Cecil Parres, CM, to William G. Ward, CM, 14 September 1971.

22. Aerial View of the Barrens

The Barrens campus at the height of seminary operations, showing the older buildings (church, Rosati Hall, Oliva Hall, and Smith Hall) on the left, moving right to the novitiate (bottom) and scholasticate buildings (top) enclosing a new campus quadrangle, and on the far upper right the academic building and recreation center.

part of the United States at the place of our beginnings, Perryville, Missouri. This is something quite dear and precious to me. It is something which transcends physical plant, academic programs, formation programs, etc. and at the same time permeates them all and breathes a life and spirit into them."[13]

Additional renovations to the student building and the community chapel were proposed in 1978, at an estimated cost of over $800,000, and consideration was given to the sale of some seminary lands to finance the project. The proposal drew a strong reaction from at least one confrere, who strongly opposed the sale of any land for development. In a letter that foreshadows later disagreements over the transfer of seminary property, Thomas Cawley argued that land "is not a possession or an asset to the community; it is a trust, a talent loaned to the community for the common good of that area . . . held in perpetuity."[14] Parres answered, "What you say about money and land is certainly true. . . . But land can become a liability as well as an asset. . . . I am not sure of this, but there may be times when you cannot afford not to sell or lease."[15]

In the meantime, the subdivision of the old western province into South, West, and Midwest provinces scheduled for 1975 raised serious questions about the future of Vincentian formation in those areas. Those questions were answered by the Provincial Assembly of 1974, which affirmed the interprovincial decision to retain common houses of formation for the next ten years, whereupon a review would be undertaken by the superiors of each province regarding renewal of the agreement.[16] St. Mary's of the Barrens Seminary enjoyed a brief resurgence by the foresight of its leaders in attempting to modernize its facilities and by the interprovincial decision to retain common houses of formation.

13. Provincial Files, DRMA—Parres Papers—Cecil Parres, CM, to William G. Ward, CM, 9 May 1972.
14. Provincial Files, DRMA—Parres Papers—Thomas Cawley, CM, to Cecil Parres, CM, 14 January 1978.
15. Provincial Files, DRMA—Parres Papers—Cecil Parres, CM to Thomas Cawley, CM, 4 March 1978.
16. Provincial Assembly MW, DRMA—Provincial Assembly 1973–74: Minutes of the Joint Provincial Assembly, 2nd Session, 25 June 1974.

Unfortunately, the continued decline in numbers of students, noted by the visiting team of the North Central Association as early as 1976 and reiterated in 1982,[17] kept the question of the future of the Barrens alive, as did continued changes in the culture and organization of the Vincentian community. A movement to close freestanding college seminaries developed across the American Catholic Church. The arguments against maintaining the old system of seminary education were summarized by an article in *America* as early as 1967:

> The "close the seminaries" apologists take the stand that it is silly for the Catholic Church to run separate undergraduate institutions for young men who want to become priests. Formidable arguments support their stand. Maintaining such institutions, they say, is unwise because in the great majority of American seminaries there can never be enough seminarians to pay the cost of a first-class educational operation. Consequently, the operation is either wildly uneconomical or not first-class. (The large number of seminaries existing without educational accreditation suggests that the latter is more often the case.) Secondly, the apologists for immediate closing of the isolated seminary would say, the "total-institution" type of seminary separates the young man from the rest of mankind at too early a stage in his development. He needs to rub shoulders with people who do not see the rest of the world as he does, whose life goals are different from his own. As he rubs shoulders, he is forced to articulate and deepen his own goals or lose them. If he loses them, the argument goes, there is no real loss; for he would either have lost them anyway or he would have been somewhat less than effective as a priest. And if he retains and deepens them, he will win other college students over to his cause.[18]

17. SMOB Files, DRMA—Academic Files: NCA Accreditation—"Advisory Visitation Report, NCA Association, April 1982," 1.
18. McNamara, "Seminary Education: Separate and Unequal," 533–34. McNamara accepted these propositions in his article and argued for the education of priestly candi-

William Hartenbach, rector of St. Mary's of the Barrens Seminary College from 1979 to 1985, recalled that the 1964 move of the theologate to Lemont, accomplished as the Second Vatican Council called for an opening of windows to the world, occasioned theoretical questioning regarding the move of the college seminary from the Barrens as well.[19] However, the sheer number of students at the time, and the expense of recreating college facilities, made such a move impractical. Hartenbach assumed he would be closing the Barrens when he was named rector in 1979. He cited the drying up of traditional sources of vocations, the continued discussions about seminary culture, the needs and desires of the three provinces involved, and the high costs of education with diminishing results in permanent community membership as the bases for his assumption.[20]

The available sources on provincial decision making regarding the status of St. Mary's Seminary in the early 1980s reveal a basic uncertainty and, sometimes, contradictory messages regarding the future of the Barrens. Hartenbach's assumption that he would be closing the seminary on his appointment to the rectorship in 1979 belies the vote of confidence given by the province at the Midwest Provincial Assembly of 1982. Participants at the Assembly, with an eye toward the upcoming renewal of the common formation agreement due in 1985, voiced continued support for continuing college formation at Perryville.[21] Indeed, some sentiment was expressed that the imminent transfer of the theology program from Lemont to Denver might increase support for the continuation of the college program at Perryville. In their preliminary comments

---

dates in existing American Catholic universities. However, Cardinal William Baum, in his 1986 report, "The State of US Free-Standing Seminaries," suggested that the graduates of free-standing college seminaries were better prepared academically for the study of theology than students from a non-seminary background and lauded the "unique" and "invaluable" contributions of college-level seminaries. In a 1994 article in *America*, Terrance W. Klein argued that, far from being shielded by isolated seminary settings, students in freestanding college seminaries "are thoroughly rooted in U.S. culture"; Klein, "U.S. Culture and College Seminaries," 18.
19. Hartenbach, interview, 10 June 2002.
20. Ibid.
21. Provincial Assembly MW, DRMA—Provincial Assembly 1982—Minutes.

regarding the 1983 Provincial Visitation of the Barrens, provincial officials noted the challenges of maintaining a full college formation program in Perryville, citing practical concerns about the rigor of the academic program, the psychological support system provided the students, and the problem of providing adequate personnel for the program. However, one visitor concluded, "It seems to me that in the theoretical order St. Mary's is not a bad place for college formation and may even be a good place. . . . In theory, I think that both the social and physical challenges can be met within the context of St. Mary's."[22]

Despite these votes of confidence, the question of the future of the Barrens remained a serious issue in the Midwest provincial council. At the end of 1983, Father Hugh O'Donnell, provincial superior, informed his council that the southern and western provinces were "seriously considering withdrawing from Perryville at the end of the *conventio* in 1985."[23] The real prospect of the nonrenewal of the common college formation agreement pressured the Midwest province to make its own decision about the future of Perryville rather than merely react to the decision of the other provinces. While the council felt it prudent to wait until the agreement expired before making a definitive decision, it was decided "that there is need for further information and examination of the Perryville program from all perspectives."[24] At its next meeting in January 1984, Father O'Donnell proposed the drafting of a statement "of the values of the program at Perryville and what that program offers our Province in college formation."[25] The ensuing council discussion focused on several areas of importance for the college formation program in general, and St. Mary's of the Barrens particularly, including "the tradition and historic roots of Perryville [and] exposure to older CMs and their life stories," as well as the "benefits of a small liberal arts program that can be tailored to our needs." More

22. MW Province Files—Miscellaneous Papers, Provincial Council.
23. MW Province Files—Minutes of the Midwest Provincial Council Meeting of 14–15 December 1983.
24. Ibid.
25. MW Province Files—Minutes of the Midwest Provincial Council Meeting of 13–14 January 1984.

negatively, the council cited the need for a "contemporary environ-
ment/atmosphere" and the expense of maintaining Perryville as an
independent program.[26]

Among the data compiled for the interprovincial governing
board of St. Mary's and the Midwest provincial council was a
report by Beth Lipsmeyer, a clinical psychologist contracted by the
seminary, on the students enrolled at the Barrens. Presented to the
provincial council at its February 1984 meeting, Lipsmeyer's report
offered a psychological profile of the student body and concluded
that, on the whole, the students were too dependent and passive
with a low sense of self-esteem and serious questions of sexual
identity.[27] The report blamed, by implication, the environment of
the isolated, freestanding seminary program at Perryville for these
psychological deficiencies but failed, as council minutes noted, to
provide "prescriptive measures that could be taken by the program
at Perryville to address issues of personal growth."[28] At the same
time, a report on "The Current State of Transition in the Church"
by Louis Brusatti, a Vincentian faculty member at St. Mary's, cited
the critical changes within the Catholic Church since the Second
Vatican Council and offered a historical and cultural context for
discussions about the future of St. Mary's. "We are again living a
transition," Brusatti wrote. "Seminaries are moving toward a system based on a collegial and collaborative model that provides a
context for personal growth and spiritual formation. This is what
we are attempting to do here as we prepare to move on."[29] Brusatti's essay ended with a poignant quote from Stephen Vincent
Ryan, provincial and superior of the Barrens in 1862 when "the
central house of the Province was moved from the Barrens to St.
Louis."[30]

If the Lipsmeyer and Brusatti reports are illustrative of the information coming to the provincial council as it pondered the future

26. Ibid.
27. MW Province Files—Lipsmeyer, "Students of St. Mary's Seminary."
28. MW Province Files—Minutes of Midwest Provincial Council Meeting of 10–11 February 1984.
29. MW Province Files—Brusatti, "Current State of Transition in the Church."
30. Ibid.

of the Barrens, it seems clear that the fate of the seminary was sealed in early 1984. Indeed, at its April 1984 meeting, the council recommended that a committee be established "to examine other options that might be available for our college formation."[31] In May, Father O'Donnell reported to the council on his meeting with provincial pastors and superiors in the aftermath of the announcement of the end of the interprovincial common formation agreement. O'Donnell indicated that "as a group they all seemed to recognize that the Seminary as it is right now cannot be maintained, e.g., enrollment is much too small for the financial investment."[32] The superiors and pastors agreed that the "final decision rests with the Provincial and his Council," although careful communication must be maintained with the entire province and, particularly, the members of the community at Perryville.[33]

As part of its efforts to collect information and maintain open communication, the provincial council solicited feedback from the entire province regarding the future of college formation at St. Mary's of the Barrens. A survey was sent to all midwestern Vincentians asking their opinions regarding the state of the college formation program, including the option of closing St. Mary's and relocating the college program. The results of the survey were discussed at the August meeting of the council and an appendix to the minutes of the meeting detailed the collective responses of the province.[34] A total of sixty-two responses were received by the council and the majority (forty-eight) agreed that "it did not seem feasible to keep our program as it is in Perryville."[35] The council acknowledged, however, that the minority opinion offered strong arguments for the maintenance of the Perryville program, with responses emphasizing the "great symbolic power" of the Barrens and offering alternatives that might keep the seminary open.

31. MW Province Files—Minutes of the Midwest Provincial Council Meeting of 5–6 April 1984.
32. MW Province Files—Minutes of the Midwest Provincial Council Meeting of 16–17 May 1984.
33. Ibid.
34. MW Province Files—Minutes of the Midwest Provincial Council Meeting of 24 August 1984, Responses of the Province to the Perryville Questionnaire.
35. Ibid.

The responses outlined in the council's summary indicate a wide variety of opinions among midwestern Vincentians regarding the decision to close St. Mary's Seminary. While some respondents questioned the timing of the decision ("why the rush?"), others suggested that the decision was long overdue given earlier studies, including the report of the Committee on the Apostolate in the early 1970s. Some respondents questioned the process followed in determining the future of St. Mary's while others supported the "best judgment of the Council." Some asked if the decision was being made "in light of our mission as a Province" and called for more clarity regarding the province's formation program in general. Some cited the expense of maintaining the Barrens while others cautioned "that it will be just as expensive elsewhere." Some called for an analysis of why "40 students have left over the past two years" while others noted that "the small number of students can be an asset in terms of education." Obviously, given the large majority supporting the decision to close the Barrens, the minority opinion was vocal and articulate. Their questions regarding the process of decision making in the province, the historical significance of St. Mary's of the Barrens, the broader identity and mission of the community, and alternative uses for the Perryville campus would be continuously posed over the next two decades as the future of the remaining works and property at the Barrens were discussed.

With the decision regarding the seminary at Perryville essentially settled, the council proceeded to organize "phase two" of the process, establishing a task force to explore alternative sites for the college formation program of the province.[36] The task force included a working committee, charged with overseeing the project and submitting a final report, an advisory committee to act as a "resource of wisdom" to be drawn on by the working committee, and a committee on "the future of Perryville" to explore future uses of the Barrens campus. An ambitious timeline called for a final report to the Provincial Council by January 1985.

---

36. MW Province Files—Minutes of the Midwest Provincial Council Meeting of 24 August 1984.

In a later correspondence with the editors of *Seminary Forum*, committee chair William Hartenbach summarized the work of the "Phase Two" committee:

> The members of the Task Force had two principal sources of information: (1) a study which had been done by our Eastern Province on the same issue in the past year; and (2) again, a questionnaire to the membership of the Province. The questionnaire was constructed in such a way as to allow the members to indicate any preference or idea they might have relative to the question. The options were quickly reduced to two—both related to educational institutions run by our community: Cardinal Glennon College in St. Louis, or DePaul University in Chicago. The Task Force, in a unanimous decision chose to recommend that the students live in a house of studies; in a split decision, the Task Force chose to recommend Cardinal Glennon College as the site for academic formation.[37]

Further insight into the mind-set and expeditious work of the committee can be gained from two documents in the provincial files relating to the task force. One paper, entitled simply "Historical Transitions," detailed the chronology of the Barrens from 1820 to 1985 and broader historical movements among the American Vincentians.[38] An "interpretation" of American Vincentian history was included in the report that emphasized the ebb and flow of historical Vincentian responses to the needs of the American Catholic Church. The Second Vatican Council, and the crisis in religious vocations that followed, presented "new Church needs" to which the Vincentians responded with a "change in mission" that included withdrawal from seminary commitments and focus on other community apostolates. An accompanying document, entitled "The Congregation of the Mission: The Age

---

37. MW Province Files—Hartenbach Papers—William Hartenbach, CM, to Adrian Fuerst, OSB, 27 February 1985.
38. MW Province Files—"Historical Transitions."

of Adaptation," called for the community to seek "new forma-
tional models to meet the needs of a changing Church and society" and repeated the historical model of institutional rise and
decay played out in the Vincentian tradition.[39] These reports represented an effort by the task force to understand the broader
implications of the closing of the Barrens as a normal response
to changing cultural needs while at the same time minimizing
the trauma of closing a seminary that had already experienced
numerous historical transformations.

The "Phase Two" task force on Perryville submitted its report to
the provincial council at its December 1984 meeting, recommend-
ing the establishment of a resident house of studies in St. Louis
to replace the freestanding seminary at St. Mary's of the Barrens.[40]
Council members asked numerous questions regarding the process
followed by the task force and the consideration of other options
and postponed the final decision on acceptance of the recommendation until its January 1985 meeting. In January, additional
questions were raised before the recommendation of the task force
was approved.[41] St. Mary's of the Barrens Seminary was officially
replaced as the site of college formation for midwestern Vincentians
by this decision.

Even before the final council decision to relocate the college,
Father Hugh O'Donnell publicly announced the closing of St.
Mary's of the Barrens Seminary and news stories appeared in various local journals, including the *St. Louis Review*, *St. Louis Post-
Dispatch*, and the *St. Louis Globe-Democrat*. The *Globe-Democrat*
article cited the declining enrollments at St. Mary's (down to
thirty-five students in its final academic year) and the decisions
of the western and southern provinces to relocate their formation
programs.[42] The article also quoted Father O'Donnell regarding

39. MW Province Files—"The Congregation of the Mission: The Age of Adaptation."
40. MW Province Files—Minutes of the Midwest Provincial Council Meeting of 17–18
December 1984.
41. MW Province Files—Minutes of the Midwest Provincial Council Meeting of 24–26
January 1985.
42. "Oldest College in Missouri Closing Down," *St. Louis Globe-Democrat*, 28 January
1985.

future uses of the Barrens campus, including its possible future as a Catholic archive and study center.[43]

St. Mary's of the Barrens officially closed with the commencement exercises of 18 May 1985.[44] Hartenbach described proudly the manner in which the seminary community accepted the transition, citing efforts to promote bonding in the community and a sense of closure among those most directly affected.[45] A review of events leading to the closing of St. Mary's supports the notion that the decision was made on the basis of a combination of practical and theoretical considerations, reflecting both the circumstances and the evolving culture of the post–Vatican II American Catholic Church and the Vincentian community.

St. Mary's of the Barrens, 1985–95

The closing of the college seminary in May 1985 did not equate to Vincentian abandonment of the St. Mary's campus or its other Perryville commitments. The order continued to own over 1,800 acres on and around the campus, with responsibility for maintaining the old academic and residence halls of the seminary. The main academic building continued to house a rich archive of American Vincentian history and museums with collections of rare books, furniture, and *objets d'art*. The acreage included a working cattle farm staffed by Vincentian brothers and a retirement center for senior Vincentians with an assisted living unit and infirmary. Finally, the campus housed the offices of the Miraculous Medal Association and the National Shrine of Our Lady of the Miraculous Medal in the historic St. Mary's of the Barrens church.

The future of the remaining works at the Barrens was determined over the next fifteen years by a confusing array of committees and task forces.[46] The history of the Barrens over this period is

---

43. Ibid.
44. For an account of student and faculty emotions on the event, see "Seminarians' Graduation a Bittersweet Event," *Perry County Republic*, May 21, 1985; and "First Seminary in the West Goes Way of Wagon Train," *St. Louis Post-Dispatch*, May 22, 1985.
45. Hartenbach, interview, June 10, 2002.
46. For details, see Janet, "Decline and Fall: Part Two."

full of uncertainty, with various and ambitious plans and proposals suggested until eventually the Vincentian provincial administration dealt with the various remaining components of the Barrens complex in a piecemeal fashion.

The original "future of Perryville" committee of 1984, established as part of the task force to implement the closing of the seminary, was composed entirely of Vincentians from the Barrens community and its work floundered in the context of the seminary's closing. Subsequently, a new committee was formed to deal with the issue of the Barrens based on "real options (including selling)" and "real research," but its charge was overwhelmed given changing circumstances, including the end of Hugh O'Donnell's term as provincial superior and preoccupation with the status of the province's other seminary commitments.[47]

Over the next seven years (1987–93) there was little real movement for systematic planning or dramatic change in the status of the Barrens. Under the leadership of Alphonse Hoernig from 1985 to 1994, the Perryville house operated with a semblance of efficiency and unity. Hoernig, himself active in local Catholic parishes, brought lay retreats to the Barrens and worked hard to gain the trust of the community. In 1988, he proposed extensive remodeling of the old community chapel at the Barrens and pushed the provincial administration to commit to some kind of investment in the future of Perryville.[48] At the same time, informal proposals were put forward by several Vincentians for the use of the Barrens campus, ranging from an ambitious plan by Charles Shelby, director of the Miraculous Medal Association, for hosting heritage and visitors' events, to ideas for the return of the novitiate program and continuing education programs for deacons and international Vincentians.[49]

---

47. MW Province Files—Minutes of the Midwest Provincial Council Meeting of 12–13 September and 13–14 October 1986. At the time, the province continued to operate Cardinal Glennon College, Kenrick Seminary, and the Lazare House of Studies in St. Louis as well as high school seminaries in St. Louis, Chicago, and Kansas City.
48. MW Province Files—Gagnepain Papers—Alphonse Hoernig, CM, to John Gagnepain, CM, 3 February 1988.
49. SMOB Records, DRMA—Administration: Future of St. Mary's—Shelby, "Proposal for the Use of the Facilities," October 1985; MW Province Files—Gagnepain Papers—Lawrence Christensen, CM, to John Gagnepain, CM, 13 July 1987, and Carl G. Schulte,

By 1993, when the Barrens celebrated the 175th anniversary of its founding, plans were announced for a systematic yearlong study known as "Mission Project: St. Mary's of the Barrens" (popularly known as the SMOB project). Launched with the directive that "the Midwest Province is not leaving or closing the Barrens," the SMOB project solicited input from midwestern Vincentians as well as professional consultants and real estate experts. Its final report recommended the establishment of a "Barrens Outreach Initiative" encompassing the work of several existing groups (Miraculous Medal Association, Catholic Home Study Service, Vincentian Studies Institute) with a new Perry County Pastoral Unit and retreat center for area clergy.[50] The provincial administration responded to the details of the SMOB report unenthusiastically, but seized onto a central insight of the project concerning the status of the Barrens. The report noted that the two "primary assets" of the Barrens were its land/location and its history/heritage of mission. None of the existing works at the site, "sometimes misnamed apostolates," constituted primary assets but were carryovers from an earlier period when they supported the work of the seminary.[51]

The task force recognized a reality that had eluded the province since the closing of the old seminary ten years earlier. The seminary had provided the unifying apostolate of the Barrens. Without the seminary, no consensus could be reached regarding the status or future of the site. As a result, the various remaining works housed at the Barrens could be considered objectively with an eye toward their ultimate disposition. That insight, of course, did not eliminate controversy or disagreement about the future, as recognized by provincial superior John Gagnepain. Gagnepain sought the advice of Robert Maloney, the superior general of the Congregation in Rome. Maloney offered sympathy and practical counsel.

> When issues are thorny and deeply felt, the tendency
> is to avoid them and delay on making decisions. Delay

CM, to John Gagnepain, CM, 1 August 1989.
50. MW Province Files—Minutes of Midwest Provincial Council Report for 15 November 1994 Meeting.
51. Ibid.

can sometimes be useful in that it enables us to develop new options and write new scenarios. But eventually, the responsible use of our resources demands that we make some hard choices. . . . I know, from our conversation, that you and your Council are already developing those options and are very sensitive to promoting our heritage and offering alternatives to the confreres who are most affected. . . . Because the question of Perryville is such a delicate one, and so many confreres have ties there, it is important that the members of the province walk along with you as the decision-making process takes place. . . . In the long run, I think that the common sense of the confreres will lead them to support you as they come to grasp the problems involved in the current situation and the reasonable alternatives that you lay out before them.[52]

The announced decisions of the provincial council regarding the SMOB report were long on general principles, short on specific details. In a March 23, 1995, summary of its decisions, the council noted their endorsement of "a series of insights gleaned from the work of the Task Force . . . [that] will now guide the future deliberations about St. Mary's."[53] Those insights included recognition of the "primary assets" of the Barrens. In addition to the personnel at the Barrens, the provincial council accepted the task force's designation of history/heritage and land/property as primary assets. Any works undertaken at the Barrens unrelated to those assets were valuable, but were not *necessarily* tied to the ongoing operation of the campus. In other words, the retirement center, farm, old seminary buildings, Miraculous Medal Association, National Shrine of Our Lady of the Miraculous Medal, programs like the Catholic Home Study Service, and the various physical assets of the Barrens were "not integral to St. Mary's of the Barrens" and their future could be determined separately and objectively, without reference to the

52. MW Province Files—Gagnepain Papers—Robert P. Maloney, CM, to John Gagnepain, CM, February 16, 1995.
53. MW Province Files—"Report to the Province from the Provincial and the Provincial Council Regarding Mission Project: St. Mary's of the Barrens, 23 March 1995," 9.

broader meaning or status of the Barrens.[54] Those works would be studied in future task forces, divorced from considerations of an overall strategic plan for the site. In the meantime, Father Gagnepain released a public statement on the future of the Barrens that envisioned an enhanced campus surrounding the National Shrine and "a reduction of residential facilities."[55]

The SMOB report appeared to have released the province from any obligation to consider the Barrens as a site of any apostolic work. In the words of the March 1995 provincial council report,

> Only with the preliminary report [by the SMOB Task Force] to the Provincial and Provincial Council were they able to say that perhaps nothing apostolic needs to continue at St. Mary's and that perhaps St. Mary's true asset is simply itself, that is, its history/heritage and its land/properties. Perhaps St. Mary's real and enduring value to the Province is its being a sort of psychological symbol for the Province, something we need and want to preserve, more for its own value and not for its being part of any apostolic endeavor.[56]

If so, the provincial council decisions of early 1995 mark a definitive break in the history of St. Mary's, perhaps even more dramatic than the closing of the seminary ten years earlier. The way was now clear for practical decision making regarding the assets of the Barrens without attachment to the health or future of any provincial apostolate.

Of course, the psychological ties of the Barrens remained strong for some confreres. The remaining residents of the Barrens felt slighted by the province's disparagement of their works. Arthur Trapp, superior of the Barrens in 1995, expressed the sentiments of the house in an April 1995 letter to Gagnepain: "I am

---

54. Ibid., 9–10.
55. MW Province Files—"Vincentians Announce Plans for Perryville, Statement by the Very Reverend John F. Gagnepain, CM, Provincial of the Midwest Province of the Congregation of the Mission, March 26, 1995."
56. MW Province Files—"Report to the Province from the Provincial and the Provincial Council Regarding Mission Project: St. Mary's of the Barrens, March 23, 1995," 8.

sitting here at The Barrens on a solitary island within a flood of anger and hurt and disgust and blame roaring 'round me, but I can't get anyone to express that to you."[57] Trapp's eloquent letter asked the provincial to "put himself" in the place of the men at the Barrens affected by the recent decisions, men seemingly told that a lifetime of work was no longer valued, that they should celebrate a heritage while denied the necessary resources, that their personal care in their declining years would be decided by external consultants. Trapp's letter put a human face on decisions that referenced abstract values, "physical assets," and institutional futures.

St. Mary's of the Barrens, 1995–2006

The provincial council's decision to accept the general principles informing the SMOB report without approving the specific details of the proposed plan ushered in a new era in the history of the Barrens. The provincial administration established a series of committees to study the separate elements identified at the Barrens—retirement center, core campus, farmlands, other services (including the Catholic Home Study Service), and other physical assets (including the library, archives, and museum collections). Overall coordination of these committees was to be assumed by the group charged with developing proposals for the "core campus." This group was to function as an implementation committee for the entire project but the right to final approval and oversight was reserved by the provincial superior and his council.

The ambiguity implicit in the administration's reserved acceptance of the SMOB report and in the multiplicity of committees established to draft proposals for the future of the various works and properties of the Barrens, always under the ultimate authority of the provincial administration, contributed to a confusing sequence of events after 1995. Committees, houses, provincial leaders, and individual Vincentians often disagreed over the specific contours

---

57. MW Province Files—Gagnepain Papers—Arthur Trapp, CM, to John Gagnepain, CM, April 1995.

of plans for the Barrens. Committees made preliminary reports and were disbanded by the administration or effectively disbanded themselves over failure to complete their tasks.

The committee established in 1995 to implement the proposals of the SMOB project report, with the development of a plan for use of the core campus and projected sale of outlying seminary lands, evoked controversy among the Vincentian community, and its commission was delayed in the summer of 1995. By that time, the implementation committee gave way to a proposed "heritage and shrine committee" chaired by MMA director Charles Shelby, which promised "the best, most exciting, mission-driven, attractive, economically viable proposal possible," but that committee, too, never materialized.[58]

In the meantime, former Barrens rector William Hartenbach was appointed provincial superior. Hartenbach professed a deep personal attachment to the Barrens but recognized the need for more practical considerations of community needs in a changing culture. In an interview published in the Perryville newspaper, Hartenbach summarized his understanding of the situation regarding the Barrens:

> Here is what the province wants. We want to be able to guarantee funding for our missions in Kenya. We want to see to it that we have the money we need to develop the central acreage where (St. Mary's of the Barrens church) and the other buildings are now. We are retaining them and they will continue to be residences for the retired and a visitor's center. All those buildings need work so we need to see to it that we have the funding for that. Along with that is the fact that one-third of our membership is over the age of 70 and we need to be concerned about retirement in other places besides Perryville. We are looking to have the income to support that.[59]

58. MW Province Files—Minutes of Midwest Provincial Council, 11–16 August 1995.
59. "Seminary Graduate Who Fought Change Now Leads Development," *Perry County Republic-Monitor*, November 27, 1997.

Hartenbach's determination to preserve the spirit over the physical reality of the Barrens led to strained relations with the Vincentian community still resident at the old campus, which commissioned a report by canon lawyer Michael Joyce on the respective rights of the house and the provincial administration. Joyce's paper effectively concluded that the provincial superior and his council were empowered to direct the works of the province, but that individual houses properly control the property attached to the house.[60]

Amid this growing controversy, Hartenbach met with members of the Barrens Vincentian community in Perryville in December 1996. The provincial superior informed the Barrens community of his plans to preserve the central campus while developing surrounding lands. Any monies raised by development were to be targeted for use in Vincentian formation programs. Finally, Hartenbach advised that the process of determining the future of the Barrens need not be a confrontational one, and he pleaded for fraternal cooperation among the community.[61] Responding to Hartenbach's pleas, the Barrens house council, with the provincial superior in attendance in April 1997, effectively ceded control of seminary lands outside the core campus to provincial authorities.[62]

The question of control of property seemingly settled, the province now moved quickly with plans to sell or develop Barrens properties surrounding the core campus. A unique plan was announced at a June 1997 press conference based on Vincentian values, sensitive to concerns for Catholic social teaching and respect for the environment.[63] The conference elicited mixed responses from the broader Perryville community, which Hartenbach predicted would welcome the opportunity for commercial development of seminary lands. Some community leaders endorsed the province's proposal

---

60. SMOB Records, DRMA—Administration: Future of St. Mary's—Joyce, "Relationship Between the Midwest Province and St. Mary's of the Barrens Seminary, 17 November 1996."
61. MW Province Files—"St. Mary's of the Barrens Summary Presentation, 2 December 1996."
62. MW Province Files—Minutes of Midwest Provincial Council, Perryville House Council Meeting of 2 April 1997.
63. "Catholic Order Wants to Develop 650 Acre Site but Control Its Use," *St. Louis Post-Dispatch*, June 5, 1997.

for development, while other residents lamented the loss of tradition implicit in any sale of property.[64] A few parish leaders questioned how development plans would affect use of the so-called picnic grove, a plot of seminary land used by St. Vincent's Parish for its annual fund-raising Seminary Picnic. Those concerns led to the establishment of the Perryville Community Park Association, a not-for-profit corporation to manage the long-term parish lease of the picnic grove.[65]

Meanwhile, the committee charged with proposing plans for the core campus completed its report in May 1998.[66] While some of the projected plans were eventually realized, the costs (amounting to over $4 million), to be borne by sale of outlying seminary properties, raised concerns in the provincial administration. Despite extensive consultation with commercial developers and some ambitious plans for combined commercial and residential developments, provincial authorities balked at earmarking the entirety of any potential sale to the core campus proposal. Hartenbach professed "sticker shock" and questioned the prudence of the plans given the changing circumstances of the Congregation.[67]

At this point, a new element entered into deliberations over the future of the Barrens property. Southeast Missouri State University, with its main campus in Cape Girardeau, planned to expand its extension activities in Perry County and queried Perryville community leaders regarding the availability of seminary facilities.[68] The possibility of utilizing core campus property, now publicly announced in the local newspaper, contradicted earlier promises to preserve the core campus for Vincentian purposes. Provincial authorities clarified that any use of campus facilities would be on a lease rather than sale basis, but the possibility doomed the prospects of the "heritage and

64. "Letters to the Editor," *Perryville Republic-Monitor*, June 12, 1997, and June 17, 1997.
65. MW Province Files—Memo, Bryan Cave, LP, to William Davidson, January 12, 1998, and Memo, Bryan Cave, LP, to Joseph Hess, CM, 6 February 1998; MW Province Files—Minutes of the Provincial Council Meeting of 9 February 1998.
66. MW Province Files—Minutes of the Provincial Council Meeting of 11 May 1998.
67. MW Province Files—Hartenbach Papers—William Hartenbach, CM, to Charles Shelby, CM, 3 June 1998. MW Province Files: Hartenbach Papers.
68. *Perryville Republic-Monitor*, September 17, 1998.

shrine" committee proposals. Hartenbach admitted the new reality and the impracticality of earlier development efforts. Ensuing negotiations with Southeast Missouri State University led to a 2000 agreement for the long-term lease of the Barrens library building.

Lease of the library building raised questions about the disposition of Vincentian properties housed in that building, including the community archives, rare book collection, and numerous donated *objects d'art*. Southeast Missouri State sought to procure those items, while Perryville community leaders lobbied for their retention in Perryville. Ultimately, the province opted to keep these properties in the Vincentian family, with the De Andreis–Rosati Memorial Archives transferred to DePaul University. Many of the rare books and other artifacts were sold at a Christie's auction in December 2001, with proceeds earmarked for the operation of Vincentian programs in Kenya and the Midwest Province.[69]

Charles Shelby now moved on behalf of the Barrens house to preserve some plan for preservation of the core campus, proposing the establishment of a St. Mary's of the Barrens Heritage Society to support campus development.[70] Shelby's proposal was rejected by the provincial council, and he countered with a trimmed-down proposal to raise $5 million to construct a modern visitor's center, demolish the old novitiate building, and landscape the surrounding grounds.[71] Hartenbach responded with a tentative and conditional approval for Shelby's plan.[72]

On July 1, 2002, Father Hartenbach concluded his six-year tenure as superior of the Midwest province of the Congregation of the Mission and Father James Swift assumed the office. At that time,

---

69. The Christie's auction netted $6 million, with records set for the sale of a first edition King James Bible ($424,000) and a first edition of Mark Twain's *Adventures of Huckleberry Finn* ($44,600); *St. Louis Post-Dispatch*, December 18, 2001.
70. SMOB Records, DRMA—Adminstrative: Future of St. Mary's—Shelby, "St. Mary's of the Barrens Shrine and Heritage Center Preliminary Plan, 14 September 1999," and "St. Mary's of the Barrens Shrine and Heritage Center Inaugural Plan, 25 October 1999."
71. SMOB Records, DRMA—Adminstrative: Future of St. Mary's—"Request to Conduct a Capital Campaign and Build Saint Mary's of the Barrens Visitor Center, Draft, 26 August 2001."
72. MW Province Files—Hartenbach Papers—William Hartenbach, CM, to Charles Shelby, CM, 9 April 2002.

efforts were still under way to sell and develop the 650 acres surrounding the core campus. A Perryville Community Park Association, including members from the Vincentian order, was founded to oversee the maintenance of the grounds for the local parish's "Seminary Picnic." Southeast Missouri State University finished renovation of the library building to accommodate extension courses beginning with the fall semester 2002, eventually partnering with Mineral Area Community College at the seminary site. The library collection was removed and books donated to the Vincentian seminary in Kenya and to DePaul University. The De Andreis–Rosati Memorial Archives were transferred to DePaul's Richardson Library. Monies from the auction of the Barrens' rare books and museum collections were earmarked for endowments to support the mission efforts of the Midwest Vincentians. The offices of the Catholic Home Study Service were relocated to rented space off the seminary grounds.

While few plans were finalized during the tenure of William Hartenbach as provincial superior, his pragmatic approach to the future of the Barrens ultimately prevailed. Father Shelby's proposed capital campaign was ultimately rejected by the provincial council, although in 2005 plans for a smaller visitors' center were approved, and the Ruth Shelby Heritage and Visitor Center was completed in 2006 with funds from the estate of Shelby's mother. In the meantime, the increasingly exorbitant costs of maintaining the old campus led the province to initiate a $10 million campaign ("The Journey Home") for demolition of outdated buildings and construction of a new Vincentian residence center. The campaign was led by a professional development director and successfully raised $5 million, with the remaining costs paid by "loans in the form of state-backed bonds."[73] The demolished buildings included the unoccupied student and novitiate halls as well as the historic buildings east of, but not including, historic Rosati Hall (the admin-

---

73. Van Dorpe, e-mail to author, October 24, 2016. Father Van Dorpe described the pressing need for action on the old campus as a "perfect storm of worn-out and outdated technology" leading to mechanical system failures that would have cost more to repair than the expense of the renovation project.

istration or "A" building). The new Apostle of Charity Residence, with graduated living quarters to accommodate both active, retired, and infirmed Vincentians, was designed to incorporate some of the distinctive architectural elements of the demolished older buildings. The new project transformed the looks of the Barrens, and the residence center was dedicated in July 2006.[74]

Conclusion

The story of the decline and fall of St. Mary's of the Barrens Seminary—a story of one American religious order coming to grips with changing circumstances necessitating hard decisions about the fate of its most historic institution—illustrates key characteristics in the contemporary history of American Catholic religious life. Since at least the Second Vatican Council, practically every element of the institutional Catholic Church has undergone a prolonged period of soul-searching and reorientation. For Catholic religious orders, the rapidly changing religious environment (declining vocations, shifting apostolic commitments, etc.) represented a veritable crisis that called for some transformation of identity or emphasis. As former Vincentian David Nygren and Sister Miriam Ukeritis have pointed out, transformation involves a model with discernible stages, from crisis through an "unfreezing" of former attitudes and search for alternative understandings and actions, to conflict and a new synthesis.[75]

The midwestern Vincentians provided a clear example of several aspects of religious transformation. As early as 1970, the report of the Vincentian Committee on the Apostolate (COTA) suggested a growing concern with the ability of the order to maintain its apostolic commitments in the middle of environmental change. The decision to close St. Mary's of the Barrens Seminary, the American motherhouse of the order and historic center of the province, was made on essentially practical grounds—the declining number of vocations and costs of maintaining an outdated physical

74. "Vincentian House Warming," *Southeast Missourian*, July 22, 2006.
75. Nygren and Ukeritis, *Future of Religious Orders in the United States*, 260.

plant rendered the decision practically inevitable. The Vincentians explained the closing, however, with reference to an interpretation of cultural and ecclesiastical history that stressed adaptation and development, ebb and flow, change and transition. Such an interpretation allowed for an internal assimilation of the transformed status of the Barrens, but failed to provide a clear direction for the future of the old seminary.

Planning for the future of St. Mary's of the Barrens after 1985 proved more problematic than the closing of the seminary. The seminary provided the central apostolate of the campus and cemented individual and congregational commitments to the institution. The loss of its unifying apostolate made it difficult to consider the future of the Barrens. Only after nearly a decade following the closure of the seminary was the province able to readjust its perceptions of St. Mary's. The SMOB report of 1995 established the principles on which future planning, however erratic and fitful, would proceed. That report focused on the Barrens as both property and heritage, with a few apostolic works in progress and a great deal of community life but no central, distinctive apostolate. Therefore, future decisions about the Barrens could be made divorced from romantic attachments to any single work.

Individual attachment to the institution of St. Mary's of the Barrens remained strong, particularly given the vitality of community life at the Barrens, which remained among the largest single communities of Vincentians in the province. These attachments contributed to conflicts with the provincial administration over the disposition of Barrens properties. The whole issue of provincial leadership and governance became embroiled in discussions over the future of the Barrens, with canon lawyers pronouncing on the rights of the house versus provincial authority and multiple committees charged with revised mandates offering alternative proposals that were met with little enthusiasm. As many testify, the Barrens still evokes strong feelings among midwestern Vincentians. Because so many Vincentians spent a significant amount of time there during their formation, the Barrens became the focus of individual emotion, both positive and negative. This welter of emotions translated into a lack of consensus over the future of St. Mary's.

In the case of the Barrens, communal identity and allegiance triumphed when the house council, at a critical moment in the planning process, submitted to provincial authority and ceded Barrens properties to the province.

The issue of congregational identity became closely tied to the fortunes of the Barrens after 1985. For the Vincentians, St. Mary's of the Barrens Seminary represented the heritage of the order and history is a prime component of corporate identity. Thus, questions of identity often focused on perceptions of the past and its role in defining the community and ordering its future. Two visions of the past collided in planning for the future of the Barrens. Father William Hartenbach, a trained historian, former rector of the Barrens, and provincial superior from 1996 to 2002, felt a keen appreciation for the Vincentian heritage at the Barrens. He hoped to celebrate the past through the Barrens but was adamant in his insistence on investing in the future. When the costs of renovating the Barrens, both in physical and human terms, became prohibitive, Hartenbach saw it as an impediment to the mission of the province and pulled back. Father Charles Shelby, a trained manager and director of the Association of the Miraculous Medal, also felt a deep attachment to the heritage of the Barrens. Shelby, however, believed that investment in the past was a sound route to recovery of a brighter future. For him, the costs of renovating the Barrens represented an investment that would pay off in greater visibility and resources available for contemporary Vincentian works. Hartenbach and Shelby, both talented and dedicated American Vincentians, represented contrasting perspectives evident in the history of the Barrens since its founding two centuries earlier. Paradoxically, the historian became the futurist and the entrepreneur became the preservationist in planning for a twenty-first-century Barrens.

Chapter Ten
CONCLUSION

> We mean to stay here as long as the Lord wants us to be here.
>
> —Raymond Van Dorpe, CM, Western Province Superior,
> 9 September 2016

The American Catholic experience in the twenty-first century is the product of over two centuries of historical development as well as more recent cultural and demographic changes. Both the history and the contemporary circumstances of American Catholicism are reflected in the present status of St. Mary's of the Barrens, which remains a physical symbol of an eventful past, an altered present, and an uncertain future.

Recent demographic data suggest that American Catholics have successfully assimilated into the broader American culture and achieved parity with non-Catholics in terms of income, education, cultural attitudes, and sociopolitical views and behaviors.[1] Catholics represent almost 21 percent of the American population and are described as "about as well educated and as wealthy as the general public."[2]

---

1. Of course, significant differences remain within the Catholic population based on ethnic origins, with the growing Hispanic Catholic community still lagging in key measures. See Pew Research Center findings, http://www.pewforum.org/religious-landscape-study/.
2. Pew Research Center, "Portrait of American Catholics on the Eve of Pope Benedict's Visit to the United States," 27 March 2008.

23. CHURCH OF THE ASSUMPTION TODAY

The Barrens church as it appears today, after a 1980 renovation that included construction of the Angelus bell tower and an Italianate façade. The Church of the Assumption served as a parish church for the Perryville community until the construction of a new St. Vincent de Paul Church in 1965. The present Assumption Church houses the National Shrine of Our Lady of the Miraculous Medal and remains a popular pilgrimage site.

Of course, as the Catholic community developed over the past two centuries, its patterns of behavior and practice changed, most dramatically so in the past fifty years. Those changes are reflected in the numbers of closed American Catholic institutions. The Center for Applied Research in the Apostolate (CARA) has compiled statistics indicating that almost 2,000 Catholic parishes were closed between 1985 and 2015 (with over 3,500 parishes—out of a total of 17,377—operating without a resident priest-pastor in 2015, up from 1,051 in 1985); over 2,400 Catholic elementary schools and 225 high schools ceased operations in the thirty-year period after 1985; the number of Catholic colleges declined from 243 in 1985 (down from 305 in 1965) to 226 in 2015; and Catholic hospitals decreased from 631 in 1985 to 541 in 2015.[3] At the same time, the self-identified Catholic population rose from 59.5 million to 81.6 million, resulting in parishes serving larger congregations, colleges teaching more students, and hospitals treating more patients.[4]

Seminary closings are more difficult to tabulate given the various levels and definitions of "seminary" (major-minor, diocesan-religious, etc.) but data reveal that the number of high school seminaries fell from 171 in 1967–68 to 16 in 1990 and major seminaries (mainly schools of theology) from 125 in 1967–68 to 39 today, with the census of graduate-level seminarians falling from a high of 8,325 in 1965 to 4,063 in 1985 and 3,650 in 2015.[5]

Institutional closings and population increases in remaining institutions reflect a number of demographic and cultural factors over the past half century since the Second Vatican Council, and the thirty years since the closing of St. Mary's of the Barrens Seminary. Included in those factors is a steep decrease in the number of Catholic priests and religious. CARA reports a 35 percent decline in

3. See the CARA website's "Frequently Requested Church Statistics" at cara.georgetown.edu/frequently-requested-church-statistics/.
4. Ibid.
5. Thanks to Sister Katarina Schuth, OSF, Professor and Endowed Chair for the Scientific Study of Religion at the St. Paul Seminary School of Divinity in St. Paul, Minnesota, for a brief summary of the often bewildering data on institutional closings. Schuth is the author of *Seminary Formation: Recent History, Current Circumstances, New Directions* (Liturgical Press, 2016). For number of graduate-level seminarians, see the CARA website above, which lists a fifty-year low population of 3,172 seminarians in 1990.

the number of American Catholic priests since 1985, with an even steeper decrease of 47 percent among priests belonging to religious orders or institutes.[6] The numbers of religious sisters fell even more dramatically, from 115,386 sisters in 1985 to 48,546 sisters in 2015.[7] Changes in American Catholic institutional culture, including closures, stem partly from necessary realignments of leadership and staffing structures. Of course, the decline in the number of priests and sisters reflects perhaps deeper cultural changes in American society and the American Catholic Church. Declining religious vocations and institutional closings may share common roots.

These trends in the broader Catholic community and in institutional Catholic history are reflected in the story of the Barrens. A 2012 article in *Forbes Magazine* touted Perryville, Missouri, as a "manufacturing oasis" with a strong economic base, low unemployment and tax rates, and progressive business and political leadership.[8] Amazingly, *Forbes* credited Perryville's economic transformation from a backwater farming and shoe factory town to a progressive "oasis" partly to its geographic location, calling it "a regional transport hub for goods and materials." Perryville, a largely Catholic town (55 percent of its population claims religious adherence as Catholic[9]) perceived historically as an isolated "backwoods" community and "border county in a border state," and occasionally derided by some observers, including Vincentians, for its unhealthy and inaccessible locale, has "made it." According to the *Forbes* article, the town has been repeatedly cited by the governor of Missouri as an economic success story.[10] In the meantime, the once thriving St. Mary's of the Barrens Seminary, frontier Catholic redoubt and cradle of bishops, is closed and its historic campus buildings largely

6. CARA, "Frequently Requested Church Statistics," reports a population of 58,632 total priests (22,707 members of religious orders) to 57,317 (22,265) in 1985 and 37,578 (11,710) in 2015.
7. Ibid. The numbers are even more telling compared to the 1965 census of 179,954 sisters. Religious brothers suffered a similar decline, from 12,271 in 1965 to 7,544 in 1985 and 4,200 in 2015.
8. Sweet, "How a Small Town in Missouri Became a Manufacturing Oasis."
9. See the 2010 County Membership Report of the Association of Religion Data Archives, http://www.thearda.com/rcms2010/r/c/29/rcms2010_29157_county_name_2010.asp.
10. Ibid.

demolished. While still an active house of the Western Province of the American Vincentian community, the Barrens is a shadow of its former self. Its decline, amidst the economic renaissance of the surrounding community, echoes the broader experience of the American Catholic Church in the twenty-first century.

So what remains of the Barrens today, and what lessons (if any) can be drawn from its rich history and relative decline? The present state of the Barrens reflects the fortunes of the Western Province of the Congregation of the Mission, which has experienced a drop in membership from around 400 priests and brothers in 1985 to 157 in 2016.[11] Of that total, thirty-three are retired Vincentians, many of whom reside in the Apostle of Charity residence on the campus of the Barrens. The remaining active Vincentians serve in parishes (thirty-five), in the province-supported mission center in Kenya (twenty-six), at DePaul University and other educational institutions (fifteen), on parish mission teams (six), in seminaries (eleven), in provincial offices (eight), in chaplaincies (four), in service to the Vincentian family (five), in studies or sabbatical leaves (six), or in various other apostolates (seventeen).[12]

In addition to the retirement center and an active farm operation (maintained by three Vincentian brothers), the Barrens houses the historic Church of the Assumption with its National Shrine of Our Lady of the Miraculous Medal, a visitor center serving over 3,000 annual visitors to the campus, and the offices of the Association of the Miraculous Medal. The Catholic Home Study Service continues to operate out of the Barrens. An extension of Mineral Area Community College in Flat River, Missouri offers courses in the refurbished academic building on campus. While the 1850 Rosati Hall (or "A" Building) remains standing, most of the other historic campus buildings were razed to make room for the modern retire-

---

11. Rybolt, *American Vincentians*, 459–67; and Van Dorpe, CM, e-mail to author, 9 September 2016. The total of priests and brothers includes twenty-six men working in the seminary maintained by the western American province in Kenya. Prospects for future growth appear limited, with three US seminarians/students reported across the Western Province in 2016, although thirty seminarians are enrolled in Kenya. NB: The western province represents a reunion of the Midwest, South, and West provinces, which had broken off in 1975 but recombined in 2010.
12. Van Dorpe, CM, e-mail to author 9 September 2016.

24. APOSTLE OF CHARITY RESIDENCE
Dedicated in 2006, this modern graduated-living center for active and retired
Vincentians was built on the site of the demolished scholasticate, novitiate, and
recreation center buildings. The residence was designed to incorporate elements
of the historic architecture of the Barrens campus.

ment center or in recognition of their age and decrepit condition.

According to provincial superior Raymond Van Dorpe, CM, the
community will continue to operate the Apostle of Charity residence for retired Vincentians and priests still active in the Perryville
region "for the foreseeable future." The Association of the Miraculous Medal plans to break ground soon on "a major landscaping
effort that will make the area between the church and the grotto
more conducive and accessible to visitors," a plan that might well
usher in "a new chapter in the history of St. Mary's of the Barrens."[13]

In the meantime, the community approaches the bicentennial
of the founding of the Barrens with mixed emotions. In the words
of Father Van Dorpe, "If you ask any Vincentian about their memories of the Barrens and how they feel about that place, you are
likely to get a variety of answers. Most of the confreres associate this

13. Ibid.

place with their seminary days. Some have wonderful memories, and some do not! However, I think almost all will admit that St. Mary's is our home and our foundation. Even those who have not been there for many years still regard it as our motherhouse."[14]

What do the memories of American Vincentians and, more significantly, the historical experience of the Barrens, have to teach the broader American Catholic Church, especially in the recent climate of institutional contraction and cultural transformation? First and foremost, the history of the Barrens reflects the necessity for change and adaptation to an evolving Catholic community. The Barrens has redefined itself often over its two-hundred-year existence. From frontier seminary serving the vast Louisiana Territory, a mission center with a thriving lay college, a dormant period following the Civil War, and revival as a multilevel internal seminary and central Vincentian house of the western United States, to a college seminary and, after its closure, a retirement residence and center for evangelization, the Barrens has adapted to the needs of the Vincentian community and the surrounding Catholic community.

In the process, the culture of the Barrens changed significantly. While some of the works housed at the Barrens moved, others adapted to the times. The lay college moved, but classes are still held on the old campus through the efforts of the local community college. The domestic missions shifted from sending priests to scattered Catholic settlements to Motor Missions in primarily non-Catholic areas and long-distance instruction in Catholic doctrine. Service as a diocesan seminary ceased, but the Barrens transformed to educate Vincentian candidates in an apostolic school and a minor and major seminary, eventually earning the coveted seal of academic accreditation, until declining numbers and provincial policies necessitated the closing of seminary operations altogether. The farm remained, shedding its slave labor pool well before the Civil War and transforming into a mechanized agricultural operation of the twentieth century. The parish moved to a new site in the city of Perryville, but Vincentian priests continue to pastor that

14. Ibid.

parish, the seminary grounds host the annual Seminary Picnic representing the largest fund-raising event for the local Catholic community, and the seminary Church of the Assumption continues to draw visitors to its shrine of the Miraculous Medal. Numbers of active Vincentians have dwindled, but the motherhouse welcomes its sons back to a state-of-the-art retirement and medical facility.

The experience of the Barrens also reflects the importance of adherence to an essential mission or spiritual "charism" in the midst of change. The spirit of St. Vincent de Paul, with its focus on humble and practical service to spiritually and materially impoverished peoples, has driven the various manifestations of the Barrens and remains as vibrant today as it was in seventeenth-century France or the nineteenth-century American frontier. While Vincentians debated the future of the Barrens throughout its long history and sometimes disagreed about the best way to utilize the institution, Vincentian values were cited by all sides. Those values inspired DuBourg to recruit the Congregation of the Mission to staff his sprawling American diocese, guided the development of the Barrens through its struggles and triumphs, characterized the course of discussions following the closure of the seminary in 1985, and led the Western Province to sponsorship of its thriving Kenyan mission. Abandonment of the essential mission values of any religious institution represents worse than an abandonment of the institution, it portends the death of the spirit underlying those institutions in the first place.

Finally, the experience of the Barrens teaches the need to maintain historical memory. Remembering and relating the history of the Barrens sheds light on the identity of the community served by the Barrens. Institutional histories tell us who we were, how we got to the present, and (by both positive and negative example) where we might go in the future. One active Vincentian priest predicts that the "graying" of the Vincentian community will result inevitably in the complete abandonment of the Barrens within the next ten years. A retired Vincentian priest still living at the Barrens suggests that "our work in this country is done." Maybe so, maybe not, but recording the story of how that work was completed remains a necessary and enlightening task. For the sake of the Barrens, the

American Vincentian community, the citizens of Perryville and surrounding regions, and the broader American Catholic community, the story of the Barrens deserves remembrance.

WORKS CITED

Archives

DRMA = De Andreis–Rosati Memorial Archives, DePaul University Special Collections and Archives, Chicago, Illinois

SMOB Records, DRMA = St. Mary's of the Barrens Seminary Records, Educational Institutions, DRMA

<u>Academic Files</u>: Curriculum, Box 26, Subseries 5.2.
    Proposed Changes, Correspondence, 1957–1965, Box 26, Folder 2.
        "Notes on Father Stakelum's Notes."
    Curriculum of Studies, 1939–1940: St. Mary's Seminary, Perryville, Mo., Box 30, Folder 4.
<u>Academic Files</u>: Faculty, Boxes 25–25A, Subseries 5.1.
    Correspondence: Dean of Students, 1932–1963, Box 25A, Folder 8.
<u>Academic Files</u>: NCA Accreditation Files and Self-Studies, Box 26–27.
    Advisory Visitation Report for North Central Accrediting Association, April 1982, Box 27, Folder 5.
    Correspondence: Edward Riley, CM, 1959–1961, Box 26, Folder 10.
    Correspondence: John P. Raynor, SJ, NCA Consultant, 1964–1966, Box 26, Folder 17.
    Correspondence: John Richardson, CM, 1959–1961, Box 26, Folder 9.
    Correspondence: North Central Association, 1962–1966, Box 26, Folder 13.
        "Institutional Self-Study, Saint Mary's Seminary, Perryville, Missouri, May, 1966."
    Correspondence and Meeting Notes: North Central Association, 1957–1961, Box 26, Folder 8.
        James A. Fischer, "Accreditation Talk with Father Reinert, SJ, in St. Louis, 20 October 1957."

"Report of Interview with Mr. Davis Madsen, Associate Secretary
        of the North Central Association: Chicago, July 5, 1961,
        Frs. Fischer and J. Falanga Attending."
Correspondence and Notes: Accreditation, 1942–47, Box 26, Folder 6.
    "By Father Fischer on trip to Chicago, June 8, 1946." Notes.
    "Report of Visit: Fr. Pius Barth, O.F.M., 1946."
North Central Association Accreditation Process, 1975–77, Box 27,
        Folder 1.
Report of Visit: Dr. William Conley, NCA Consultant, 1962, Box 26,
        Folder 15.
Report of Visit: Evaluation Team; Dr. John Bannan and Rev. Francis
        C. Brennan, 1982, Box 27, Folder 4.
Report of Visit: John Horner and Joseph Pendergast, 1966, Box 26,
        Folder 20.
Report of Visit: John P. Raynor, SJ, NCA Consultant, 1964, Box 26,
        Folder 18.
Administration: Future of St. Mary's: Charles Shelby Files, Box 15.
        Joyce, Michael. "Relationship Between the Midwest Province and
                St. Mary's of the Barrens Seminary, 17 November 1996."
        "Request to Conduct a Capital Campaign and Build Saint Mary's
                of the Barrens Visitor Center, 26 August 2001."
        Shelby, Charles. "Proposal for the Use of the Facilities of St.
                Mary's of the Barrens, October 1985."
        Shelby, Charles. "St. Mary's of the Barrens Shrine and Heritage
                Center Preliminary Plan, 14 September 1999."
        Shelby, Charles. "St. Mary's of the Barrens Shrine and Heritage
                Center Inaugural Plan, 25 October 1999."
        Shelby Charles. "St. Mary's of the Barrens Summary Presentation,
                2 December 1996."
Administration: Superior's Correspondence, Box 6.
        G. C. LeFevre: Provincial, Marshall Winne, Box 6, Folders 3–7.
        "Curriculum Saint Mary's Seminary." Undated.
        "Duties Assigned to the Personnel of Saint Mary's Seminary."
                Undated.
Buildings and Grounds, Box 79 and 79A.
        Hoernig, Alphonse. "Birth of a Water System," 1990, Box 79A, Folder 12.
        Martin, Daniel. "Projected Repairs and Improvements, St. Mary's
                Seminary, Perryville, August 30, 1954." Typewritten copy,
                Box 79, Folder 5.

"Space Recommendations for St. Mary's Seminary Library and Classroom Building." Undated photocopy, Box 79, Folder 5.

"Perryville Library-Classroom Building." Undated photocopy, Box 79, Folder 5.

Governance: Domestic/House Council Minutes 1993–2004, Box 5C.

Governance: Visitations, Box 3.

    Ledger Book 1842–87, Folder 1.

    Ledger Book 1894–1961, Folder 2.

History: Anniversaries: SMOB Reopening of St. Mary's of the Barrens (60th), Box 1A, Folder 4.

History: General Histories 1906–1968, Box 1, Folder 1.

    Bozuffi, Alceste. "The Servant of God: Felix De Andreis, Priest of the Mission." English translation. Perryville, MO, 1930. Typewritten manuscript.

    Musson, William. "Historical Sketches of the Western Province (1888–1935)."

    Faris, John. "In Retrospect." 7 December 1946.

Student Activities, Box 60.

    "Camp St. Vincent, January 1983," Box 60, Folder 1.

    Camp St. Vincent: Correspondence, Box 60, Folder 2.

    Rybolt, John. "Camp St. Vincent." Undated typewritten copy, Box 60, Folder 1.

Student Activities: Publications, Box 66–67.

    The DeAndrein vol. 1–19 (1930–1949), Box 66.

    The DeAndrein vol. 20–35 (1949–1965), Box 67.

Students: Diaries, Box 44 and 53.

    Record of Principle [ital.] Events, 1859–1864, Box 44, Folder 2.

    Record of Principle Events, 1864–1866, Box 44, Folder 3.

    Record of Principle Events, 1886–1890, Box 44, Folder 4.

    Scholasticate Diary, 1890–1927, Box 53, Folders 1–5.

Provincial Files, DRMA

Fischer Papers = Reverend James A. Fischer, 1962–1971.

O'Donnell Papers = Reverend Hugh O'Donnell, 1978–1987.

Parres Papers = Reverend Cecil L. Parres, 1971–1978.

Ryan Papers = Rev. Stephen V. Ryan, 1857–1868.

Smith Papers = Reverend Thomas J. Smith, 1879–1905.

Stakelum Papers = Reverend James W. Stakelum, 1950–1962.

Winne Papers = Winne, Reverend Marshall, 1938–1950.

Personnel Files, DRMA

Fischer, James A.
  Osiek, Carolyn. "Interview with James. A. Fischer, May 2,1997." Box
    1, Folder 3.
Lynch, John
  "Building Supply Contract (1848)," Box 1, Folder 10.
  Letter to the Director of Seminaries in Paris (1850), Box 1, Folder 5.
Rolando, James
  Ryan, William. "Brief Biographical Notes: James Rolando." Typewrit-
    ten manuscript, Box 1, Folder 1.
Souvay, Charles Leon*, Box 5.
  Rosati, Joseph. *Memoire sur l'establissement de la Congregation de la
    Mission aux Etats-Unis d'Amerique.* Copy of an original in the
    Congregation of the Mission's Roman Provincial Archive,
    Folders 8–10.
  Rosati, Joseph. "Testimonial Given to Rev. J. M. Odin, CM." 8 Sep-
    tember 1824, Folder 16.
Timon, John. "Father Timon's Narrative of the Barrens." Handwritten
    original, Box 1, Folder 4.

**Provincial Assembly MW, DRMA = Provincial Assembly Records
of the Midwest Province, 1843–1997, DRMA**

Provincial Assembly 1973–1974: First Session, Box 7.
  Committee on Apostolate, Common Life, and Prayer Life, 1973–74,
    Folder 17.
Provincial Assembly 1973–1974: Second Session, Box 8.
  "Report on Self-Study, Joint Provincial Assemblies, 1973–74." Min-
    utes, 1974, Folder 25.
Provincial Assembly 1982, Box 10.
  Minutes, 1982, Folder 4.

**GCUSA, DRMA = Correspondence: General Curia (Paris) and
USA, DRMA Microfilm Collection #2, Box 4.**

MW Province Files = Midwest Province Provincial Files (Earth City, MO)
Brusatti, Louis. "The Current State of Transition in the Church."
    Undated, unpublished paper.

*The Souvay Files were previously a separate collection, but now have been incorporat-
ed into other collections.

"The Congregation of the Mission: The Age of Adaptation." Unsigned, undated.

Gagnepain, John. Letters/Papers.

Hartenbach, William. Letters/Papers.

"Historical Transitions." Unsigned, undated.

"Ideas of Midwest Confreres for the Future of SMOB." Undated.

Lipsmeyer, M. Beth. "The Students of St. Mary's Seminary: Psychological Profile, Developmental Task of Adolescence and Relevant Research." Unpublished paper. (January 1984).

Memo, Bryan Cave, LP, to William Davidson, 12 January 1998.

Memo, Bryan Cave, LP, to Joseph Hess, CM, 6 February 1998.

Minutes of Midwest Provincial Council Meetings.

Miscellaneous Papers, Provincial Council.

"Report to the Province from the Provincial and the Provincial Council Regarding Mission Project: St. Mary's of the Barrens, 23 March 1995."

"Vincentians Announce Plans for Perryville, Statement by the Very Reverend John F. Gagnepain, CM, Provincial of the Midwest Province of the Congregation of the Mission, March 26, 1995."

Interviews and E-mails

Derbes, Louis, e-mail to D. Steele, 11 November 2002.

Hartenbach, William, interview with author, 10 June 2002.

Paulus, Sandy, e-mail to author, 4 November 2015.

Schuth, Katarina, e-mail to author, 11 July 2016.

Van Dorpe, Raymond, e-mail to author, 9 September 2016.

Van Dorpe, Raymond, e-mail to author, 24 October 2016.

Vincentian Serial Publications

Annales de la Congregation de la Mission. Vol. 4 (1838).

Annales de la Congregation de la Mission. Vol. 15 (1850).

De Andrein (1930–65)

Newspapers

Chicago Tribune (1986)

Perry County Republic (1985)

Perry County Republican (1924)

Perry County Republic-Monitor (1997–98)

St. Louis Globe-Democrat (1985)
St. Louis Post-Dispatch (1997, 2001)
St. Louis Times-Democrat (1905)
Southeast Missourian (2005–6)
Weekly Perryville Union (1864)

Published Primary Sources

Anderson, Galusha. "The Missouri Oath of Loyalty of 1865." Excerpted
    and introduced by G. E. Rule. *Civil War St. Louis*, posted Feb.
    2001. www.civilwarstlouis.com/History/Oathofloyalty.htm
    (accessed March 16, 2017).
Association of Religion Data Archives. "U.S. Congregational Membership:
    County Reports." http://www.thearda.com/rcms2010/select-
    County.asp (accessed March 16, 2017).
Baer, Campion. "Development of Accreditation in American Catholic
    Seminaries, 1890–1961." PhD diss., University of Notre Dame,
    1963.
Brackenridge, Henry Marie. *Views of Louisiana: Containing Geographical,
    Statistical and Historical Notices of That Vast and Important Portion
    of America.* Baltimore: Schaeffer and Maund, 1823.
Center for Applied Research in the Apostolate. "Frequently Requested
    Church Statistics." cara.georgetown.edu/frequently-requested
    -church-statistics/ (accessed March 16, 2017).
Cummings, Jeremiah W. "Our Future Clergy: An Inquiry into Vocations
    to the Priesthood in the United States." *Brownson's Quarterly
    Review* 17 (Oct. 1860): 497–515.
De Andreis, Felix. *Frontier Missionary: Felix De Andreis, C. M., 1778–1820:
    Correspondence and Historical Writings.* Edited and introduction by
    John Rybolt. Chicago: Vincentian Studies Institute, 2005.
Dunand, Marie Joseph. "Diary of the Reverend Father Marie Joseph
    Dunand." Translated by Ella M. E. Flicke. *Records of the American
    Catholic Historical Society* 26, no. 4 (Dec. 1915): 328–45, and 27,
    no. 1 (March 1916): 45–64.
"Father Smith, Pioneer Provincial." *De Andrein* 34, no. 1 (1963): 11–12.
Kennerly, William Clark, as Told to Elizabeth Russell. *Persimmon Hill: A
    Narrative of Old St. Louis and the Far West.* Norman: University of
    Oklahoma Press, 1948.
Pew Research Center. "A Portrait of American Catholics on the Eve of
    Pope Benedict's Visit to the United States." March 27, 2008.

www.pewforum.org/2008/03/27/a-portrait-of-american-catholics-on-the-eve-of-pope-benedicts-visit-to-the-us/.

———. "Religious Landscape Study." www.pewforum.org/religious-landscape-study/.

Rosati, Joseph. *Life of the Very Reverend Felix De Andreis, C.M.: First Superior of the Congregation of the Mission in the United States and Vicar General of Upper Louisiana*. St. Louis: B. Herder, 1900.

———. "Recollections of the Establishment of the Congregation of the Mission in the United States." Six Parts. Edited by Stafford Poole. *Vincentian Heritage Journal* 1, no. 1 (1980): 67–95; 2, no. 1 (1981): 33–54; 3, no. 1 (1982): 131–60; 4, no. 2 (Fall 1983): 109–39; 5, no. 1 (Spring 1984): 103–31; 5, no. 2 (Fall 1984): 107–44.

Rozier, Firmin A. *Rozier's History of the Early Settlement of the Mississippi Valley*. St. Louis: G. A. Pierrot and Son, 1890.

Ryan, Stephen V. "Early Lazarist Missions and Missionaries: Read Before the U.S. Catholic Historical Society, May 8, 1887." In *Three Centuries of Vincentian Missionary Labor, 1617–1917: The Centenary of the Congregation of the Mission in the United States*. Perryville, MO: Miraculous Medal Association, 1917.

Sadlier's Catholic Directory, Almanac and Ordo for the Year of Our Lord 1883: With Reports of the Dioceses in the United States, British America, Ireland, England, and Scotland. New York: D. J. Sadlier and Co., 1883.

Timon, John. "Barrens Memoir." Edited and Annotated by John Rybolt. *Vincentian Heritage Journal* 22, no. 1 (2001): 45–105.

Vincent de Paul. *Correspondence, Conferences, Documents*. Vol. 11, *Conferences*. Edited by Marie Poole. New York: New City Press, 2008.

Secondary Sources

Anello, Robert. *The Hand of God at Work in Adult Catholic Priestly Formation: Holy Apostles College and Seminary, 1956–1995*. Franklin, WI: Self-published, 2015.

Barclay, Thomas S. "The Test Oath for Clergy in Missouri." *Missouri Historical Review* 18, no. 3 (Apr. 1924): 345–81.

Baum, William. "The State of U.S. Free-Standing Seminaries." *Origins* 16, no. 18 (1986): 313–25.

Bayard, Ralph. *Lone Star Vanguard: The Catholic Reoccupation of Texas*. St. Louis: Vincentian Press, 1945.

Beal, John P., James A. Coriden, and Thomas J. Green. *New Commentary on the Code of Canon Law*. New York: Paulist Press, 1999.

Berger, Peter. *The Sacred Canopy: Elements of a Sociological Theory of Religion.* Garden City, NY: Doubleday Press, 1967.

Bianchi, Eugene C. *Passionate Uncertainty: Inside the American Jesuits.* Berkeley: University of California Press, 2002.

Brekus, Catherine A. "Catholics in America." *Christian History Magazine* 102 (2012). www.christianhistoryinstitute.org/magazine/article/catholics-in-america/.

Carey, Patrick W. *Catholics in America: A History.* Westport, CT: Praeger, 2004.

———. *Orestes A. Brownson: American Religious Weathervane.* Grand Rapids, MI: William B. Eerdmans, 2004.

———. *People, Priests and Prelates: Ecclesiastical Democracy and the Tensions of Trusteeism.* Notre Dame, IN: University of Notre Dame Press, 1987.

Carmel, Mary. "Problems of William Louis Dubourg, Bishop of Louisiana, 1815–1826." *Louisiana History: The Journal of the Louisiana Historical Association* 4, no. 1 (Winter 1963): 55–72.

Centennial History of Perry County, Missouri, 1821–1921. Perryville, MO: Perry County Historical Society, reprint edition, 1984.

Crews, Clyde F. *American and Catholic: A Popular History of Catholicism in the United States.* Cincinnati, OH: St. Anthony Messenger Press, 2004.

Cronin, Patrick. *Memorial of the Life and Labors of Rt. Rev. Stephen Vincent Ryan, D.D., C.M.: Second Bishop of Buffalo, New York.* Buffalo, NY: Buffalo Catholic Communications Co., 1896.

D'Antonio, William V., Michelle Dillon, and Mary L. Gautier. *American Catholics in Transition.* Lanham, MD: Rowman and Littlefield, Publishers, 2013.

Deuther, Charles. *Life and Times of Right Reverend John Timon, D.D., First Roman Catholic Bishop of the Diocese of Buffalo.* Buffalo, NY: Published by the Author, 1870.

Dichtl, John R. *Frontiers of Faith: Bringing Catholicism to the West in the Early Republic.* Lexington: University Press of Kentucky, 2008.

Dolan, Jay P. *The American Catholic Experience: A History from Colonial Times to the Present.* Garden City, NY: Doubleday Press, 1985.

———. *In Search of an American Catholicism: A History of Religion and Culture in Tension.* New York: Oxford University Press, 2002.

Dosen, Anthony. *Catholic Higher Education in the 1960s: Issues of Identity, Issues of Governance.* Charlotte, NC: Information Age Publishing, Inc., 2009.

Duggan, Lawrence G. *Armsbearing and the Clergy in the History and Canon Law of Western Christianity.* Woodbridge, UK: Boydell Press, 2013.

Easterly, Frederick. *The Life of Rt. Rev. Joseph Rosati, C.M.: First Bishop of St. Louis, 1789–1843.* Washington, DC: Catholic University of America Press, 1942.

Editorial Staff. "The American Vincentian Experience: Reflection on Mission." In *The American Vincentians: A Popular History of the Congregation of the Mission in the United States, 1815–1987*, edited by John Rybolt, 433–50. New York: New City Press, 1988.

———. "A Survey of American Vincentian History: 1815–1987." In *The American Vincentians: A Popular History of the Congregation of the Mission in the United States, 1815–1987*, edited by John Rybolt, 5–96. New York: New City Press, 1988.

Endres, David J. *American Crusade: Catholic Youth in the World Mission Movement from World War I Through Vatican II.* Eugene, OR: Pickwick Publications, 2010.

Faherty, William B. "In the Footsteps of Bishop Joseph Rosati." *Italian Americana* 1, no. 2 (Spring 1975): 280–92.

Farrelly, Maura Jane. "Catholicism in the Early South." *Journal of Southern Religion* 14 (2012). http://jsr.fsu.edu/issues/vol14/farrelly.html.

Fiand, Barbara. *Refocusing the Vision: Religious Life Into the Future.* New York: Crossroad Publishing, 2001.

Fisher, James T. *Communion of Immigrants: A History of Catholics in America.* New York: Oxford University Press, 2006.

Foley, Patrick. "Missionaries Extraordinaire: The Vincentians from St. Mary's of the Barrens." *Vincentian Heritage Journal* 22, no. 1 (2001): 1–10.

Foley, William E. *The Genesis of Missouri: From Wilderness Outpost to Statehood.* Columbia: University of Missouri Press, 1989.

Gallen, James M. "John Bannon: Chaplain, Soldier and Diplomat." *The Christian Banner* 15, no. 1 (1999). Online at Civil War St. Louis: http://www.civilwarstlouis.com/History/fatherbannon.htm.

Garraghan, Gilbert. "The Trappists of Monks Mound." *Illinois Catholic Historical Review* 8, no. 2 (Oct. 1925): 106–36.

Gillis, Chester. *Roman Catholicism in America.* New York: Columbia University Press, 1999.

Gleason, Philip. "Boundlessness, Consolidation and Discontinuity Between Generations: Catholic Seminary Studies in Antebellum America." *Church History* 73, no. 3 (Spring 2004): 583–612.

————. "From an Indefinite Homogeneity: Catholic Colleges in Antebellum America." *Catholic Historical Review* 94, no. 1 (Jan. 2008): 45–74.

————. *Keeping the Faith: American Catholicism Past and Present.* Notre Dame, IN: University of Notre Dame Press, 1987.

Grace, Thomas. "Growth and Development of St. Mary's of the Barrens: Oldest Institution of Higher Learning West of the Mississippi." Master's thesis, DePaul University, 1966.

Greeley, Andrew. *The Catholic Revolution: New Wine, Old Wineskins, and the Second Vatican Council.* Berkeley: University of California Press, 2004.

Harney, John. "Enshrining the Mission: The Bishop Sheehan Memorial Museum and Vincentian Visions of China." *American Catholic Studies* 126, no. 3 (Fall 2015): 45–69.

Hennesey, James J. *American Catholics: A History of the Roman Catholic Community in the United States.* New York: Oxford University Press, 1981.

Hubrick, Barbara. "Perry County Through the Civil War." *Perry County Heritage* 17, no. 1–2 (1999): 1–24.

Janet, Richard J. "The Decline and Fall of St. Mary's of the Barrens: A Case Study in the Contraction of an American Catholic Religious Order, Part One." *Vincentian Heritage Journal* 22, no. 2 (2001): 153–81.

————. "The Decline and Fall of St. Mary's of the Barrens: A Case Study in the Contraction of an American Catholic Religious Order, Part Two." *Vincentian Heritage Journal* 25, no. 1 (2005): 1–30.

————. "The Era of Boundlessness at St. Mary's of the Barrens, 1818–1843: A Brief Historical Analysis." *Vincentian Heritage Journal* 31, no. 2 (Nov. 2012): 65–102.

————. "St. Mary's of the Barrens Seminary and the Vincentians in Southeast Missouri." Master's thesis, Southeast Missouri State University, 1979.

Kehoe, Richard. "Becoming a Bishop and Remaining a Vincentian: The Struggles of Archbishop John Joseph Lynch, C.M." *Vincentian Heritage Journal* 13, no. 2 (1992): 127–50.

Klein, Terrance W. "U.S. Culture and College Seminaries." *America* 170 (June 1994): 16–21.

Marienburg, Evyatar. *Catholicism Today: An Introduction to the Contemporary Catholic Church.* New York: Routledge, 2014.

Marlett, Jeffrey. *Saving the Heartland: Catholic Missionaries in Rural America, 1920–1960.* DeKalb: Northern Illinois University Press, 2002.

Massa, Mark. *The American Catholic Revolution: How the Sixties Changed the Church Forever.* New York: Oxford University Press, 2010.

———. *Anti-Catholicism in America: The Last Acceptable Prejudice.* New York: Crossroad Publishing, 2003.

McCullen, Richard. "Father Richardson: An Appreciation." *Vincentian Heritage Journal* 17, no. 2 (1996): 79–82.

McDannell, Colleen. *The Spirit of Vatican II: A History of Catholic Reform in America.* New York: Basic Books, 2011.

McDonald, Lloyd Paul. *The Seminary Movement in the United States: Projects, Foundations and Early Development, 1784–1833.* Washington, DC: Catholic University of America Press, 1927.

McDonough, Peter, and Eugene C. Bianchi. *Passionate Uncertainty: Inside the American Jesuits.* Berkeley: University of California Press, 2002.

McGreevy, John T. *Catholicism and American Freedom: A History.* New York: W. W. Norton and Co., 2003.

McKenna, Patrick. "The Catholic Motor Missions in Missouri." *Vincentian Heritage Journal* 7, no. 1 (1986): 97–134.

McKeown, H. C. *The Life and Labors of Most Reverend John Joseph Lynch, D.D., Cong. Miss., First Archbishop of Toronto.* Montreal and Toronto: James A. Sadlier, 1886.

McNamara, Robert J. "Seminary Education: Separate and Unequal." *America* 116, no. 14 (Apr. 1967): 533–34.

Melville, Annabelle M. *Louis William DuBourg: Bishop of Louisiana and the Floridas, Bishop of Montauban, and Archbishop of Besancon, 1766–1833.* 2 vols. Chicago: Loyola Press, 1986.

Messmer, S. G. "Two Interesting Communications from the Most Reverend Archbishop of Milwaukee." *Catholic Historical Review* 2, no. 2 (July 1916): 182–88.

Mills, Billie. "An Introduction to the Civil War at St. Mary's of the Barrens." *Perry County Historical Society* 15, no. 1 (1997): 22–33.

Morris, Charles R. *American Catholics: The Saints and Sinners Who Built America's Most Powerful Church.* New York: Times Books, 1997.

"National Register of Historic Places Registration Form: St. Mary's of the Barrens Historic District." July 18, 1995. dnr.mo.gov/shpo/nps-nr/95001041.pdf (accessed March 16, 2017).

Nygren, David, and Miriam Ukeritis. *The Future of Religious Orders in the United States: Transformation and Commitment.* Westport, CT: Greenwood Press, 1993.

O'Connell, Daniel. *Furl That Banner: The Life of Abram J. Ryan, Poet-Priest of the South*. Macon, GA: Mercer University Press, 2006.

Okwuru, Christian. *Responsibilities and Significance of the Congregatio pro clericis in the Life and Ministry of the Diocesan Clergy*. N.p.: Xlibris, 2012.

O'Rourke, Timothy. *Maryland Catholics on the Frontier: The Missouri and Texas Settlements*. Parsons, KS: Brefney Press, 1973.

———. *Perry County, Missouri: Religious Haven in the Trans-Mississippi West*. Parsons, KS: Brefney Press, 1979.

O'Toole, James. *The Faithful: A History of Catholics in America*. Cambridge, MA: Belknap Press, 2010.

Parrish, William F. *A History of Missouri*. Vol. 3, *1860–1875*. Columbia: University of Missouri Press, 1973.

Pasquier, Michael. *Fathers on the Frontier: French Missionaries and the Roman Catholic Priesthood in the United States, 1789–1970*. New York: Oxford University Press, 2010.

"Perry County Population Figures, 1830–1990." *Perry County Heritage Journal* 12, no. 2 (1994): 76–78.

Poole, Stafford. "An Active and Energetic Bishop: The Appointment of Joseph Glass, C.M., as Bishop of Salt Lake City." *Vincentian Heritage Journal* 15, no. 2 (1994): 119–62.

———. "Ad Cleri Disciplinam: The Vincentian Seminary Apostolate in the United States." In *The American Vincentians: A Popular History of the Congregation of the Mission in the United States, 1815–1987*, edited by John Rybolt, 97–162. New York: New City Press, 1988.

———. "A Brave New World: The Vincentians in Pioneer America." *Vincentian Heritage Journal* 14, no. 1 (1993): 141–52.

———. "The Diplomatic Missions of Bishop Joseph Rosati, C.M." *Catholic Historical Review* 91, no. 4 (Oct. 2005): 633–87.

———. "The Educational Apostolate: Colleges, Universities, and Secondary Schools." In *The American Vincentians: A Popular History of the Congregation of the Mission in the United States, 1815–1987*, edited by John Rybolt, 291–346. New York: New City Press, 1988.

———. "The Founding of Missouri's First College: St. Mary's of the Barrens, 1815–1818." *Missouri Historical Review* 65, no. 1 (Oct. 1970): 1–22.

———. *A History of the Congregation of the Mission, 1625–1843*. Perryville, MO: St. Mary's Seminary, 1973.

———. "Notable Vincentians (8): Aloysius Meyer." *Vincentian Heritage Journal* 18, no. 1 (1997): 93–100.

————. *Seminaries in Crisis.* New York: Herder and Herder, 1965.

Poole, Stafford, and John E. Rybolt, trans. and ed. "Notice Concerning the Origin, Progress, and Current State of the Mission of the Congregation of the Mission in the United States of America (1838)." *Vincentian Heritage Journal* 9, no. 1 (Spring 1988): 89–99.

Poole, Stafford, and Douglas Slawson. *Church and Slave in Perry County, Missouri, 1818–1865.* Lewiston, NY: Edwin Mellen Press, 1986.

Rabble, George. *God's Almost Chosen Peoples: A Religious History of the American Civil War.* Chapel Hill: University of North Carolina Press, 2010.

Rahill, Peter J. "St. Louis Under Bishop Rosati." *Missouri Historical Review* 66, no. 4 (July 1972): 495–519.

Reda, John. *From Furs to Farms: The Transformation of the Mississippi Valley, 1762–1825.* Dekalb: Northern Illinois University Press, 2016.

Renouard, Jean Pierre. "Itinerary and Elements of Vincentian Spirituality." Third Asian Vincentian Institute, Motherhouse, Paris. (September–December 2006). *FamVin Vincentian Encyclopedia.* famvin.org/wiki/Itinerary_and_Elements_of_Vincentian_Spirituality (accessed March 16, 2017).

Richardson, John. "Father Richardson: Some Incidents in His Early Life." *Vincentian Heritage Journal* 17, no. 2 (1996): 69–71.

Riforgiato, Leonard R., and Dennis A. Castillo. *The Life and Times of John Timon (1797–1867): First Bishop of Buffalo, New York.* Lewiston, NY: Edwin Mellen Press, 2006.

Rothensteiner, John. *History of the Archdiocese of St. Louis in Its Various Stages of Development from A.D. 1763 to A.D. 1928.* 2 vols. St. Louis, MO: Blackwell Weilandy Co., 1928.

Ryan, Frances, and Edward Udovic, eds. *Vincent de Paul and Louise de Marillac: Rules, Conferences, and Writings.* New York: Paulist Press, 1995.

Rybolt, John, ed. *The American Vincentians: A Popular History of the Congregation of the Mission in the United States, 1815–1987.* New York: New City Press, 1988.

————. "American Vincentians in 1877–78: The Maller Visitation Report (1)." *Vincentian Heritage Journal* 18, no. 1 (1997): 57–83.

————. "American Vincentians in 1877–78: The Maller Visitation Report (2)." *Vincentian Heritage Journal* 19, no. 2 (1998): 245–82.

————. "Christmas Novena." *Vincentian Heritage Journal* 6, no. 2 (1985): 257–69.

———. "Joseph Rosati, C.M. (1789–1843): Pioneer American Bishop."
    Vincentiana 48, no. 2 (2004): 394–403.

———. "Kenrick's First Seminary." *Missouri Historical Review* 71, no. 2
    (Jan. 1977): 139–55.

———. "Seminary Education in the Louisiana Territory: The Vincentian
    Contribution." http://works.bepress.com/john_rybolt/34.

———. "St. Vincent College and Theological Education." *Vincentian Heri-
    tage Journal* 7, no. 2 (1986): 291–322.

———. "Three Pioneer Vincentians." *Vincentian Heritage Journal* 14, no. 1
    (1993): 153–68.

———. *The Vincentians: A General History of the Congregation of the Mis-
    sion*, Vol. 3, *Revolution and Restoration (1789–1843)*. New York:
    New City Press, 2013.

———. *The Vincentians: A General History of the Congregation of the Mis-
    sion*, Vol. 5, *An Era of Expansion (1878–1919)*. New York: New
    City Press, 2014.

———. "Works of Devotion, Evangelization and Service." In *The American
    Vincentians: A Popular History of the Congregation of the Mission in
    the United States, 1815–1987*, edited by John Rybolt, 401–32. New
    York: New City Press, 1988.

Sanders, Sharon, and Diana Bryant. *Our Dear Brother Joseph: The Life of
    Joseph Lansman*. Cape Girardeau, MO: Cape Girardeau Genealog-
    ical Society, 1999.

Schauinger, J. Herman. *Cathedrals in the Wilderness*. Milwaukee, WI: Bruce
    Publishing, 1952.

———. *Stephen T. Badin: Priest in the Wilderness*. Milwaukee, WI: Bruce
    Publishing, 1956.

Schneiders, Susan. *Finding the Treasure: Locating Catholic Religious Life in a
    New Ecclesial and Cultural Context*. Vol. 1, *Religious Life in a New
    Millennium*. Mahway, NJ: Paulist Press, 2000.

Schroeder, Susan. "Seminaries and Writing the History of New Spain: An
    Interview with Stafford Poole, C.M." *The Americas* 69, no. 2 (Oct.
    2012): 237–54.

Schroeder, Walter. *Opening the Ozarks: A Historical Geography of Missouri's
    Ste. Genevieve District, 1760–1830*. Columbia: University of Mis-
    souri Press, 2002.

Shaw, Russell. *American Church: The Remarkable Rise, Meteoric Fall, and
    Uncertain Future of Catholicism in America*. San Francisco: Ignatius
    Press, 2013.

Slawson, Douglas. "The Ordeal of Abram J. Ryan." *Catholic Historical Review* 96, no. 4 (Jan. 2010): 678–719.

———. "Thirty Years of Street Preaching: Vincentian Motor Missions, 1934–1965." *Church History* 62, no. 1 (Mar. 1993): 60–81.

———. "The Vincentian Experience of the Civil War in Missouri." *American Catholic Studies* 121, no. 4 (Winter 2010): 31–60.

Spalding, Martin. *Sketches of the Life, Times, and Character of the Rt. Rev. Benedict Joseph Flaget, First Bishop of Louisville, Kentucky.* Louisville, KY: Webb and Levering,1852.

The Spanish Land Grants of Our Own Perry County, Missouri. Perryville, MO: Perry County Historical Society, 1994.

Steinfels, Peter. *A People Adrift: The Crisis of the Roman Catholic Church in America.* New York: Simon and Schuster, 2003.

Sweet, Ken. "How a Small Town in Missouri Became a Manufacturing Oasis." *Forbes*, 3 August 2012. www.forbes.com/sites/kensweet/2012/08/03/how-a-small-town-in-missouri-became-a-manufacturing-oasis/#4fa51d0d51cf.

Tentler, Leslie Woodcock, ed. *The Church Confronts Modernity: Catholicism Since 1950 in the United States, the Republic of Ireland, and Quebec.* Washington, DC: Catholic University of America Press, 2007.

Tucker, Phillip Thomas. *The Confederacy's Fighting Chaplain: Father John B. Bannon.* Tuscaloosa: University of Alabama Press, 1992.

Udovic, Edward. "Go Out to All the Nations! The Foreign Mission Apostolate: 1914–1987." In *American Vincentians: A Popular History of the Congregation of the Mission in the United States, 1815–1987,* edited by John Rybolt, 347–400. New York: New City Press, 1988.

Varacalli, Joseph A. *Bright Promise, Failed Community: Catholics and the American Public Order.* Lanham, MD: Lexington Books, 2001.

———. *The Catholic Experience in America.* Westport, CT: Greenwood Press, 2006.

White, Joseph M. "The Diocesan Seminary and the Community of Faith: Reflections from the American Experience." *U.S. Catholic Historian* 11, no. 1 (Winter 1993): 1–20.

———. *The Diocesan Seminary in the United States: A History from the 1780s to the Present.* Notre Dame: University of Notre Dame Press, 1989.

———. "Perspectives on the Nineteenth-Century Diocesan Seminary in the United States." *U.S. Catholic Historian* 19, no. 1 (Winter 2001): 21–35.

Wills, Garry. *Bare Ruined Choirs: Doubt, Prophecy and Radical Religion.* Garden City, NY: Doubleday and Co., 1972.

Wineapple, Brenda. *Ecstatic Nation: Confidence, Crisis and Compromise, 1848–1877.* New York: HarperCollins, 2013.

Wittberg, Patricia. *The Rise and Decline of Catholic Religious Orders: A Social Movement Perspective.* Albany: State University of New York Press, 1994.

Wroblewski, Sergius. "The Intellectual Climate in Seminary Life." In *Seminary Education in a Time of Change*, edited by James Michael Lee and Louis J. Putz, 233–53. Notre Dame, IN: Fides Publishers, 1965.

INDEX

Page numbers in *italics* refer to illustrations.

A

academic accreditation, 184–87
  and the Barrens, 186–200
  and Catholics schools/seminaries,
    186, 190–91
  See also North Central Association
academics and curriculum develop-
    ment at the Barrens, 53. *See also*
    academic accreditation
  early seminary curriculum, 64–65
  faculty/alumni scholarship, 203–10
  lay college, 64
  major-minor seminary delineation,
    184, 195
  1939–40 seminary curriculum,
    184–85
  1966 seminary curriculum, 196
  1982 seminary curriculum, 198–200
  reforms, 136–38, 185, 187–89, 191
  summer school, 174–75, 197–98
  tradition v. innovation, 182
American Catholic Church
  Americanism (heresy), 6–7, 128
  Americanization of, 6, 21, 36, 66–
    67, 109, 147
  beginnings and early history, 14,
    19–20, 73
  and Civil War, 101–2, 115
  demographics, 21st century, 244,
    246–47
  and education, 186
  and foreign missions, 158–59
  general history, 3, 5–7
  and immigration, 81–82
  institutions and institutional his-
    tory, 3, 5–6, 20, 35–36, 147, 246,
    250–52
  19th century (antebellum period),
    35, 81–82, 85
  1884–1962, 127–31, 171–72
  post–Vatican II, 215–18, 241
  Romanism/Romanization, 6, 129–30
  slavery, attitudes toward, 102
  religious communities, tensions in,
    216–17, 241
  Third Plenary Council of Baltimore
    (1884), 129, 137, 150
  21st century, 244, 246–47
American Catholic colleges, 8, 35,
    54–55, 186
American Vincentians: A Popular History,
    68
Apostle of Charity Residence (Barrens),
    241, 248–49, *249*
apostolic school (Barrens), 133,
    133n16, 135–36, 140, 142

B

Badin, Stephen, 30, 30n19
Bardstown (KY), 24, 29–30
Barbier, Francis, 109
Barnwell, William, 133, 138n34, 139
Barr, William, 139
Barrens foundation contract (1815),
    27–28, 51–52, 55
Barrens seminary
  closing of (1985), 223–30
  relations with Barrens Settlement/
    Perryville, 16–17, 31, 53–54, 237–
    38, 247–48
Barrens Settlement (later Perryville,
    MO), 8, 11
  Catholicity, 24–25, 55–56, 56n, 69
  demographics, 69

Barrens Settlement, *continued*
  founding and early history, 14–16
  isolation of, 15–16, 91
  name of, 14–15, 15n12
  offer of land to DuBourg, 29–30
  relations with seminary and Vincentians, 15–17, 31, 53–54
Barry, William J., 67
Barth, Pius, 186–87, 187n50, 189
Bishop's Mill (Barrens), 85
Boccardo, Angelo, 73
Bonaparte, Napoleon, and fortunes of Vincentians, 12, 22
Brackenridge, Henry, 15n14
Brennan, Francis C., 198
Brennan, William, 180–82
Brusatti, Louis, 225
building/construction of Barrens campus. *See also individual buildings*
  Apostle of Charity Residence (2006), 241, 248–49, *249*
  Bishop's Mill, 85
  Church of the Assumption (1837), 11, 56, 84, *94*, *141*, 146, *166*, *245*, 248, 251
  demolition of buildings, 240–41
  early plans and construction, 30–31, 62
  Finney Library (1954), 144–45, *188*
  fire in college buildings (1866), 240–41
  growth, 1888–1962, 140–47
  Kulage Hall/scholasticate building (1931), 143
  maintenance/repair needs, 174, 240n73
  National Shrine of Our Lady of the Miraculous Medal (1930), 146
  Novitiate Building (1927), 143, *183*
  Oliva Hall (1898), 142
  pre–Civil War era buildings, 83–85
  master plan, proposed (1952), 144–45
  recreation center (1956), 145
  renovation plan (1971), 219, 221
  Rosati's Sacristy/Rosati cabin, *57*, 141, 146
  Rosati Hall (1850), 84–85, 140, 248
  Smith Hall (1892), 142
  state of campus in 1888, 13
  state of campus in 2016, 248–49
  Thomas Shaw description of, 140–41
Byrne, Peter, 138

C
Camp St. Vincent, 151–52
Carey, Patrick, 82, 127–28
Catholic Home Study Service, 11, 208, 233, 240, 248. *See also* Confraternity Home Service
Catholic Students Mission Crusade, 157, 159, 165
Catholic University of America, 174–75
Cawley, Thomas, 221
Cellini, Francis, 62, 72, 72n39
Center for Applied Research in the Apostolate (CARA), 246–47
Church of the Assumption (Barrens), 11, 56, 84, *94*, *141*, 146, *166*, *245*, 248, 251
Civil War
  and American Catholic Church, 101–2
  and American religion, 101
  in Missouri, 105, 110–11, 114–16
  in Perryville, 105, 112–15
  at St. Mary's of the Barrens, 105–6, 108, 110–16
Clet Correspondence Guild, 160
Cold War, 172–73
Committee on the Apostolate (COTA), 217–18, 227, 241
Confraternity Home Service, 157–58, 164–65. *See also* Catholic Home Study Service
Congregation of the Mission (Vincentians), 4
  adaptability of, 17, 228–29
  American mission, founding and fortunes of, 4–5, 7, 9,11–12, 14, 16, 65, 93, 131–32, 228, 248
  apostolates, 55
  and Barrens Settlement, 15–17
  bishops, 4, 58–60, 93, 95, 200–203
  brothers, 68
  contract with DuBourg (1815), 27–28, 51–52, 55
  division of American province, 100, 124, 131–32, 219, 221
  foreign missions, 158, 201–3

founding and European roots, 9, 12,
21–22
and French Revolution, 22
General Assembly of 1835, 76–77
General Assembly of 1968/69, 8, 217
Midwest (USA) Provincial Assembly
of 1974, 221
Midwest (USA) Provincial Assembly
of 1982, 223
parishes/parochial work, 55–56
post–Vatican II, 217
recruitment by DuBourg, 25–28
and secular politics, 108–9, 112, 116
seminaries, 53, 58, 65, 119, 136–37,
192, 218–19
and slavery, 103–4
and spirituality, 12, 42, 68–69, 251
Conley, William H., 194
Consalvi, Ercole, 27
Crosson, Frederick J., 197
Cummings, Jeremiah W., 67, 67n22
Cummings, John, 118–19

D

Daughters of Charity, 12
De Andrein (newspaper), 148, 153–54,
156–57, 160–61, 163, 172–73
De Andreis, Felix, *26*
on American conditions, 67
assessment of, 40–42
cause for canonization, 39
death, 42
early life, 25–26
quoted, 19
recruitment to American mission,
26–28
at Ste. Genevieve, 29, 57
at St. Louis, 31, 41, 52
role at the Barrens, 38–39, 41–42, 52
as Vincentian superior, 61
De Andreis-Rosati Memorial Archives
(DRMA), 152–53, 239–40
Demion, Constance, 136
demographics (Barrens enrollment and
population)
antebellum/Civil War era population, 83
Civil War, effects of, 105–6
declining enrollment, late 20th
century, 199

early years, 47–49, 72
1886–1903 population, 133, 135–36
lay college, 63
post-1945 growth, 173–74
slave population, 104
21st century (2016), 248
Dichtl, John, 20
Doheny, Estelle, 145n51, 170, 176, 201
Donovan, Joseph, 204
Drake Constitution, 117. *See also* ironclad oath
DuBourg, William, *23*
assessment of, 40
and the Barrens Settlement, 29–30
as bishop of Louisiana, 23–24
on De Andreis, 42–43
on division of Louisiana diocese, 75
early life, 22–23
New Orleans, problems with church
28n14
and proposed Louisiana seminary,
74–75
and recruitment of Vincentians,
25–27, 51
role at the Barrens, 8–9, 38–40, 54, 71
and Rosati, 44
and slavery at the Barrens, 103
transfer of see to St. Louis, 28, 30
Dukehart, Cyril, 190
Dunand, Marie Joseph, 25, 29–30

F

faculty at Barrens, 168–69, 189, 191,
194, 196
Fallon, Lester, 155–57, 205
Faris, John, 133, 138
farm at the Barrens, 11, 54, *181*, 233,
248, 250
Fiat, Antoine, 131, 137
Finney, Joseph, 148–50, 177–79
Finney Library (Barrens), 144–45, *188*
Finney, Thomas O'Neil, 139, 159
Fischer, James A., *180*
and academic accreditation, 186–87,
189–93
as Barrens superior, 180–82
biography of, 205
as provincial superior, 205–06
as scholar, 206
Flaget, Benedict, 28n15, 28–29, 61

Franzelin, Giovanni, 150
French Revolution, effects on Vincentians, 12, 19, 21–22
frontier (American) conditions, and Catholic missionaries 4–5, 20–21, 62, 65–66, 68
fund-raising at the Barrens, 176–79

G

Gagnepain, John, 232, 234
Glass, Joseph, 200–01
Gleason, Philip, 8, 35–38, 50–51, 54–55, 60, 62, 67, 71, 92
Great Depression, 163

H

Hartenbach, William, 223, 228, 230, 236–40, 243
Hayden, John, 98, 121
Hayden, Sarah, 30–31, 62
Hess, Henry, 143
Hoernig, Alphonse, 231

I

identity/role of the Barrens, 10–11, 51–53, 60, 85
importance of the Barrens
    adherence to mission and memory, 251–52
    and Gleason model of American Catholic development, 36–38
    as microcosm of American Catholic narrative, 3–7, 9, 17–18, 244, 250
    as microcosm of antebellum era Catholic history, 83
    as microcosm of American Catholic "triumphalism," 127, 172, 211
    as microcosm of early American Catholic experience, 21
    as model for adaptation/change, 7, 16, 250–51
    as reflection of Catholic experience in Civil War, 102–3
    as reflection of post–Vatican II trends/tensions, 216
Inglesi, Angelo, 73
institutional history as microcosm, 3
Internal Revenue Service (and Barrens fund-raising), 176–77
ironclad oath, 117–19

J

Joyce, Michael, 237

K

Kennerly, William Clark, 61, 64
Kenrick, Peter Richard, 45, 75–76, 117
Kenrick Seminary, 76, 138
Kulage Hall (Barrens), 143
Kulage, Maria Theresa, 143, 143n44

L

Labouré, Catherine (saint), 11, 148
Lansman, Joseph, 85, 142
lay education at the Barrens, 11
    apostolic school, 133
    closure of lay college, 89
    college building, 84
    college building fire of 1866, 88–89
    college curriculum, 64
    college extension programs, 21st century (Mineral Area College and Southeast Missouri State University), 238–39, 248
    growth and support of college, 63–65
    lay college revival of 1850–66, 88
    lower school/academy, 56, 89, 120, 122
    move of lay college to St. Vincent (Cape Girardeau) in 1843, 87
    reputation of, 64. *See also* Kennerly, William Clark, and Rozier, Firmin
    suspicions of, 87
    threatened suppression of college, 47–48
    undifferentiated nature of college, 54–55
leadership of the Barrens, 37–51, 92–100, 179–82
LeFevre, Cyril, 167 (quoted), 167–71, 178
Leven, Stephen, 155
Lilly, Joseph, 204–5
Lindbergh, Charles, 162–63
Lipsmeyer, Beth, 225
Louisiana Territory, 9, 23
Louws, Cornelius, 173
Lukefahr, Oscar, 208–9
Lynch, John, 60, 84, 96–7

M

Madsen, David, 193
Maller, Mariano, 106, 110
    biography, 92–93
    praised by Ryan, 93
    as visitor, 93
    visitation report on Barrens (1877),
        99, 122–23
Maloney, Robert, 232–33
Martin, Daniel, 174, 177–82, 185
McCarthy, Daniel, 115, 123
McClinton, William, 179n42
McMenamy, Patrick, 106–8, 116
Menti Nostrae, 130, 186
Meyer, Aloysius, 89
Miraculous Medal Association, 11, 146–
    50, 176–77, 209, 230, 233, 248
Misner, Paul, 202
"Mission Project: St. Mary's of the Bar-
    rens" (SMOB Report), 232–36, 242
missions/missionary work/outreach
    programs at the Barrens
    Barrens Outreach Initiative (1994), 232
    Catholic Students Mission Crusade,
        S. V. Ryan Unit, 156–57, 159–61
    Clet Correspondence Guild, 160
    Confraternity Home Service, 157
    early mission work, 11, 48, 57–58
    establishment of regional parishes,
        89–90
    post-1945 internationalization of
        Barrens, 173
    Miraculous Medal Association, 148–
        50, 248
    motor missions, 155–58
    outreach programs (2016), 248
    Sheehan Museum, 160–62
    Vincentian Foreign Mission Society,
        159–61
    See also Confraternity Home Service;
        Catholic Home Study Service;
        Miraculous Medal Association;
        motor missions; Catholic Students
        Mission Crusade, S.V. Ryan Unit;
        Religious Information Bureau
Monte Citorio (Rome), 22, 25
Moore, Isidore, 24
motor missions, 11, 155–56, 158
Musson, William, 132n15, 133–34, 138

N

North Central Association of Colleges
    and Schools (NCA), 174, 181, 185–
    87, 189–200, 222
novena, 149, 153
Novitiate Building (Barrens), 143, *183*
Nozo, Jean- Baptiste, 77, 89–90
Nugent, Francis, 138
Nygren, David, 241

O

O'Callaghan, Malachy, 134–35
O'Connell, Michael, 175–76, 180–82
Odin, Jean-Marie, 47, 47n32, 60, 148
O'Donnell, Hugh, 224, 226, 229
Oliva, Angelo, 56, 62, 142
Oliva Hall (Barrens), 142
Our Lady of the Miraculous Medal, 11

P

Pansza, Ralph, 199
Parres, Cecil, 219, 221
Pasquier, Michael, 20
Penco, Anthony, 95–96
Perryville (MO), *14*, 14–15, 56
    and Civil War, 82–83, 104–5, 112
    early growth/immigration, 82
    Forbes article (2012), 247
    post–Civil War growth, 119
    slavery, 82, 82n4
    21st century, 247
Perryville Community Park Associa-
    tion, 238, 240
Pius VII (pope), and foundation of the
    Barrens, 26
Pius XII (pope), and Barrens curricu-
    lum, 130
Poole, Stafford, 65, 90–91, 103–4, 203–
    4, 207–8
Price, Sterling, 114
problems/challenges at the Barrens
    adaptability/assimilation, 7, 17, 52,
        61, 63, 68–70, 73
    administrative problems, 47, 100, 123
    authority issues/relations with bish-
        ops and Vatican, 74–75, 90–91,
        107, 129
    departure of formation programs,
        85–87, 98, 108, 120–21, 219
    early challenges/deprivations, 31, 39

problems/challenges, *continued*
  episcopal appointments, 58, 60, 93, 95
  external demands, 49, 77
  finances, 53–54, 71–72, 106–7, 122, 134–35, 175–78
  identity issues, 5, 233–35, 243
  internal divisions/tensions, 47, 68, 169–71, 174, 237
  isolation/neglect, 5, 9, 15, 91, 107, 121, 133–34
  Maller 1877/78 visitation, 122–23
  mixed student population, 37, 49, 62–63
  numbers, lack of, 72–73, 197, 222, 227
  post–Civil War retrenchment, 90–92, 119–21
  rival institutions, 75–77, 169
  sectionalism and Civil War, 83, 107–12, 116–17
  student development issues, 225
property of Barrens, disposition of (1995–2016), 221, 230, 232, 236–40, 242

Q

Quigley, John, 106, 108, 112
Quinn, Charles, 203

R

Rabble, George C., 101–2
Raynor, John P., 194–95
Reinert, Paul, 190
Religious Information Bureau, 11, 157
Richardson, James, 185, 210–11
Richardson, John, 190–91, 210
Riley, Edward, 189–90
Ritter, John, 177
Rolando, James, 98–99
Rosati cabin (Barrens), *57*, 141, 146
Rosati Hall (Barrens), 84–85, 140, 248
Rosati, Joseph, *37*
  arrival at Barrens Settlement, 30–31
  assessment of, 45–46
  at Bardstown, 29
  as bishop of St. Louis, 42–45, 47, 58
  commission of missionaries, 57–58
  on conditions at the Barrens, 62, 72
  on De Andreis, 42
  death, 45

  on division of Louisiana diocese, 75
  and DuBourg, 44, 74
  early life, 43
  and lay college at Barrens, 63–64
  quoted, 35
  recruitment for American mission, 27
  role at the Barrens, 38–39, 43–44, 54, 66
  role in broader church, 45
  St. Louis seminary plans, 75–76
  on seminary program, 65
  and Tornatore, 46–47
  as vicar-general of Louisiana, 43
Rosetti, John, 73–74
Rozier, Firmin, 64
Ryan, Abram, 3, *87*, 108–11, 116
Ryan, S. V. Unit (Catholic Student Missions Crusade), 159–61
Ryan, Stephen Vincent, *86*
  and Abram Ryan, 110
  at the Barrens, 97
  biography, 97
  as bishop of Buffalo (NY) 60
  and changes at the Barrens, 86–87, 91–92, 98, 120
  and Civil War, 106, 111–12, 114–15, 116–18
  and consolidation of apostolates, 90
  on ironclad oath, 118
  on Maller, 93–95
  on parishes, 90
  quoted, 81, 101
  as visitor, 98, 120
Rybolt, John, 43, 46, 50, 69–70, 89, 209–10

S

Saint-Lazare, 12–13, *13*, 22
St. Boniface Parish (Perryville, MO), 89
St. Louis (MO), 16, 29
St. Mary's Parish (Barrens Settlement/Perryville, MO), 11, 56–57, 89, 250–51
St. Vincent's College (Cape Girardeau, MO), 76–77, 87, 107, 121, 133
Salhorgne, Dominique, 46–47
Schroeder, Walter, 15n12, 24–25, 69
Schuth, Katarina, 246n5
Sedes Sapientiae, 186, 191
seminaries, Catholic

and Catholic Students Mission Crusade, 159
closings of, 246
curriculum of, 64–65, 129–30, 136–37, 182, 184–85
in early America, 4, 51, 54–55, 58
"free-standing," controversy regarding, 222, 223n18, 225
mixed, 7, 9, 36–37, 62–63
pontifical, 179n43
post–Vatican II, 222, 225
reforms of, 128–31, 137, 147, 150
Shaw, Thomas, 127 (quoted), 140–41
Sheehan, Edward, 202
Sheehan (Edward T.) Memorial Museum, 160–62
Shelby, Charles, 231, 236, 239–40, 243
Sicardi, Carlo Domenico, 26–27, 52
slaves/slavery
and American Catholic Church 102
at the Barrens, 102–4
in Perry County (MO), 103, 105
Poole and Slawson, *Church and Slave in Perry County, Missouri*, 103–4
Slawson, Douglas, 103–4, 108–9
Smith, Thomas, *132*
biography, 100
on division of province, 100, 131
resignation, 139
St. Mary's of the Barrens, regard for, 123–24, 135
on seminary formation program, 137
Smith Hall (Barrens), 142
Southeast Missouri State University, 238–40
Souvay, Charles, 152, 201n88
Spanish Civil War, 163–64
Spanish land grants, 14, 17, 17n16, 24
Stakelum James, 177
standardization of Barrens status/programs, 167–71
Steines, Nicholas, 142
student activities at the Barrens, 147–54, 162–65, 196
Swift, James, 240

T

Third Plenary Council of Baltimore (1884), 129, 137, 150

Timon, John, *38*
Americanizing tendencies, 69–70
assessment of, 50
on Barrens Settlement, 54n53
as bishop of Buffalo (NY), 50, 60
controversies and criticism, 49–50
early life, 48
and growth of Congregation in U.S., 58
missionary work, 48, 57, 68
parishes, 89
reforms of, 65–66
role at Barrens, 38–39, 48
on slavery, 104
as visitor, 48 -49, 76–77
Tornatore, John, 46–47, 73, 109
Trapp, Arthur, 234–35
Trappists, 25n10

U

Ukeritis, Miriam, 241

V

Varacalli, Joseph, 19
Vachetta, Carlo Antonio, 153
Van Dorpe, Raymond, 240n, 244 (quoted), 249–50
Vatican Council II, 6, 172, 228
Vawter, Bruce, 206–07
Vincent de Paul (saint), 9, 12, 22, 42, 155
Vincentian (magazine), 160, 160n84
Vincentians. *See* Congregation of the Mission
Vincentian Foreign Mission Society (VFMS), 159–61, 173

W

Weekly Perryville Union, 105
White, Joseph M., 128–29
Wills, Garry, 215
Winne, Marshall, 152, 175, 179
World War II, 164

About the Author

Richard J. Janet currently serves as professor of history at Rockhurst University in Kansas City, where he has taught since 1985. He received the PhD in modern European history from the University of Notre Dame. Janet is the author of numerous articles, essays, and reviews (both scholarly and popular). His work on the history of the Congregation of the Mission in the United States is supported by the Vincentian Studies Institute of DePaul University.